BPI BRANCH

JAN   2010

B RICH, M.
The king of oil : the secret lives of
Marc Rich
Ammann, Daniel.
33341005080824

D0742555

WITHDRAWN

The KING *of* OIL

The
KING *of* OIL

THE SECRET LIVES OF
MARC RICH

DANIEL AMMANN

St. Martin's Press

New York

Alameda Free Library
1550 Oak Street
Alameda, CA 94501

THE KING OF OIL. Copyright © 2009 by Daniel Ammann. All rights reserved.
Printed in the United States of America. For information,
address St. Martin's Press, 175 Fifth Avenue, New York, N.Y. 10010.

www.stmartins.com

Library of Congress Cataloging-in-Publication Data

Ammann, Daniel.
    The king of oil : the secret lives of Marc Rich / Daniel Ammann.
        p. cm.
    ISBN 978-0-312-57074-3
    1. Rich, Marc.   2. Petroleum industry and trade—United States—Biography.
3. Tax evasion—United States.   4. Criminal justice, Administration of—International
cooperation.   I. Title.
    HD9570.R53A55 2009
    381'.42282092—dc22
    [B]   2009016926

First Edition: October 2009

10   9   8   7   6   5   4   3   2   1

To Irene and to Emilie

CONTENTS

Contents

Contents

Contents

ACKNOWLEDGMENTS

I couldn't have written this book without the help and the advice of dozens of people I didn't know when I started. These oil and commodities traders, who had worked with Marc Rich in one capacity or another during the last forty years, shared their thoughts and their memories with me, opened doors and documents, and explained the technicalities of trading and financing. They tried to show me the big picture, and they revealed their little secrets. Most of them want to keep a low profile and don't wish to read their names in a book. I thank you all for trusting me so much without knowing me before.

Arthur Klebanoff was the best agent and counselor imaginable: highly professional and motivated, truly knowledgeable, and with a good sense of humor. Phil Revzin, Senior Editor at St. Martin's Press, believed in this project from the moment we talked about it for the first time. Roger Köppel, the owner and editor-in-chief of my journalistic home *Die Weltwoche*, generously granted me a long leave of absence from my position as Business Editor. I owe them my sincere appreciation.

Several friends and colleagues took the time to ask the right questions and to review, discuss, and improve the manuscript. They proved their friendship by being critical.

Among those who helped me, in various ways, to realize this book, my heartfelt thanks go (alphabetically) to Avner Azulay, Stefan Barmettler, Simon Brunner, Peter Hänseler, Pia Hiefner Hug, Christian König, Thomas Kramer, Michael Krobath, Monika Meili, Isaac Querub, Karin and Christoph Rothenhöfer, Ursula Santo Domingo, Jun Sarbach, Danny Schaechter, Peter Schildknecht, Doris and Jakob Schildknecht, Markus Schneider, Stefan and Lydia Spohr, Christine Steffen, Gabriele Werffeli, André A. Wicki, Jodok Wicki, Mark Willard and Tradukas, Bruno Ziauddin, Dave Zollinger, and Alain Zucker. I wish to mention particularly Hans Jörg Brun, without whose support and insights this book would not exist.

My deepest gratitude goes to my parents Margrit and Josef Ammann-Mahler, who always believed in me and taught me to make up my own mind. And most of all to Irene Schildknecht Ammann, the best wife, and to Emilie, the best daughter, for their love, for their encouragement, and for their (much needed) patience.

The KING *of* OIL

The UNDISPUTED KING of OIL

O il. Black gold. The "world's most controversial resource" has created the mighty dynasties of the Rockefellers and the Gettys.[1] It has tempted dictators such as Saddam Hussein into acts of aggression and brought down emperors such as the shah of Iran. Even today, countries are prepared to go to war to secure access to this strategically important resource. Without oil, there would not be an airplane in the sky or a car on the road. Without oil, hospitals would cease to operate and shopping centers would remain empty. Our modern economy is unthinkable without oil. Oil is the world's most important source of energy. More important, it is the most important commodity of an industrial society. We live in the Age of Oil. We are "hydrocarbon man," whose very survival would be impossible without oil.[2]

The spot market for oil was surely one of the most lucrative ideas of the twentieth century. Back when Marc Rich first began to snatch away a part of the global oil trade from the mighty oil corporations, crude oil cost $2 per barrel. In summer 2008 a barrel went for a record $140.[3] Marc Rich's undertaking was revolutionary—and highly successful. In the 1970s, Rich and a handful of trusted partners single-handedly managed to break the cartel of Big Oil, a cartel that dominated every aspect of the oil trade from the well to the gas pump. They created the first fully functioning, competitive market. They invented the spot market. Thanks to the oil trade, Rich—who came to the United States as a poor Jewish refugee boy—became one of the world's richest and most powerful commodities traders. He advanced to become the "undisputed King of Oil," as one of his longtime associates referred to him.

The high point of Rich's power was soon followed by his fall from grace, a fall that cost the billionaire his reputation, his wife, and his company. Marc Rich is not known the world over as a result of his amazing entrepreneurial achievements, which were many. His name does not ring a bell because he was a unique pioneer of globalization, which he was. His name is not bound to the realization of the American dream, even though he rose from a penniless European Holocaust survivor to become one of the richest men in America by the strength of his own will.

Despite his fabulous wealth, Rich lost control over his own name. Today the name Marc Rich means the billionaire trader who fled the United States in 1983 to avoid charges of tax evasion and making illegal oil deals with Iran during the hostage crisis. Marc Rich stands for the controversial last-minute pardon he received from President Bill Clinton in January 2001, "one of the most disgusting acts of the Clinton administration," as *Forbes* magazine wrote.[4] Marc Rich stands for doing business "with just about every enemy of the United States," according to Rep. Dan Burton, chairman of the House Committee on Government Reform from 1997 to 2002.[5]

Who is this man who led a life of high stakes and high risks? Who is this man who saw wars and revolutions not as curses but as business opportunities? Who is the real Marc Rich, the man who managed to elude the agents of the most powerful nation on earth for nearly twenty years?

Although he is one of the most important and most controversial commodities traders of the twentieth century, only one biography has been written about him, nearly twenty-five years ago, and is now outdated.[6] Perhaps this lack of coverage has something to do with the 1983 criminal proceedings that made Rich into the persona non grata that he is today. More likely it is because Rich is considered the most secretive trader of the notoriously furtive commodities trading community. For years, no one had ever seen a photograph of him. The media had to resort to artists' sketches for their reports. He systematically avoided reporters. Rich gave his last interview of significant length over twenty years ago. As a result, no one has ever succeeded in getting to know the real Marc Rich. No one has ever been able to find out his secrets.

Three years ago I decided to do just that.

"Dear Mr. Rich," I wrote in a letter in December 2006, in which I asked him for a meeting. "My aim is to get to know you better—your values, your thoughts, and your motivations." I included a long list of questions.

I wanted him to know that I did not intend to avoid the delicate subjects. I wanted to ask him why he thought it was right to do business with Ayatollah Khomeini's Iran, with Fidel Castro's Cuba, or with apartheid South Africa—with corrupt, violent, and racist governments. I wanted to hear him speak about the charges of tax evasion, which he was accused of by none other than Rudolph W. Giuliani. I wanted to know why he did not return to the United States and defend himself in court. I wanted to know why he was finally pardoned by President Bill Clinton. I wanted to ask him how he came to terms with the death of his daughter, whom he was unable to visit in the United States during her illness. Of course, I also wanted to know why and how he of all people was so successful.

In all truth, I did not expect a response. Rich had never answered these questions before. That is why I was so surprised when he agreed to a meeting. Perhaps he was pleased by the fact that as a journalist I had been following his story for over ten years. I had always tried my best to remain fair and balanced. Each time I wrote an article about Rich, I gave him the opportunity to make a statement. It came as an even greater surprise when Rich agreed to my demands for total control over the contents of this book. I insisted on the "final cut privilege." I did not want to write an "authorized account"—I wanted to do all of my own research, and naturally I wanted the freedom to write the things that he might not wish to read. Rich agreed to my terms, but he had one condition. He wanted to read my manuscript before it was sent to the publisher so that he could have the opportunity to point out any mistakes. I accepted his request on the condition that I would not be required to make changes to my manuscript if I thought I was right. After having read the manuscript, his comment was as short as it could possibly be. He thanked me in a letter for writing "a balanced report" and didn't ask for any changes at all.

My many long conversations with Rich were an important source of information for this book. As you'll see, he answered all the questions I had wanted to ask, and many more. It was the first time he had ever spoken about any of these subjects, and he only refused to answer my questions when he thought he might have a legal reason for doing so. He spoke openly about his dealings in the world's troubled regions and admitted to having made deals with Iran, South Africa, Angola, and Cuba. He spoke for the first time about the legal case against him—insisting that he never evaded paying taxes and had never broken any laws.

I interviewed dozens of oil and commodities traders from the United States, Africa, Europe, and Asia who had worked with Rich in one capacity or another during the last forty years. They told me about the milestones in Rich's life, his most important business partners, and his decisive business deals. They introduced me to the intricacies of the commodities trade. I had to accept the fact that most of them wished to remain anonymous. Commodities traders, I learned, take more pains to avoid publicity than even Swiss bankers. In this business—which often brings together clients who officially will have nothing to do with one another—discretion is one of the most important prerequisites for success. I read countless—sometimes confidential—documents concerning Rich's case and his companies.

In order to find out more about the private Marc Rich, I spoke with his daughters Danielle and Ilona as well as with his close friends, including the legendary hedge fund pioneer Michael Steinhardt. My conversation with Denise Rich, a very impressive woman, was of particular significance. She spoke frankly about her life with her former husband, their bitter divorce, and her role in obtaining Rich's pardon. Ursula Santo Domingo—Rich's first secretary, a Spanish marquesa—told me of Rich's early days as a trader. A former officer of the Israeli intelligence service, Mossad, provided insight into Rich's very special relationship to Israel and the crucial services he provided to the Jewish state. Finally, the attorneys Jack Quinn—Bill Clinton's former White House counsel—Robert F. Fink, and André A. Wicki tried to convince me of how flawed the case against their client actually was.

Naturally I spoke with Rich's opponents, such as his "nemesis," Morris "Sandy" Weinberg Jr., who as a young assistant U.S. attorney for the Southern District of New York led the investigation into Rich's dealings and wrote the indictment against him.[7] I spoke with former U.S. Marshal Ken Hill, who for fourteen years secretly sought to detain—or even kidnap—Rich. I spoke to members of the judiciary and diplomats in the United States and Switzerland who told me off the record what they could not tell me publicly. I spoke to competitors and former employees who had fallen out with Rich.

The result of all the conversations and research is an epic story of power, morality, amorality, and ingeniousness in which many things are not as they appear. It is a story in which private lives collide with global politics. It is the saga of Marc Rich.

The BIGGEST DEVIL

I t is one of the coldest mornings of the year in St. Moritz, and I'm walking to my car. The snow crunches under my feet, and my breath hangs before me in a cloud of mist. It is eight degrees below zero Fahrenheit in the world's oldest and most glamorous ski resort, and I can almost hear the air crackling. I have to scrape away a thick layer of ice from my car windows before I get in. I curse quietly under my breath to hide my nervousness, and I hope the car will start despite the bitter cold. "Please," I beg, as I turn the key. The man I have arranged to go skiing with in the Swiss Alps hates nothing more than people being late. This much I already know. Speaking of his ex-wife, when I once asked him about his divorce, he said, "She is always late. Always."[1] There was no irony in his voice.

Arriving late is not an option. Not here and not now. In half an hour I am going to meet Marc Rich, the twentieth century's most powerful, most important, and most notorious oil trader. No one before and none since has ever been as successful as Rich, and none has stirred up such strong emotions around the world. Friends and colleagues admire him for his unique genius that virtually revolutionized international trade. Enemies despise him and consider him an unscrupulous profiteer who would sell his own grandmother—if the deal was good enough. It seems as if Marc Rich, now seventy-four years old, can only be seen in terms of black or white. The fact that he was pardoned by Bill Clinton in January 2001 has changed nothing. In fact, it had the opposite effect. The pardon, considered one of the "most notorious" in United States history, is seen by many of Rich's opponents as proof that he can buy anything, even immunity from the president of a superpower.[2]

I want to find out who this man really is beyond all the clichés and simplifications. How did Marcell Reich, a poor Jewish refugee boy from Belgium, become Marc Rich, "one of the wealthiest and most powerful commodities traders ever to have lived," as the *Financial Times* put it?[3] How did he and a handful of business partners seem to appear out of nowhere and go on to dominate global trade in oil and other commodities? What were the crucial decisions, the milestones in his unlikely career? How far did he have to go in order to reach them? What were his limits? What were his greatest successes and his worst defeats? What drives him on? What can be learned from his entrepreneurial skills?

I am lucky. My black Opel starts with a turn of the key. Only the speakers seem to have a tough time with the extreme temperatures. Mick Jagger's voice sounds strangely dull: *Please allow me to introduce myself / I'm a man of wealth and taste.* It is just before 8:00 A.M., and the streets are full of snow. There is not a person in sight. I drive carefully past the frozen Lake St. Moritz toward the luxurious Suvretta House, the best hotel in town. Within a span of a few days, the hotel will be taken over by the international jet set and European gentry as a fitting location for their Christmas and New Year's celebrations. Nestled among the snow-covered fir trees, the hotel seems tranquil and serene on this particular morning. A group of snowmen with red carrots for noses stands quietly by the hotel entrance.

Mick Jagger's voice echoes from the speakers. Forty years later, the Rolling Stones song "Sympathy for the Devil," written in the very symbolic year of 1968, can be heard again on nearly every radio station. I turn right and head toward the lower terminus of the Suvretta ski lift, where I am to meet the "biggest devil"—the exact term that Marc Rich used to describe himself. "I was painted as the biggest devil," he said to me without the least bit of self-pity during our last conversation in his office in the town of Zug. Those who are familiar with Rich's matter-of-fact style know that he is not prone to exaggeration.

A. Craig Copetas, who wrote the first and hitherto only biography of Rich nearly twenty-five years ago, called him "the veritable Prince of Darkness."[4] Rich was stylized as the personification of evil, the ruthless villain, and the capitalist monster whose fingers are "sticky with the blood, sweat, and tears of the Third World."[5] Over the years, the name Marc Rich became a symbol for greed and unscrupulousness, a chilling code that stands for everything that is wrong with "real-world capitalism."

There is a precise date for the day on which Marc Rich lost control over his own name. On September 19, 1983, a Monday, a young and ambitious United States attorney for the Southern District of New York appeared before the media. Trying hard to hide his glee, Rudolph W. "Rudy" Giuliani feverishly announced "the biggest tax fraud indictment in history." He read aloud from the indictment to the bewildered journalists and camera teams. The *New York Times* saw the need to describe the situation as an "unusual public display."[6]

Giuliani accused Rich, then forty-eight, of a total of fifty-one crimes.[7] In addition to tax evasion to the tune of at least $48 million, Rich was accused of racketeering, conspiracy, and trading with the enemy—the gravest crimes of which an upstanding citizen can be accused. It was alleged that Rich had been trading in Iranian crude oil and had ignored the U.S. embargo against Iran at a time when Americans were held hostage in Tehran. In the law library of the U.S. attorney's office, Giuliani announced that Rich and his business partner Pincus Green could spend the rest of their lives in prison for their crimes. The two businessmen had already absconded with their families to Switzerland, where the headquarters of Marc Rich + Co. AG, founded ten years prior, was located.

Since then, investigators have frequently referred to the affair as "the biggest tax fraud in American history," politicians have often described

Rich as a "billionaire fugitive," and journalists have written articles about "the most wanted white-collar criminal in U.S. history"—a Google search for this wording places Marc Rich right at the top of the list.[8] Understandably, the accusation of trading with the enemy weighs most heavily in public opinion. As the Republican Congressman Chris Shays stated when he summarized the public's mood, "A traitor to [his] country, to our country."[9] For many, Marc Rich is quite simply an enemy of the state.

The biggest devil. I was amazed to hear these words from Marc Rich himself. He may have his strengths, but volubility is not one of them. He speaks quite deliberately and succinctly, usually in only two or three sentences. I had been warned of this. If I could manage to get anything more than a "no," "yes," or "why," I could be happy with the results. He speaks English with a barely noticeable German accent, his father's language, and with an unexpectedly soft voice. While talking he looks you straight in the eyes and scrutinizes your reaction. His handshake is as firm as his conviction that reporters mean trouble.

Meeting Marc Rich

I first met Marc Rich some months before our St. Moritz ski date. We were sitting in his office on the top floor of a run-of-the-mill steel-and-glass building next to the Zug railway station. To get up here, where you can enjoy the view from the large windows over the town's commercial center and the gently rolling hills of the surrounding countryside, you have to pass through a highly sophisticated security system. In the building's foyer, next to a popular gym, cameras keep track of visitors taking the elevator. Lawyers and asset managers have their offices here. On the fifth floor the visitor is confronted with an opaque door of frosted glass; the plaque reads MARC RICH GROUP. When you ring the bell you are aware another camera is scrutinizing you. The automatic door opens. Now you are trapped in a kind of glass cubicle, where the receptionist on the other side of a glass door inspects you. It would come as no surprise to discover the glass doors were bulletproof. Only after the first door has closed does the second door open, and you enter the company offices.

In the waiting room, there is a small glass table and two black leather LC2 chairs designed by the Swiss artist and architect Le Corbusier. "Marc Rich Group, good morning," an assistant says on her telephone, although German is usually spoken in Zug, and it is actually already late afternoon. I remember one of his most loyal traders once said to me that "the sun never sets in Marc Rich's empire," a reference to King Charles V of Spain (1500–1558), Holy Roman Emperor, who ruled over a world empire thanks to the discovery of America in 1492 by Christopher Columbus. "Marc was the undisputed King of Oil."

An assistant leads me through labyrinthine corridors decorated completely in white to Rich's office. There are paintings by Miquel Barceló and Antony Tapies on the walls. A sand-colored carpet muffles the sound of footsteps. Just before I reach the director's office, I notice two burly men behind a room divider sitting at their computers and looking rather bored. "Drivers," the assistant says in answer to my question. "Security," Marc Rich later confirms. The two bodyguards, who never leave his side, even when he goes across the street for lunch, remind me of the time when the American government had set a bounty on his head. It was the time when Rich was hunted the whole world over by agents and adventurers, and he only rode in an armored Mercedes.

A small effective team of specialists led by a former Mossad officer provided for Rich's security. They were clearly very successful, as the American agents who wanted to kidnap him in Switzerland and spirit him out of the country were never able to detain him. "He paid very well for security. He had the money to buy what he needed. It was like tackling a country," Ken Hill told me in Florida. As a U.S. marshal, Hill had tried for fourteen years to capture Rich. (We'll hear his story in chapter 12.)

"Which reproach hurts you most?" I ask in Rich's office to get the interview rolling.

"Which reproach are you referring to?" Rich asks in response.

Whenever he thinks a question is imprecise, he likes to answer it with a question of his own. He's sitting behind a long wooden desk and writing a note on a white leather desk mat. As always, he's wearing a dark blue suit with a white shirt and a red tie. He has a cold and is drinking a cup of chicken broth. There is cigar smoke in the air, as there was during almost all of our meetings. A half-smoked Cuban Cohiba lies in a crystal ashtray. This is one of the few pleasures that Rich could never have enjoyed in the United States. Since February 7, 1962, Cuban cigars—and all other Cuban products—have been forbidden there. That was the day John F. Kennedy imposed a trade embargo against Cuba by executive order—and, as a passionate cigar smoker, he had press secretary Pierre Salinger buy up all available stocks of his favorite type of cigar in Washington, D.C., beforehand.[10]

Rich's desk is dominated by a large computer screen, and real-time currency exchange charts and stock indexes flash across it. The two books next to the screen grab my attention—the newest edition of the compendium *Metal Traders of the World* and *My Life*, Bill Clinton's autobiography. Photographs of moments in Rich's life are closely bunched together on a sideboard, mostly photographs of his daughters Ilona and Danielle and of his grandchildren. At the front of the collection there is a photograph of his second daughter, Gabrielle, together with Bill Clinton and Al Gore. Gabrielle died of leukemia in 1996 at the age of twenty-seven. Another photograph shows Israeli prime minister Ehud Olmert embracing Rich. On the wall, in simple wooden frames, there are two certificates for honorary doctorates that Israeli universities awarded to Rich in 2007. As we'll see, it was mainly due to the intercession of Israeli politicians on Rich's behalf that Bill Clinton finally agreed to grant him a pardon. Israel owes Rich a debt of gratitude for many reasons, including the provision of crucial clandestine service, as I will show later.

"You bought Iranian oil from the Ayatollah Khomeini while the mullahs were holding American embassy employees hostage," I answer his question. "You did business with Fidel Castro's Cuba despite the

U.S. trade embargo. You delivered racist South Africa oil while the black population suffered under the laws of apartheid. You are considered the greatest tax fraudster in the history of the United States."

He looks at me and says in a soft voice, "I heard it so often that I became immune to it."

"To be painted as the biggest devil, as you put it, must hurt," I insist.

"No," Marc Rich says.

The last curt answer came only after a long, telltale pause. It was one of the few times in our conversations that his answer did not sound convincing. Several friends had assured me that the accusations had hurt him deeply.

As if he sensed my skepticism, he gave me a sphinxlike smile and suddenly asked me, "Do you ski?"

I nodded, surprised. "Every Swiss knows how to ski. I first stood on skis at the age of three." I might have sounded a bit too self-confident.

"Show me how good you ski," he said and proposed we go skiing together just before Christmas.

Charming and Cunning

I'm the first one to arrive at that empty parking lot at the bottom of a ski lift, where I wait for Rich on an icy-cold December morning. I had come to know him over the previous few months—monosyllabic, yet outspoken; charming, yet cunning; highly focused despite his seventy-four years of age. Perhaps most astonishing, the man who thinks as highly of publicity and journalists as a vegetarian does of a pork sausage, a man who gave his last previous interview of significant length while the Berlin Wall was still standing—this man answered nearly every question I had for him, even the most delicate ones.

Marc Rich's story is both typically American and typically Jewish. Parts of the saga can be seen as the embodiment of the American dream, a classic dishwasher-to-millionaire fantasy. Marcell Reich, the Jewish boy-refugee from Antwerp, barely escaped certain death in the Holocaust. In the spring of 1940, he fled from Belgium with his family, the day the Nazis marched into the country. Penniless and unable to speak a word of English, the young Reich fled to Morocco by freighter and, with a great deal of luck, finally reached the United States. Under the name of Marc Rich, he entered the world of trade—one of the few lines of business that Jews have been allowed to pursue over the centuries. People soon began to speak of a wunderkind. With remarkable skill, talent, determination, and endurance, he made himself into the most successful commodities trader of his time. He then ran so afoul of the law that he landed on the FBI's Most Wanted list. The United States government offered a high reward for his capture and chased him all over the world.

Rich's is one of the most amazing careers of the twentieth century, a career that is tightly woven with great events in world history: Fidel Castro's revolution in 1959; the decolonization of Africa in the 1960s; the Yom Kippur War and the oil shock of 1974; the fall of the shah of Persia and the seizure of power by the Ayatollah Khomeini in Iran in 1979; apartheid South Africa in the 1980s; and the crumbling of the Soviet Union in the 1990s. Marc Rich and his business partners were on the scene when these events happened. Thanks to their know-how, their hard work, and their considerable aggression, they were able to react to these events to their benefit more than their competitors ever could. Most important, however, Marc Rich is an epochal pioneer of globalization and an architect of the modern system of commodities trading. His name will be forever connected with an economic revolution—he is the inventor of the spot market, without which modern oil trading would be unthinkable. Whenever you fill your tank with gasoline, you make a trade "on the spot." The driver needs gasoline, accepts the price on offer, and can fill up the tank, pay, and drive away with no further obligations. This was the great exception to what was standard procedure in the international oil-trading business right up until the beginning of the 1970s. Only around 5 percent of the world's oil was freely traded according to the law of supply and demand, whereas the other 95 percent changed hands according to long-term contracts and at fixed prices. Since World

War II, the global oil market had been dominated by the "Seven Sisters," the leading international oil companies.[11]

This cartel of multinational oil companies took its strongest beating from Marc Rich + Co. AG, a small company founded in the Swiss town of Zug in 1974. It is as if a small software company were to suddenly wrestle away Microsoft's market position. In next to no time, Marc Rich and his four business partners managed to achieve what all commodities traders admire and strive for:[12] They created a new market for products that until then either had been traded in very small amounts or had not been traded at all. They managed to create an independent distribution system that bypassed the Seven Sisters. Rising demand leads to higher prices for consumers, and Rich can be found at the very beginning of the oil boom that followed. He began trading modest amounts of Tunisian crude oil at the end of the 1960s. Then a barrel of crude oil cost $2 (the price hit a record $147 in July 2008 but fell back as far as $35 in February 2009), the Club of Rome's *Limits to Growth* had not yet been written, and hardly anyone had ever heard of peak oil, a term that describes the worldwide decline in oil production.[13]

Rich also sparked the emancipation of the oil-producing countries. Increased competition among the multinational oil companies meant that producers could now demand more for their natural resources than ever before. Isaac Querub, Rich's longtime colleague and confidant, went so far as to compare him with the father of Communism: "You can say in a way that Marc Rich was the Karl Marx of the oil-producing countries. In the same way that Karl Marx made all the workers become aware of their class and their interests, Marc made all of the oil countries aware of their interests in a way. It was a revolution, no doubt about it."

"He Was Our God"

Less than ten years after it was founded, Marc Rich + Co. AG was the largest and most profitable independent oil-trading company in the world, even though the company's two most important partners—Marc Rich and Pincus Green—were being pursued by the most powerful nation on earth. No one could avoid dealing with Marc Rich + Co. "By the mid-1980s, we were already trading one million barrels of crude per day," says Rich. Marc Rich + Co. soon became the largest commodities trading company in the world, trading not only oil but also all types of metals and minerals from aluminum to zinc. "In metals, it's now Marc Rich and the forty dwarfs," a competitor said, reflecting a sentiment somewhere between respect and resignation.[14] An oil trader in England, who had worked for Rich for many years before successfully going into business for himself, once told me without any hint of irony, "Marc was a titan, no, more than that. He was our God. When he called to congratulate you on a profitable trade, it was like God called you."

From the "biggest devil" to "God"—there can be no greater span when it comes to evaluating a person. Pitch black or snow white. Why is Rich so polarizing? How does he manage to stir such emotions? There is a psychological explanation for this phenomenon: It is easy to pigeonhole Rich. We can ignore the ambiguities and complexities of Rich's person, as well as the ambiguities and complexities of the oil trade in general. If we demonize Rich—or if we make him appear larger than life—we make it easier for ourselves to forget the moral and political contradictions of our own actions.

Most commodities come from countries that are not beacons of democracy and human rights. "The resource curse" and "the paradox of plenty" are the terms economists and political scientists use to describe the fact that countries that are rich in oil, gas, or metals are usually plagued by poverty, corruption, and misgovernment.[15] If commodities traders want to be successful, they are forced—much like journalists or intelligence agents, who will take their information from any source—to sit down with people that they would rather not have as friends, and they apparently have to resort to practices that are either frowned upon or downright illegal in other parts of the world.

"When in Rome, do as the Romans do," an oil trader once said in response to one of my questions. He had spent a lot of time in Nigeria, one of the most corrupt countries in the world, which just happens to possess immense oil reserves. I wanted to know what he meant. "If you want to get pregnant, you can't stay a virgin," he said. Of course, he admitted, he had paid bribes in order to receive contracts. "[Marc Rich's] trading empire was based largely on systematic bribes and kickbacks to corrupt local officials," alleged the House Committee on Government Reform, which carried out an investigation into the circumstances surrounding Rich's pardon.[16] The oil trader in Nigeria does not accept this charge. "We would be neither as successful nor would we still be in business if we had only paid bribes. More importantly, we offered our customers a better service than our competitors." Rich himself does not deny having authorized bribes (see chapter 14).

The Final Frontier

"I'm driven by what drives most people: ambition," Rich said to me. "Mankind has developed through ambitions. Some wanted to climb higher, some wanted to run faster, some wanted to fly, others to dive. I wanted to succeed in business." His final frontier was the earth's crust and the treasures it contains. In order to achieve his ambitions, he traded with anyone who would trade with him, be they dictators or democrats, communists or capitalists. Born Jewish, he supported Israel and nonetheless made deals with the Iranian Islamists who wanted to destroy the Jewish state. Even South Africa's apartheid regime could count on him. This all made him one of the richest men in the world—and a bogeyman to all political camps. The Left sees him not as Marx but as an exploiter of the third world. The Right considers him a traitor for doing business with Iran and Cuba. Both sides see him as the greatest tax fraudster of all time. He maintains his innocence and insists that he never broke any laws. His lawyers provide long explanations detailing how all of his business dealings were perfectly legal under Swiss law, but public opinion remains unmoved by this argument—not to mention the American politicians who are convinced that the opposite is the case. "It is clear that Rich built his fortune doing business without legal, ethical, or even moral restraints," the House Committee on Government Reform concluded.[17]

Rich, who of all people always maintained that his company acted "apolitically," sank ever deeper in the political meat grinder. His trading with Iran after Khomeini's seizure of power remains his mortal sin, but American politicians also get angry about his alleged dealings with Muammar el-Qaddafi's Libya "even after U.S. oil companies completely withdrew from the country."[18] They denounce him for selling grain to the Soviet Union after the United States had enacted an embargo against the country following its invasion of Afghanistan in 1980. They rage over the fact that he traded copper, sugar, and oil with Cuba despite the Kennedy embargo. "Mr. Rich was publicly reported to have traded with just about every enemy of the United States they have had over the last twenty years, and many of those countries were embargoed," says Dan Burton, the influential chairman of the House Committee on Government Reform when its report on Rich was written.[19]

Anti-Semitic Stereotypes

The capitalist without a country who makes deals with the enemy. The speculator who creates nothing of his own but only acts as an intermediary while profiting from others. The "bloodsucker of the Third World," as Rich was once referred to in the Swiss parliament. The perfidious profiteer, who would rather leave his own country and give up his citizenship than pay taxes. Many critics may not be aware of the anti-Semitic stereotypes that resonate throughout these accusations. More than a few of my interviewees see this as at least one of the reasons why Rich was so persecuted while other oil companies that acted in a similar fashion were treated much more leniently.

"I don't really like to use the word 'anti-Semitic,' because you can say for any type of criticism that this or that is anti-Semitic. Usually it is just not true, but in Marc's case this was a really big problem," Avner Azulay said to me. The former officer of Israel's Mossad intelligence service is one of Rich's closest friends and was influential in gaining his pardon. "He was a parvenu. Not from the U.S. establishment—and Jewish. I have no doubt about it: A part of the American establishment, the WASP elite, is anti-Semitic," says another one of Rich's longtime companions, who closely witnessed his case from the very beginning.

An anti-Semitic angle to the whole affair? "Could be," Rich himself says. "I was an easy target: one individual, making a lot of money, Jewish." Sandy Weinberg, the assistant U.S. attorney who initiated and heavily influenced the criminal proceedings against Rich, took a sip of Perrier from a bottle and raised his voice for the first time. He strongly rejected the charge of anti-Semitism. "My father was a Jew from Brooklyn. He was discriminated against as a Jew," he angrily told me while we were sitting in his office on the thirteenth floor of the Bank of America Building, which provides a fantastic view of Tampa that reaches toward St. Petersburg.

"Survival is Rich's chief commodity," a journalist for *Fortune* once aptly wrote.[20] This could be Rich's motto. The experience of having to flee his home in Belgium had a great effect on Rich. He does not like talking about it, but he confirms my suspicion. "The forced emigration instilled in me a strong desire for independence." "Independence" is a word that Rich often uses, and he uses it again when I ask him what his unimaginable wealth means to him. "Wealth always means independence."

He has the typical mentality of the immigrant who has to do everything himself and who wants to show everyone that he can make it. He was hungry for success and ambitious enough to work his way up from a small apartment at 4404 Holly Street in Kansas City, Missouri, to a ten-room apartment on Park Avenue in Manhattan. "He is motivated by an athlete's drive to think faster, work harder, and achieve more than others," says the private banker Karl Reichmuth, who has known Rich well for many years.

Top performance was Rich's instrument in gaining recognition, esteem, and—if not love—respect, as a young refugee who spoke not a word of English, as a Jew in the Diaspora all on his own, and as an only child who wanted to please the father he so admired. His close friend Michael Steinhardt, the legendary hedge fund pioneer, expressed it best, when he received me in his Madison Avenue office in Manhattan. Steinhardt is a man like a panda bear with a silver mustache and a very low and calm voice. His office on the seventeenth floor offers a view of the ice rink in Central Park and contains marvelous artworks. There are ancient Judaica like silver menorahs and Torah boxes. There are photomontages by the famous German artist John Heartfield, né Helmut Herzfeld, who was satirizing Adolf Hitler and the Nazis with his gripping work. Steinhardt shows the seminal picture of the white dove of peace spitted on a bayonet in front of the League of Nations building in Geneva. "Succeeding in business became a function of Marc's life," he then says about his friend. Over the years, success became an end in itself; it became the true meaning of life.

His Greatest Strength

"His greatest strength?" Ursula Santo Domingo repeated my question. We were sitting in her apartment in an upscale neighborhood on the outskirts of Madrid. The elegant marquesa with German roots was Rich's first secretary. She has known him for more than forty years. Later their families became friends, and they sometimes went on vacation together. "He is what we call *superdotado* in Spanish, a gifted individual. His greatest strength is surely the fact that he does not give up until he has achieved his goal. He could work on something day and night until it finally worked out. He never thought of anything else except work. You cannot achieve what he has achieved if you only work eight hours a day and keep your weekends free."

All successful commodities traders, Marc Rich included, are aware that they are living their lives on a knife edge. There is a very fine line between riches and ruin, between right and wrong, between success and loneliness. A South American oil trader told me of being hired by Rich in the 1970s. "Marc picked up a knife with his left hand and ran his right index finger over the edge of the blade. He said, 'As a trader you often walk on the blade. Be careful and don't step off.'" If one believes Rudy Giuliani and his assistant, Sandy Weinberg, then Rich really did step off in the early 1980s. "We didn't have a good case, we had an overwhelming case," Weinberg told me. However, Giuliani and Weinberg never had to prove in court how good their case actually was. As Rich elected not to return to the United States, the trial never took place and he was never convicted—or acquitted.

One aspect of Marc Rich's career that was virtually forgotten during the entire affair was his unique entrepreneurial success. For starters, he is more than just a profiteer and boycott breaker. It was not Rich's alleged tax evasion that made him the twentieth century's most dominant trader. When I asked how he had managed to achieve so much, he answered with the standard trader's joke, "Buy low, sell high." Then he added in a more serious tone, "The ingredients are hard work, hard work, and hard work—and good collaborators. Obviously a little bit of luck helps also." These are surely important elements of success, but they cannot provide a good explanation for the sheer scale of his remarkable achievements.

It is because I want to speak to Rich about all of these things that I am waiting in the Suvretta ski lift parking lot in St. Moritz on a cold early morning. We had agreed to meet at eight thirty, and not a minute later a grass green car pulls up and Marc Rich climbs out. It is not one of those Mercedes, BMWs, or Jeep SUVs that are so fashionable among the jet-set crowd but an unimposing Subaru Legacy with Lucerne plates that has obviously seen a few years. One of the burly men I had met in Rich's office is sitting behind the wheel. The bodyguard turns out to be a kind of butler. He helps Rich unload his skis.

If a journalist were to happen to observe this rather unspectacular scene, he or she could never imagine who was standing here. Rich is wearing a black helmet with ski goggles, a bright red jacket, and blue ski pants. A look at his feet reveals the true ski aficionado—if your ski boots prove comfortable, you keep them forever. He is, as every year, accompanied by his daughters Ilona and Danielle with their families. It is obvious that he enjoys their company. "Please stay here, don't go yet. I miss you every day," he says on the chairlift to Danielle, who is leaving for the States the next day. "I have to go back to New York. Mother would be very sad if I didn't come back to her," Danielle answers. "Call her and tell her to come here," Rich insists. Danielle shakes her head. "You know she has a history in St. Moritz. I don't think she would feel at ease here." This short conversation sums up the entire story. Rich met Gisela Rossi, an attractive German woman, in 1992. In the end she turned out to be a reason for divorce (see chapter 16).

The first half of the 1990s was a time when everything suddenly seemed to be going wrong. Marc Rich was free, but the American government's pursuit was beginning to take its toll. For Rich, who loved traveling and traveled often, Switzerland was like a golden cage. In almost every other country in the world he was in danger of being picked up by American agents and brought back to the United States. He was isolated. A number of potential business partners wanted to have nothing to do with him—at least officially—as most did not want to play games with the American government. Commodities prices were dropping deeper and deeper across the board. After the end of apartheid, the sanctions against South Africa were gradually lifted, and the country no longer had to pay a premium to obtain Rich's oil.

His good friends say he was often insufferable back then. He drank a lot, surrounded himself with bad advisers, and made a few bad decisions that cost him a lot of money and, in the end, his company. On top of it all, his divorce from his first wife, Denise, became a bitter and expensive battle that was fought out in the limelight of the media. The scars ran deep. For years after the divorce, the two never spoke. Those who know the details say that it was not easy for Denise to campaign for her ex-husband's pardon. St. Moritz, once the place of happy family vacations, was now the place where their marriage had begun to crumble. No wonder that she had little desire to return there.

Skiing in St. Moritz

The ski resort of Corviglia on the mountain above St. Moritz is not only one of the largest but also one of the most attractive resorts in the Alps. Rich owns a three-story chalet on Suvretta Hill, which has the most exclusive and most expensive real estate in the area—a villa recently changed hands here for an estimated $70 million. Rich's chalet is equipped with an indoor pool where he goes to swim every morning. In the winter he spends almost every weekend here. He is an excellent skier who masters every run with elegance, even at seventy-four. He is sportive as ever, still likes to play tennis, and works out twice a week with a personal trainer.

While the super-rich may enjoy being flown by helicopter up to the mountain's summit, Rich stands in line with ordinary people at the chairlift. On the slopes, a vigilant observer would notice his two companions, one skiing in front of Rich, the other behind. The two bodyguards are carrying radios and heavy backpacks—you never know. Although he is still suffering from a cold, Rich is indefatigable as he makes his way down the slope. The moment he is in the chairlift he starts to work—on the phone to business partners all over the world, easily switching back and forth between English, Spanish, French, and German. When I ask him which language he is most comfortable with, he answers with a shake of his head and a sweep of his hand. He spoke German with his father and French with his mother. He often speaks Spanish with his daughters, who grew up in Spain, and in business he most often speaks English.

These days Rich is heavily involved in the real estate business, and the subprime mortgage crisis is keeping him busy. He owns some land in Spain, the European country hit worst by the crisis, which is not of the best quality. He bought it a few years ago for $30 million in the hope that its value would rise during the prevailing real estate boom. Now the value of the land is melting like snow in the spring sun. The banks are looking to get out. On the phone in the ski lift, Rich gives short and snappy instructions and asks a few questions. "How many percent do we have? Who's got the lead? We're not going to throw good money after bad. Good-bye." After hanging up, he talks openly about the deal with his daughter Danielle and her husband, Richard. It does not seem to bother him at all that I am sitting next to him in the chair-lift and can hear everything.

After a morning of skiing, he invites me to his chalet for lunch. Stepping out of the lift that takes you from the garage to the third floor of his house, you are immediately struck by the fairy-tale view of the snowy mountains and lakes of the Upper Engadine Valley. The furnishings in the house display impeccable good taste. It is a happy mix of modern furniture and modern art that provides a fitting contrast to the chalet's traditional wooden interior. Two bright large sofas dominate the spacious room. On the table between the sofas there are bronze animal sculptures from Bolivia and a mountain of monographs covering the entire history of art from Diego Velázquez to Joseph Beuys and Philip Taaffe. On the walls are works by Miquel Barceló and Keith Haring. The whole chalet smells like a florist's shop. Everywhere there are gorgeous flower bouquets in green vases left over from Rich's birthday—roses, tulips, lilies; all of them white, his favorite color.

We are joined by his girlfriend Dolores "Lola" Ruiz, whom he calls *"mi más bella flor"* (my most beautiful flower). What at first sounds perhaps a bit affected turns out to be something quite different when I discover who Lola really is. The Spanish-Russian intellectual with a degree in philosophy is writing a book about her famous grandmother Dolores Ibárruri Gómez, the legendary secretary-general of the Communist Party of Spain. During the siege of Madrid in the Spanish Civil War (1936–39), she coined the slogan *"¡No Pasarán!"* which soon became a global antifascist rallying call. Her nom de guerre was "La Pasionaria," the passion flower. Ernest Hemingway immortalized her in *For Whom the Bell Tolls*, his novel about the Spanish Civil War, which was made into a film with Gary Cooper and Ingrid Bergman. One of La Pasionaria's most often quoted lines goes "It is better to die on one's feet than to live on one's knees." Reformulated, the line fits her granddaughter Lola's partner quite well: It is better to go down in freedom than to spend a single day in an American prison.

After a lunch of chicken with potatoes and green beans, I sit with Rich on the sofa in front of the panorama window. We drink a 2000 Rioja Imperial Reserva from CVNE, Rich's favorite wine. "It's a clean wine," he says curtly. The heavy wine, pressed from Spanish Tempranillo grapes, is not a status-symbol wine from Bordeaux. In St. Moritz you can buy a bottle for roughly thirty dollars. A fugue from Johann Sebastian Bach sounds from the speakers, and a frozen Lake Silvaplana sparkles before us in the rattling cold. The glimmering blue Piz Corvatsch casts its shadow over the valley.

"My father." Rich answers my question without hesitation. "My father is definitely the person who influenced me most. We fled from Belgium, and he managed to build up an important business from zero." He then begins to tell me a story—a story of poverty and riches, power and morality, politics and genius. His story, and in many ways the story of oil in the past and the future.

a JEWISH FATE

David Reich bought his first automobile, a used black Citroën, on Wednesday, May 8, 1940. He sensed that very little time remained for himself and his small family. Only wealthy people were able to afford a car at that time, but David Reich was by no means rich. The thirty-eight-year-old shoe retailer spent virtually his entire savings on the used vehicle, yet the purchase did not fill him with pride. Not at that point in history. Not as an Orthodox Jew in Belgium.

The writing on the wall was clear enough for those who wanted to read it. The German *Wehrmacht* had just overrun Denmark and Norway, and eight months previously, in September 1939, Nazi Germany had invaded Poland. It was the beginning of World War II, which was soon to develop into the biggest and deadliest conflict in human history. It was probably only a matter of days until the German troops would also attack France via Belgium. By the spring of 1940 it was easy to predict what would then happen to a Jewish family. The racist Nuremberg Laws, which systematically discriminated against and disenfranchised the Jews, had already been in force in Germany since 1935. Books by Kurt Tucholsky, Upton Sinclair, Sigmund Freud, Anna Seghers, and Lion Feuchtwanger had been publicly burned. Jews were effectively excluded from economic, political, and social life in the German *Reich*. Following legal discrimination and the expropriation of Jewish property, the *Kristallnacht* in November 1938 signaled the start of their physical persecution as well.

Adolf Hitler's notorious speech on January 30, 1939, the sixth anniversary of his takeover of power, was heard on radios and seen in the weekly newsreels in cinemas. The words tumbled out of the dictator's mouth in the Reichstag as he screamed, staccato, "If international finance Jewry within Europe and abroad should succeed once more in plunging the peoples into a world war, then the consequence will be not the Bolshevization of the world and therewith a victory of Jewry, but on the contrary, the destruction of the Jewish race in Europe."[1]

David Reich, an energetic man possessed of a simple elegance who was the father of a bright five-year old boy, had stopped deluding himself by May 8, 1940. He had already witnessed too much, having personally experienced anti-Semitic persecution, as had his parents and grandparents. He was born in 1902 into an Orthodox Jewish family in the Galician shtetl of Przemyśl among the foothills of the Carpathian Mountains. Pshemishl, as the town was then known in Yiddish, belonged to the Austro-Hungarian Empire but is now situated in southeastern Poland on the border with Ukraine. When the Austro-Hungarian monarchy fell during World War I, there were once more terrible pogroms against the Jews in Galicia. David Reich fled with his parents and relatives toward Western Europe.

He started a new life from scratch twelve hundred kilometers from the place of his birth, in Frankfurt in the German *Reich*. It was an experience he shared with many European Jews, and an experience that ingrained itself in the collective memory of the Jewish people. In many Jewish households a suitcase packed with the essentials was always kept ready at hand, in order to leave at a day's notice "if it starts again." After Adolf Hitler was named chancellor of Germany on January 30, 1933, which also brought ultimate power to the Nazis, David Reich soon found it was time to get out that suitcase. Once more he was to leave his home, never to return, as he had done with Pshemishl.

In this fateful year of 1933 that would lead Germany to its greatest catastrophe, he met a petite, attractive woman called Paula "Pepi" Wang. Born in 1910 in Saarbrücken, she fascinated him, not least with her boundless energy. She was a woman who knew what she wanted and was not afraid to say it. The couple married and decided to settle in Antwerp, a Belgian town of special significance for Jews. Antwerp was at that time (and is now once again) one of the great centers of European Jewry. The city on the river Scheldt is a commercial center with a glorious past and boasts one of the largest ports in the world. The French historian Fernand Braudel described it as "the centre of the entire international economy" in the sixteenth century.[2] Portuguese ships unloaded their precious cargos there, whether pepper from India or cloves from Zanzibar. It was an international, cosmopolitan town of traders and businessmen from the major trading nations all unified in their desire to make a profit. It was also an extremely tolerant town that permitted the development of a large Jewish community. David S. Landes characterizes Antwerp as a center of industrial, commercial, and mental progress used to economic, intellectual, and spiritual diversity.[3]

The city to which David and Paula Reich emigrated in late 1933 was the most important center for the global diamond trade. Eighty percent of the world's finished diamonds were produced and traded here.[4] Of all the diamond businesses, 90 percent were in Jewish hands, but David Reich did not have either the luck or the right contacts to get a foothold in this lucrative business. He thus practiced one of the few professions that had been open to European Jews for centuries: trade. He worked harder than most and traded everything that could be sold, first scrap metal and then fabric, before concentrating on shoes. "David was always on the move. He was very dynamic and had lots of ideas," a family friend told me. Antwerp was a town that imbued its inhabitants with a mercantile mentality.

Their income was sufficient to ensure a modest lifestyle—an apartment in the inner city, three meals a day, and an occasional trip to the movies. Today it would be called lower middle class. Their little paradise was complete when Paula Reich gave birth to a boy on the afternoon of

Tuesday, December 18, 1934. They called him Marcell, after Mars, the Roman god of war. His middle name was David, after his father.

Marcell David Reich, who was later to make a name for himself as Marc Rich, was born into a devout Orthodox family that adhered to kosher rules and said Hebrew prayers. His father was a learned man, strict with himself and with his family, and uncompromising when it came to discipline, hard work, and religion. He was a demanding father whom Marc adored. He was also a reliable, honest man who could be trusted implicitly. Paula, his mother, was an astute, intelligent, and subtly ironic woman of French stock with a natural air of authority about her. Throughout her life she had two heroes: her husband and her son Marc. Friends of Marc remember her as a typical "Jewish mother"— caring, encouraging, and overprotective. Young Marc grew up bilingually, speaking his father's native German at home as well as his mother's French. He attended Tachkemoni School in downtown Antwerp, a Jewish school that still exists near Pelikaanstraat, the town's world-famous diamond center. He loved Selma, his German nanny, with all his heart.

The Escape from the Holocaust

It could have been a decent life, but then it did "all start again." It was once more time to get out the packed suitcase. By May 8, 1940, there was real cause to fear that the Nazis would bring the whole of Europe to its knees, and so David Reich spent virtually everything he had in order to buy the used black Citroën. It was a prudent move, for Nazi Germany commenced its push westward two days later. On Friday, May 10, 1940, at 5:35 A.M. the Low Countries were attacked by the *Wehrmacht*, and the *Luftwaffe* bombed the port of Antwerp.

"My father put us all in the car. My mother, my nurse Selma, myself. We started to drive away. I saw the German planes. I heard the bombings," says Marc Rich. We sit in his office in the Swiss town of Zug and drink coffee. We talk about his childhood, his relationship to his parents, and what has influenced him. The German attack and the hasty getaway are his first real memories—the fear, the confusion, the uncertainty. The trauma of flight and loss of home were etched into the mind of the five-year-old boy.

Thousands of Belgians tried to save themselves that day by heading into France. David and Paula Reich, with Marcell and Selma, were also driving south in great haste. The French border was less than a hundred miles from Antwerp. They made the terrible discovery at the border that the officials would not permit Selma, the non-Jewish German nanny, to enter the country. France had been at war with Germany since September 1939, and no amount of discussion could persuade the authorities to change their minds. Selma had to be left behind at the Belgian border and was forced to get by as best she could on her own.

Their escape to France saved the Reich family from the Holocaust. Almost as soon as the Nazis captured Antwerp eight days later on May 18, 1940, between six thousand and ten thousand Jews were rounded up.[5] The Jews were deprived of their property, their businesses were liquidated, and their institutions were banned. It was all part of Hitler's plan to systematically exterminate European Jewry in its entirety. Out of the estimated fifty-two thousand to fifty-five thousand Jews still living in Belgium in 1940, twenty-five thousand had been deported by the end of the war to Eastern Europe, where they were murdered in the death camps, primarily in Auschwitz.[6]

Nazi Germany seemed invincible in the spring of 1940, and the German word *Blitzkrieg* was soon understood in every language. The Germans overran Belgium, Luxembourg, and Holland within a matter of days. They attacked France in early June, and the first German soldiers were posing for photographs in front of the Arc de Triomphe in Paris on June 14.

Casablanca

Driving the black Citroën, David Reich took his family down to Marseille in unoccupied southern France. He hoped to find a ship in the country's largest port city that would take them away from Europe, although very few countries were still prepared to take Jewish refugees in the summer of 1940. Australia was accepting refugees, but a passenger ship sailing "down under" was out of the question, as it was beyond the family's means. However, after weeks of waiting Reich finally found a cargo ship, the *Monviso,* that was traveling to Australia and would take on Jewish refugees for a few francs.

The *Monviso* left Marseille on a Saturday. That was reason enough for several refugees to forgo the journey that would have saved their lives. "Since the boat was leaving on a Saturday, which is Shabbos, they refused to go and stayed behind," remembers Marc Rich. Devout Jews were forbidden from using means of transport on the Sabbath. However, David Reich knew that the Sabbath laws may be broken to safe a life, and this was definitely one such case.

The family slept below deck on improvised hammocks strung between pipes. The passengers were fed meat from goats kept in an enclosure on deck. The freighter may have been cramped, uncomfortable, dirty, and reeking of oil, but it nevertheless saved the Reich family from the Nazi gas chambers. A photo from that time shows little Marcell in shorts and sandals standing next to his parents and looking exceptionally happy. His mother, wearing a headscarf and smiling shyly into the camera, is standing in the middle. His father is wearing glasses, a white shirt, and white shorts. A man is seen hugging a crying child in the background. Almost all of the ship's passengers were destitute Jews.

The *Monviso,* however, did not get very far. It had just crossed the Straits of Gibraltar and started heading south when it was stopped off the Moroccan coast near Casablanca. Officials refused to let the ship continue and detained the refugees. Marc Rich and his family were initially held for a few days on the freighter before being interned in a refugee camp in Azemour, south of Casablanca. Their dream of finding a new life in Australia, far away and safe from the Nazis, abruptly fell apart.

Three months went by, and then four. The longer they were interned in the camp, the less likely it was that the Rich family would be set free.

It was a traumatic experience for Marc to be held prisoner, guarded by grim policemen. He could sense his father's helplessness.

The family was finally saved by three skills possessed by Marc's father. David could speak German, Yiddish, and French, which made him a sought-after translator in the camp. His down-to-earth, determined approach won the trust of his fellow internees, who elected him as their representative. Most important, this position enabled him to make contacts among the Moroccan authorities, who accepted him as an intermediary. He consequently managed to achieve a freedom of movement that he would not otherwise have enjoyed as an internee. He was allowed to travel to Casablanca regularly in order to negotiate with officials and was finally permitted to contact his sister, who had moved to the USA some years before. She worked for a Christian organization, which granted her access to U.S. Secretary of State Cordell Hull in Washington.

This contact turned out to be the Reich family's ticket to freedom. The sister managed to obtain visas permitting her brother and his family to enter the United States. Instead of traveling to Australia as planned, the Reich family was unexpectedly allowed to go to America, a country that had strictly limited immigration when it passed the 1924 Immigration Act. Instead of traveling below decks on an oily freighter, the family was now booked on a regular passenger ship. The SS *Serpa Pinto* was "nice and comfortable," recalls Marc Rich.

"We Lost Everything, but We Survived"

One spring day in 1941, months before Pearl Harbor, the American entry into the war, and the Babi Yar massacre, a small Jewish boy from Antwerp stood at the railing of an oceangoing steamship.[7] He looked at the Statue of Liberty and the skyline of New York in excitement. He had never seen a skyscraper before and could not speak a single word of English. A twist of fate had ensured that Marcell David Reich was allowed to enter the United States. There were two reasons for his survival: first, an accumulation of what were in themselves unfortunate events, and second, the foresight and skill of his father. "We lost everything," says Marc Rich, "but we survived." It was the greatest success—certainly the most important one—of David Reich's life. At the time, it was the very definition of success for European Jews: survival. Only one in ten Jews survived the persecution in Galicia, where the Reich family once lived. If David Reich had not moved first from Przemyśl to Frankfurt, then on to Antwerp, before fleeing to Marseille, his chances of survival would have been slim. As it turned out, the Reichs were now lucky survivors in the Promised Land.

Marcell Reich, alias Marc Rich, would always retain the mentality of a survivor and refugee; he would always be "different." His determination to succeed is rooted in this mentality, as well as his feelings of uprootedness. This determination is further strengthened by his experience as a Jew living in the Diaspora, as well as by the fact that he was an only child. Research has revealed that only children score significantly better in achievement motivation and personal adjustment than siblings.[8]

A dossier compiled by the U.S. Marshals Service on Marc Rich contains a strange piece of information stating that the Reich family apparently moved directly from the steamship SS *Serpa Pinto* to Manhattan's exclusive Fifth Avenue. In reality Rich initially lived with his parents at his aunt's house, the same aunt who had secured their visa. She lived in Crestwood, New York, a neighborhood in Yonkers where there was a substantial Jewish community. They then embarked upon an odyssey that lasted years. The family first moved to Philadelphia before moving on to Kansas City and back to New York, this time to Queens, and finally ending up in Manhattan.

"He Was Small, He Had an Accent, and He Was Jewish"

Marc Rich recalls that he attended twelve different schools in twelve years. This fact made it even more difficult for him, as a refugee and an only child, to find friends. He remained a loner who was left to his own devices, a force of habit that developed with time into a characteristic. Rich would always be an outsider, someone who neither belonged to the establishment nor wanted to. He was someone with a nothing-gets-me-down attitude who had something to prove. "You cry a little and then you move on," he replies when asked how he deals with defeat.

In February 1943 the Reich family changed their name to the more American-sounding Rich—and Marcell was henceforth known as Marc. However, the Riches were still Europeans at home, where they mainly spoke French and German with each other. A year later they moved to 4404 Holly Street in Kansas City, Missouri. They lived in a cramped apartment on the second floor of a brick building situated in a fairly unglamorous neighborhood in the south of the city. The Rich family became American citizens on February 14, 1947. For the first time since fleeing from Galicia, they had a real home.

The few classmates who remember him in Kansas City recall that Marc Rich was an unobtrusive, quiet boy who participated very little in social activities. The family mainly kept to itself. Marc attended the E. F. Swinney Elementary School, Westport Junior High School, and finally Southwest High School. He took classes in Hebrew in the evenings and on weekends. He appears in the class photo of the 1949–50 Southwest High School yearbook but is not listed as belonging to any clubs or sports teams. One classmate, Elaine Fox, says, "I remember he was small, he was quiet and he had lots of black, wavy hair. I think one of the reasons he was quiet was because he was different. He had an accent and he was Jewish."[9]

He was the "quietest kid in Camp Osceola," recalls author Calvin Trillin, who shared a tent with Marc Rich in the Missouri Ozarks in 1949. Rich would later perfect the strategy of keeping a low profile and being discreet. Trillin (who unlike Rich has made it into the school's Hall of Fame) was impressed that Rich spoke more languages than any other Boy Scout in the camp. Incidentally, the two tentmates did not discuss crude oil prices or arbitrage deals around the campfire. "If a reporter asked me whether Marc Rich ever cornered the market in any commodities at Osceola . . . , I would know that the only serious commodity at Camp Osceola was something called Chigger Rid, which sometimes stopped the itching of chigger bites, although not usually."[10]

David Rich ran the Petty Gem Shop, a jewelry store he had opened in 1946. Instead of playing with other children, eleven-year-old Marc hung around and helped out in his father's shop. "I did everything and anything. I put price tags on the jewelry and helped to clean and sell it." The wheeling and dealing, the bargaining and selling appealed to him. It was there, in his father's little shop on East Eleventh Street in Kansas City, that he started to develop an interest in business.

Business was good; indeed, it was so good that David Rich expanded into wholesale trading and set up Rich Merchandising. He was a typical trader, always full of ideas and always on the lookout for new business. René Trau, Marc Rich's cousin in Antwerp, recalls when his uncle David came to visit shortly after the war. "He was full of business ideas; import toy cars, export cosmetics, open banks in Bolivia." He sold precious stones, car parts, burlap bags, and tobacco. Through trading burlap bags he made contacts in South America, especially Bolivia, where the bags were used for packing tin concentrate, potatoes, or sugar. He frequently flew to La Paz, the capital of a country torn apart by inner conflicts, civil wars, and revolutions. David Rich joined with partners in setting up Sidec Overseas (which exported agricultural products to the United States), a travel agency, and, in the late 1950s, the American Bolivian Bank, the country's leading private bank.

His Biggest Influence

"My father had a knack for success and an uncompromising work ethic," says Marc Rich, and the admiration can still be heard in his voice. Thanks to his father's increased income, they were able to move out of the cramped apartment and buy a redbrick house at 429 East Seventy-second Street in the late 1940s. It cost $18,000 at the time (approximately $160,000 in today's money).[11] David Rich soon received a call from Eric

"Maxie" Korngold, a distant cousin from the Bronx. Aware of David's experience dealing in burlap bags, he suggested that he should start working for the Melrose Bag & Burlap Company. The Rich family moved to Forest Hills in Queens, a neighborhood with a traditionally large Jewish population.

Within a few years the company had been transformed into a trading concern, and it later set up headquarters on Manhattan's exclusive Sutton Place. Its main activity was importing Bengali jute to be used in the manufacture of burlap bags. David Rich once more demonstrated his perfect sense of timing, for the early 1950s was the best time to invest in jute: Troops from Communist North Korea crossed the 38th parallel into South Korea on June 25, 1950, thus marking the beginning of the Korean War. The United States and fifteen other foreign nations intervened with UN approval in order to repel the aggressors. The three-year war offered David Rich a stroke of luck. The army needed a large quantity of burlap for making sandbags, and demand outweighed supply. The Melrose Bag & Burlap Company hit the jackpot when it became a prime defense contractor.

Marc Rich worked in his father's office before and after school. The booming burlap business taught the teenager two lessons: Products can be sold for a better price when there is a shortage, and crises and wars can also offer business opportunities. Rich says his father gave him security when he needed it most, whether he was fleeing from Europe, in the Moroccan internment camp, or in the new and unknown world of the United States. His father was to remain his lifelong role model. Marc would always emulate him. He wanted to prove that he had really made it, even when he had already earned hundreds of millions of dollars. The desire to make his father proud would always be one of the driving forces in Marc Rich's life.

He also never forgot how his father achieved his success. He made contacts, established trust, worked hard, was reliable, and adjusted quickly to changing circumstances, and he had no qualms about seizing a business opportunity when he found one.

Thanks to the family's increasing prosperity, Marc Rich was able to leave Forest Hills High School and attend a private school in Manhattan. He presided over the French club at the private Rhodes Preparatory School, located at 11 West Fifty-fourth Street—a school that was later attended by Dan Brown, James Caan, and Robert De Niro. Rich graduated early in 1952, having skipped a year. At the age of eighteen he made a note of his dream job in his high school yearbook: business. His 1952 report card describes him as "purposeful," "actively creative," "strongly controlling," "deeply and generally concerned," "assumes much responsibility," and "exceptionally stable."[12]

He enrolled at New York University in fall 1952 to study marketing but soon realized that he wanted practical experience rather than theoretical learning. A German Jewish acquaintance of his father's secured him a job interview at Philipp Brothers, then the world's largest trader in raw materials. Rich could not have known that Philipp Brothers would provide him with what very few people ever succeed in finding: his vocation.

4

The AMERICAN DREAM

Marc Rich had mixed feelings when he walked into Philipp Brothers headquarters for the first time in spring 1954. The building was situated on Pine Street, which runs parallel to Wall Street in Manhattan's financial district. It was the year in which the French would lose the pivotal battle of Dien Bien Phu in Vietnam, and President Dwight D. Eisenhower would announce his domino theory, warning against a Communist takeover of power in Southeast Asia. The Korean War had ended the previous July with the permanent partition of the country.

Rich had been reluctant to accept an apprenticeship at the world's largest and most highly regarded commodities trading company. He had just turned nineteen when he began working in the mailroom for forty dollars per week. "I'm a postboy now. This is beneath my dignity," he thought to himself when he was assigned the tedious task of sorting telex messages. "After all, I have a high school diploma, and I went to university." He had no alternative. Anybody who wanted to work at Philipp Brothers began in the mailroom, regardless of whether he had only attended elementary school or had graduated from college. There was very little indication on that spring morning that Marc Rich would soon become one of the most successful university dropouts of all time.

The tried and tested German tradition of the apprenticeship has hardly changed since the Middle Ages. The *Lehrling* (apprentice) is taught the trade from scratch by his experienced *Meister* (master), and in return for this on-the-job training he works for a modest wage. In times gone by the apprentice was effectively a member of the master's family, with the older man taking on the role of guardian or father figure for the younger.

"It's a family business" was how one veteran trader explained the advantages of the traditional system to me. "Who gives a damn about diplomas? We all knew each other. The boss at the top knew the youngest apprentice. You quickly got to know who had particular strengths and weaknesses, and who had a talent for what. Your father or a family friend could get you in through the door, but then you had to prove that you were good, in fact even better than the others. There was no patronage system that would let a dud rise up through the ranks; it was all based on your own performance."

Philipp Brothers functioned according to this principle. The company was founded by the German brothers Oscar and Julius Philipp, who began trading metals in Hamburg in 1901. Oscar Philipp set up a branch of the business in London in 1909, and in 1914 a cousin risked the move across the Atlantic to the United States. The company headquarters was later moved to New York in the wake of the world wars, and it was not long before Philipp Brothers became the largest commodities trading company in the world.

A Jewish Tradition

European Jews—particularly German Jews such as Oscar and Julius Philipp—had dominated the trade in metals since the nineteenth century. For centuries Jews in Europe had suffered from discrimination. They were unable to become farmers, as they were forbidden from owning land. As they were excluded from the craft guilds, they were unable to become craftsmen. The Catholic Lateran Council of 1215 stated that Jews were barred from taking on official functions. In other words, Jews were not allowed to carry out the most important economic activities of the time. They were, however, permitted to perform one function that was proscribed for medieval Christians: making loans with interest.

Thus the Jews became moneylenders and traders in the absence of any other options. "That is the malice of the anti-Semites," a strictly devout commodities trader explained to me. "We were forced into trading, and now we are denounced as the greedy Jews, who only care about money." Trading had one further, sad advantage for the Jews, the trader said. "If you don't have land, a farm, or a fixed profession, you can pack quickly if someone comes along tomorrow to send you away, if they've really got it in for you." If it starts again.

Gradually, those who were more successful started importing and exporting precious metals and stones, frequently over large distances. The demand for metals and other commodities from distant countries increased along with the growth of industrialization in the eighteenth and nineteenth centuries. This meant that the metal trading business was primarily in Jewish hands because Jews had the necessary know-how and international connections. Jews were also well represented in the important traditional mining regions, which were mainly situated in German-speaking Central Europe, in eastern Germany, Bohemia, Poland, Austria, and Hungary.

It is one of the ironies of history that the persecution and expulsion of the Jews is what made such an efficient trading community possible. King Edward I of England expelled the Jews in 1290, and the French monarchs Philip IV and Charles VI chased them from fourteenth-century France. The mass murder of Jews reached a high point with the pogroms in Germany and Central Europe between 1347 and 1353 at a time when the Black Death was raging across the Continent. Sephardic Jews were forced to leave Spain in 1492. By the onset of the modern era, the Jewish Diaspora was greater than that of any other people. The scattered

Jews had a trading tradition that was second to none and sufficient confidence to enable trade over large distances and periods of time. It was a society that succeeded in continually renewing itself from within. Its members had known each other for eons, enjoyed family and religious ties, and shared the same values and work ethic. This degree of social control created a sense of loyalty and trust that a business deal would be conducted honestly and reliably.

Any economic network is largely dependent on trust if it is to function well. As economists put it, a high degree of trust lowers the costs of transactions and compensates for a lack of information. According to the American philosopher Francis Fukuyama, trust is a key prerequisite for prosperity.[1] It will become apparent in chapter 7 that trust was to be one of Rich's secrets to success.

When Rich joined the company in 1954, Philipp Brothers still essentially consisted of a tightly knit group of German-Jewish immigrants. The names of the major players who were active in the company provided an indication of their heritage: Ludwig Jesselson, Adolfo Blum, and Henry Rothschild. They were all pioneers of economic globalization who helped write trading history. These men became mentors to Rich, whose family was known in trading circles and whose father came from the tragedy that was Germany—just as they did. He had the best teachers in the business. Most important, Rich had the strength of will and the patience to listen, observe, and learn.

The First Trade

The mailroom may have initially appeared to be a dull place, but an ambitious, clever trainee was able to pick up a lot about trading there. Telex messages containing fascinating information arrived from all over the world. Who's buying? Who's selling? From where to where? At what price? What's the margin? It was a crash course in pricing strategies. One metal trader from Rich's early years at Philipp Brothers recalls that he "was just an amazingly fast student. You'd teach him something, and he'd learn it the first time—no questions asked."[2] Accustomed as the traders were to long working hours and weekends full of overtime, they were struck by the young man's talent and commitment. The word was soon out that Rich was a hard worker, a reputation not easily acquired in such circles. "I was working hard and long hours," remembers Rich, who only had one thing on his mind at that point: to get out of the mailroom and start trading. "My bosses took notice and gave me more challenging work. The real learning came after the mailroom, in the traffic."

After a few months in the mailroom, the traffic department was the second stage for all apprentices in the learning-by-doing system at Philipp Brothers. Rich recalls how he started off by shadowing the traffic manager. He was later sent to the docks by himself to supervise the goods being unloaded, inspect the weight and quality, and check the invoices. He finally began to handle the trading transactions. "I handled shipments of merchandise and metals, covered insurance, and arranged for payments with letters of credit," recalls Rich.

So Rich learned how to become a commodities trader from the ground up. After two years he became a junior trader, and Henry Rothschild soon took him under his wing. Rothschild, who was not a member of the banking family, was born in Bochum, Germany, entered the commodities business when he was sixteen, and had previously done business with Marc Rich's father. He is described as a shy, taciturn, and quick-thinking analyst. The master and apprentice were kindred spirits when it came to their similar ways of thinking.

Rothschild was an extremely demanding boss who was responsible for the South American market at Philipp Brothers and for developing the firm's expanding network in Europe. He increasingly delegated the day-to-day business to Rich, who effectively became his assistant. "I was fascinated by the size of the market," explains Rich. "Take oil or aluminum. You can find those materials in almost any product you touch. The whole world needs them, from east to west and north to south." It was a fascination that would remain. The first commodity he personally traded was Bolivian tin.

To Create a Market

Rich was soon being referred to as a wunderkind at Philipp Brothers. "From the beginning he was an astute and very knowledgeable trader," says one eyewitness. There was one main reason for his success—he had specialized in a niche product, one that in the mid-1950s was only traded in minute quantities: mercury.

Talk to commodities traders and sooner or later you will hear an expression that is inevitably spoken in a tone of reverence: "to create a market." It is a trader's lifelong goal to match producer with consumer and find a buyer for a commodity that has previously only been traded very little. An exceptional commodities trader requires one skill above all else in order to create a new market for a commodity: the capacity to analyze a situation thoroughly and recognize trends quicker than the competition. Who is sitting on a commodity without recognizing its complete potential? How do technological developments or political events such as wars affect the demand for commodities? Crude oil, to take an example, was processed for lamp oil and tar for centuries before its monetary and strategic value was changed drastically by the invention of the gasoline engine in the late nineteenth century.

Many good commodities traders have never succeeded in creating a market, yet Rich managed to do so while he was still a junior trader. It was a coup he pulled off time and again, most resoundingly with crude oil. One of his greatest talents was seeing what others failed to see. "He is a visionary," Rich's friend and former employee Isaac Querub told me. In the opinion of one trader who worked with him in Africa, "Marc Rich was a man of genius." Ursula Santo Domingo adds, "He sees things before others even begin to think about them." "To see the opportunity is the most important thing as a trader," Rich told me. We spoke about the importance of contacts in this business—access to the "man with the key," as the decision makers are so quaintly called in Africa. Rich's answer surprised me. "The analysis is more important than the relationships," he said.

Rich first created a new market for a commodity in the mid-1950s. He began to develop an interest in mercury when he was still only twenty-one years old. At the time mercury was used predominantly in thermometers, batteries, and detonators; trading was consequently limited, and the prices were low. Rich searched for available mercury with a determination that impressed his colleagues. Having analyzed the global political situation, he had come to the conclusion that mercury would soon be in great demand, which meant that there was business to be made.

The cold war was on the verge of escalating in the mid-1950s. The Communists, led by Mao Tse-tung, had seized control in China in 1949. The Korean War had erupted in 1950 and continued until the summer of 1953. In June 1953 Soviet troops had crushed an uprising in East Germany. The year 1956 saw the Suez Crisis, when Gamal Abdel Nasser of Egypt nationalized the Suez Canal and was opposed by Great Britain, France, and Israel. The Soviet Red Army marched into Hungary in the same year to defeat the popular uprising against the Soviet-backed government.

When Rich started trading in mercury, all the indications were pointing to war. "He called any producer who had the slightest connection to mercury in order to buy the stuff," remembers a colleague. He located his first source at the Spanish mining company Consejo de Administración de las Minas de Almadén y Arrayanes, which is known as Mayasa today. Before long he had established good relationships with producers and consumers and was regarded as an expert in the mercury trade.

Meanwhile, the demand for the commodity soared. The United States government, with Republican President Dwight D. Eisenhower at the helm, commenced a rearmament program that saw the air force and army increasing their stocks of mercury by over 50 percent. The United States bought commodities in huge amounts. Mercury had only been used for batteries since the mid-1940s, but now the market was booming. Due to their longer life spans, mercury batteries were mainly used in military equipment such as walkie-talkies, metal detectors, and other electronic devices.

Sensitive Assignments

Rich was now the man to see when it came to mercury. It was his first business coup, and it earned significant profits for Philipp Brothers. The young dealer had not been at Philipp Brothers very long, yet this success strengthened his position enormously within the company. It was proof to his superiors that he had the talent to spot opportunities, the courage to grasp them, the patience to successfully conclude a deal, and enough common sense to avoid excessive risks.

When the manager of the Bolivian office of Philipp Brothers had to travel back to England because his mother was having an operation, it was immediately clear who would replace him. Henry Rothschild sent Rich for six months to the same South American country where David Rich had also done business. Bolivia was a dangerous place known for its political and economic instability. A nationalistic movement had brought about a revolution in 1952, and the country's large mines had subsequently been nationalized. The South American country has been an important source of silver, tin, and tungsten since the sixteenth century. Rich not only learned perfect Spanish in La Paz, Bolivia, he also picked up the essentials of doing business in politically volatile countries. He was evidently very adept in his dealings. A partner at the time relates how he always kept the risks under control und managed to establish good contacts thanks to his quiet, modest style.

Following his success in Bolivia, Philipp Brothers sent its rising star to South Africa for the first time in 1958. At that point the country was still in the Commonwealth, and the trade boycott against the apartheid regime had not yet begun. It was a journey to his first defeat. Rich thrashed out the details of the sale of a manganese ore mine for months on end, and he remembers the negotiations as being "very tedious, very long." In the end, after six months of negotiating, "I couldn't conclude the purchase. I had to come home with empty hands." He did not hear a single word of criticism from his mentors Rothschild and Jesselson. They both knew that Rich would profit from the experience.

Despite this single setback, he had clearly demonstrated his capacity for sensitive assignments. He had proved that he could stay calm in chaotic situations. He was persistent and innovative without ever becoming foolhardy. More than anything else, he was enterprising and resourceful. Those were exactly the qualities that Philipp Brothers was counting on in early 1959. A bearded revolutionary was in the process of rewriting history in Cuba. Philipp Brothers, which had enjoyed close business ties with the Batista regime, was not amused. It needed a troubleshooter.

Fidel Castro's Cuban Revolution

Ernesto "Che" Guevara and his fellow rebels marched into Santa Clara on New Year's Eve 1958. The loss of the last government-held town before Havana sent a signal to the Cuban dictator Fulgencio Batista, who fled to the Dominican Republic that night with a handful of his henchmen. Fidel Castro's revolutionary forces entered Havana on January 8, 1959, after more than two years of guerrilla fighting.

The reaction from the country was overwhelmingly positive, especially among the *campesinos*, the subsistence-level farmers. The army and police went over to the rebels within hours. Calm returned to Havana twenty-four hours after the takeover. Castro and his comrades in arms were welcomed by jubilant crowds. While the people had become ever poorer, the Batista clique had become wealthy by exploiting the country and its natural resources. Estimates put the dictator's fortune at dozens of millions of dollars. Batista had come to power in 1933 aided by the United States, which had supported his military dictatorship with a mutual assistance pact. The U.S. government only withdrew its backing when the Batista regime was in its death throes, unable to guarantee the economic stability of the country any longer.

Fidel Castro and Che Guevara, who would later become Cuba's minister of industry, embarked upon a program of nationalization of mines and industries—a development that came as a serious shock to Philipp Brothers. Although the company saw itself essentially as a trading corporation with no industrial infrastructure or investments, it had begun to prefinance production in several countries. In return it was rewarded with exclusive, long-term contracts. It was a policy that Marc Rich would later hone to perfection. (See Chapter 14.)

The revolution's leaders froze one such loan that Philipp Brothers had made to Cuba—a substantial loan of $1.2 million for a pyrite mine. To put it in context, Philipp Brothers recorded $6 million in pretax profit in 1959. What was to be done? Rothschild immediately suggested sending his young assistant Marc Rich to Havana. The company had a tradition of placing significant trust in young employees and assigning them to extremely difficult tasks. Rich was familiar with the Latin American mentality and by now spoke fluent Spanish.

So the twenty-four-year-old Rich flew to Havana shortly after the revolution in order to negotiate with the new regime. The ensuing talks were to drag on for six months. His negotiating style was determined yet civil. He used all the tricks in the wily trader's book. He knew that he had to find a solution that was agreeable to both sides. "It's only a good deal when the two signatories are laughing together at the table. That's the only way a partnership can have any future. Otherwise it's the only deal you'll make," he explained to me.

Rich analyzed the situation. What did Castro and his government need most of all? They needed hard currency. They needed international contacts. They needed jobs. Castro must want to continue production at the pyrite mine, which would both ensure jobs and bring currency into the country. Rich thus devised a creative solution that initially appeared foolhardy. "I offered to inject fresh money," he tells me on a ski lift between descents in St. Moritz. "The Cubans liked the idea. It allowed them to continue with the pyrite mine. I was able to recover the entire amount of our initial investment."

Castro aroused a great deal of sympathy at the start of the revolution, even in the United States. In contrast to Che Guevara, whom Rich remembers as "energetic and lively," he did not behave like an orthodox Marxist or a friend of the Communist Soviet Union. Yet the regime soon revealed its ideological inflexibility. Rich grew increasingly skeptical as he witnessed political developments in Cuba with his own eyes. "I don't understand why they became Communists," he tells me on the ski lift. "OK, they wanted to change what the corrupt Batista regime had done, but I saw how the Communists took over everything with an iron fist. There was virtually no opposition; people just accepted it." He shakes his head in disbelief and repeats, "I don't understand how they got taken in by Communism. It was so bad for people."

"Cuba really put Marc Rich to the test," an acquaintance told me. "What can he do, what can't he do. Does he have ideas? Is he creative? Can he handle the pressure?" Rich's critics place the emphasis elsewhere. Biographer A. Craig Copetas quotes an anonymous "former traffic manager" who was supposed to have said, "Marc cut his teeth in Havana, and the experience shaped his character because it taught him that being illegal was okay under certain conditions."[3]

Despite the embargo, Rich never stopped trading with the Cuban regime. The Cohiba cigars he smokes with such pleasure are not the only evidence of this. Rich flew regularly to Havana until the February 1962 trade embargo. Cuban business was subsequently conducted via the Madrid office. The most important raw materials Rich traded with Cuba up to the mid-1990s were initially pyrite and copper. These were followed by manganese ore—important for steel production—and nickel. His company later bought sugar from Cuba and delivered Venezuelan or Russian oil. Rich once even chartered the *Monviso,* the same freighter on which he had escaped with his parents from France to Morocco, to transport pyrite from Cuba to Italy. In 1991 a Cuban defector claimed that Rich's company had conducted negotiations with Fidel Castro's son about mining uranium in Cuba.[4] Rich denies this claim and maintains the talks revolved solely around lead and zinc deposits.

After Cuba, Rich was the man to watch at Philipp Brothers; he was the company's rising star. Over the next few years he moved around the globe, staying six months in India, six months in Amsterdam, always on the lookout for a deal as he traveled from Congo-Brazzaville to Senegal ("There wasn't a lot of business in Africa," he notes). It was the age before mass tourism, and flying was an exclusive and extremely expensive activity. Rich loved the travel, the independence, and the adventure. He loved sniffing out business opportunities. It was exactly the kind of lifestyle that Rich had yearned for as a young student. He needed a challenge. In 1964, Ludwig Jesselson, the head of Philipp Brothers, offered Rich, at the age of thirty, the position of Madrid office manager. Rich did not hesitate for a second.

Friends in Fascist Spain

Marc Rich is a reserved, levelheaded man. Like every good trader, he has his emotions tightly under control. He keeps his feelings to himself and does not indulge in excessive enthusiasm. Yet when he speaks of Spain he sounds like a teenager recalling his first sweetheart. It was love at first sight, and Rich finally felt as if he were in his element. He felt an instant attraction to the Spanish way of life, which still influences his own lifestyle. He likes eating lunch in the afternoon and dinner late in the evening. "I liked Spain so much that I became Spanish," he tells me in his chalet in St. Moritz. "It's a wonderful country. You have the desert, mountains, green flatlands, the sea all around, music, arts, everything."

While he spends much of the winter on the pistes of St. Moritz, in summer he is frequently drawn to his sumptuous property in Marbella. The $9.5 million villa was built in Moorish style by a student of Frank Lloyd Wright. The Moroccan coast is visible on clear days. He fell in love with his future wife Denise in Spain, and two of his three daughters would be born there. Denise Rich told me that their happiest times were in Madrid. Spanish is still one of the family's languages. "When we left Spain I didn't want my daughters to lose Spanish, so we continued to speak the language," he told me. He still employs Spanish-speaking domestic staff.

A painting by the Spanish painter Antonio Quirós (1912–84) hangs in Rich's Swiss office. He initially saw it in the first apartment he rented in Madrid in 1964, and he liked it so much that he bought it. The apartment was in the Torre de Madrid, at the time the tallest building in Europe. The Philipp Brothers offices were in the same building. Rich had chosen the location carefully. It meant that he lost no time traveling to work and could be in the office whenever necessary.

"We worked very, very hard. Marc's capacity for work is incredible," recalls Ursula Santo Domingo. She first met him forty-five years ago, after he had advertised in the newspaper for a secretary. "He invited me to an interview on a Saturday. The whole company was empty. Not a soul was there except Marc Rich. I later found out that he worked every Saturday, and every Sunday, too. He thinks about business twenty-four hours a day." Fifteen-hour days beginning at 7:00 A.M. and ending at 10:00 P.M. were the rule rather than the exception. As a joke, Rich would greet colleagues who arrived for work at 8.30 A.M. with a casual "Good afternoon."

Spain in 1964 was an exciting place to be. The country had been ruled with an iron fist by Generalissimo Francisco Franco's fascist government since the end of the Spanish Civil War in 1939. Spain remained politically and economically isolated until 1955 and was even denied membership in the United Nations. The peninsula became strategically important during the cold war thanks to its proximity to the Strait of Gibraltar. The 1960s brought an unexpected economic boom that catapulted Spain from a predominantly rural country to an open, modern industrial society. The "Spanish miracle" was sparked by radical liberal economic reforms and aided by massive public investment in infrastructure, while technocrats supplanted the old fascist Falangists in the government.

One of these technocrats was Alfredo Santos Blanco, a forty-year-old professor of economics employed at the Ministry of Industry. He became of one Rich's most important contacts and an excellent opener of doors. "Through my friendship with Alfredo I was able to have many more connections," Rich tells me. When Rich first met Santos Blanco he was the president of Minas de Almadén y Arrayanes, the state-run cinnabar, or mercury ore, mines Rich had done business with before. The largest cinnabar reserves in the world were situated near Almadén, and it had been mined since ancient times for its mercury content. The Fuggers, the famous German banking and trading dynasty, owned the concession for the mines in the sixteenth and seventeenth centuries. Today the mines are virtually exhausted. Santos Blanco was of enormous importance for Rich's career, as the next chapter will show. Without him, Rich would not have been so successful at such an early stage.

The fact that the Jewish businessman and the ultra-Catholic professor should become friends remains one of the paradoxes in Marc Rich's life. It is certainly surprising that Rich had such a great love for fascist Spain. Francisco Franco owed his victory in the Spanish Civil War mainly to support from Nazi Germany. Although Spain remained officially neutral during World War II, it openly sympathized with Adolf Hitler's National Socialists and permitted German submarines and warplanes to be resupplied in Spain. Franco claimed to be a friend of the Arab nations, and he neither recognized Israel nor strived for diplomatic relations. He permitted the Palestine Liberation Organization (PLO) to open an office in Madrid in 1974. Israel was not recognized by Spain until 1986.

Even though he enjoyed very close connections to Israel, Rich was apparently not concerned about Franco's policies. "Marc didn't care about it," one old friend in Spain who worked with Rich at the time told me. "He didn't care about politics, only about business and making money. This is one of Marc's strengths." This type of neutrality has proved to be an advantage to Rich's success in business, although some might label his attitude amoral.

In the 1960s Rich was, as the Spanish friend told me, "extremely successful in Spain." The Philipp Brothers office in Madrid at the time controlled what we would now call the emerging markets. South America, including a Cuba subject to the American embargo, was one such market. Africa, which was going through a wave of decolonization in the late 1950s and early 1960s, was another. Emerging markets in Africa included Congo, Algeria, and Nigeria, countries rich in natural resources that were to play a special role in Rich's business dealings. Even the Middle East, not yet of great significance for Philipp Brothers, was overseen from Madrid. "The difficult regions were handled by Madrid," one participant told me. They included many areas of conflict, new countries without established structures, and inexperienced regions lacking mercantile know-how. Above all, they were all countries with deposits of every natural resource to be found under the earth. They were also countries with an increasing awareness of the value of their natural resources.

American Hero

The 1960s was one of the twentieth century's greatest periods of expansion for commodities traders. Economies were booming in Europe, the United States, and Asia. The decade saw a rapid development of technologies that culminated in the first moon landing in 1969. There was a tremendous spirit of optimism all over the world.

Rich knew the importance of seizing opportunity when it presented itself. He transformed Madrid into one of the most powerful offices in the company. That was not least thanks to the team of hungry young employees he had hired. "Marc didn't care about your origins or your education," I was told by a Spaniard who had been hired by Rich and stuck with him through thick and thin. "He was looking for people ready to work, ready to travel, ready to be loyal to the company, ready to earn money." They traveled to up-and-coming third world countries that were on the lookout to sell commodities in exchange for much-needed hard currency. "It was a very good experience because in Spain we traded everything from alumina to zinc," Rich tells me. "I got experience with all the commodities, and I enjoyed it."

By the end of the 1960s, Marc Rich had made it. From his humble origins as a child refugee from the Nazis, he had risen through the ranks of society by hard work. He became one of the most influential office managers at one of the world's largest commodities traders. Now he was taken seriously as a businessman by fascist ministers in Spain and Cuban revolutionaries alike.

Only in the United States could such a career have ever been possible. Marc Rich was living the American dream. He embodied deeply held American values such as courage, persistence, risk-taking, team spirit, and, of course, hard work. The United States was proud of its successful son. There was great respect for the American who had snatched the commodities trade from the Europeans.

European countries had dominated world trade in raw materials since the late Middle Ages. The northern Italian city-states of Venice and Genoa dominated trade before giving way to the Portuguese and Spanish from the fifteenth century onward. Beginning in the seventeenth century, it was the Dutch trading fleets that ruled the waves until the arrival of the British. Before World War I, over 60 percent of world trade was still in European hands.[5] Trade became increasingly American, not least thanks to companies such as Philipp Brothers and traders such as Marc Rich. Rich was soon deemed a historically significant figure and labeled "a genius in the formerly European dominated metals market."[6]

The trade in metals was only the start. The real revolution began with crude oil.

5

The CRUDE AWAKENING

The revolution started as revolutions usually do—quietly and unspectacularly. Alan Flacks, who directed a small office in Milan for Philipp Brothers, flew to Tunis in the summer of 1969. He had heard by chance that Tunisia was interested in selling its oil to an independent trader for the first time. Only five years had passed since oil had been discovered in Tunisia, which was one of the first of the African nations to achieve independence. Now the country was auctioning twenty-five thousand metric tons of crude oil for immediate delivery. Flacks purchased the oil and sold it to an Italian refinery. He had already found a willing buyer when he bought the oil, making the trade a risk-free, fast-profit deal. Traders call such deals "back-to-back trades." The dealer purchases a commodity and immediately sells it on to a prearranged buyer.

Although Marc Rich was thrilled when he got word of the deal in Madrid, he was at the same time deeply disappointed that it was Flacks who had managed to bring off the deal and not him. For quite some time, Rich had been trying to find a means of trading oil using Philipp Brothers' worldwide organization. At that time oil was never traded on the open market, which meant that oil was not a commodity in the classical sense. He first began thinking of openly trading oil during the Six-Day War in June 1967. Egypt's President Nasser had disrupted Israeli shipping when he ordered the blockade of the Gulf of Aqaba in May 1967. This cut off the port of Eilat from the rest of the world. Most of Israel's oil was imported through Eilat, which provided Israel's sole access to the Red Sea. When Egypt, Jordan, and Syria began massing troops at the Israeli border, Israel launched a daring preemptive strike. On the morning of June 5, Israeli jets attacked the opposing air forces, successfully destroying all of the enemies' planes. Thanks to Israel's resulting air superiority, within only a few days its forces were able to occupy the Sinai Peninsula, the Golan Heights, the Gaza Strip, the West Bank, and East Jerusalem.

The World's First Oil Embargo

The Six-Day War produced the world's first oil embargo. Analysts had been discussing the "oil weapon" for years, and this weapon was now primed and ready for use. The most important Arab oil-producing nations—Algeria, Iraq, Kuwait, Libya, and Saudi Arabia—pledged to stop supplying oil to countries that were friendly to Israel: the United States, Great Britain, and to a certain extent Germany, which had established diplomatic relations with Israel in May 1965. The embargo might have been effective, as three-fourths of Western European oil demand was met by imports from the Middle East and North Africa.[1]

Yet the embargo was an ineffective weapon. The United States, Great Britain, and Germany met their import shortages with oil from non-Arab sources. Venezuela increased production, as did Iran and Indonesia. The loss of income meant that the real losers were actually the boycott's organizers. Within two months after the oil embargo had been announced, they resumed deliveries to the affected countries. However, the Egyptians continued to block the Suez Canal, through which the majority of the oil from the Persian Gulf destined for Europe passed, until 1975. The paradoxical effect of the two-month boycott was that, due to increased production, there was now a greater supply of oil than there was demand for it.

This state of affairs sounded like a wonderful opportunity to a resourceful trader like Marc Rich, and while he was in Spain he realized that there was money to be made in trading oil. He had already discussed the idea with Alfredo Santos Blanco, his economist friend who worked in the Spanish ministry of labor. Fascist Spain, which did not recognize Israel, maintained excellent relations with the oil-rich Arab world. Rich was determined to take advantage of this special situation, but then along came Alan Flacks in 1969 and threatened to steal this new market from under his nose. Rich was lucky in that Philipp Brothers was not organized along a strict set of rules—there was no "first come, first served" rule, for example. Whoever had better ideas, better contacts, or just better luck was the one who could make the deals. Displaying the same persistence and determination that would always set him apart from other traders, Rich set out to take on the oil business.

"Oil was a product that was moved in huge quantities and had a big value, but it hadn't been traded in a transparent and competitive market. I just thought it should be possible to trade oil despite the Seven Sisters," Rich told me. "If I see a situation in the market and it makes sense to me, then I do something about it."

The Seven Sisters

"The Seven Sisters" was the nickname for the seven companies that dominated the world's international oil trade in the mid-twentieth century: the Americans Chevron, Esso (Standard Oil of New Jersey), Gulf, Mobil, and Texaco, British Petroleum, and the Anglo-Dutch Shell.[2] In the 1960s, the world of oil was quite different from what it is today. Oil was not traded according to free-market principles, and there was very little latitude for price dynamics. Oil-producing nations sold nearly all of their oil to the Seven Sisters at fixed prices agreed upon far in advance (up to two years), and only around 5 percent of crude oil was traded freely according to the laws of supply and demand. Whoever wanted to buy oil had to deal directly with the corporations. Only rarely did the major oil corporations trade on short notice on the open market—when they wanted to sell a temporary surplus or to correct an unexpected shortage, for example.

The Seven Sisters' domination of the global oil trade after the Second World War extended vertically as well as horizontally. They controlled every aspect of production and distribution, ranging from extraction at the well, refining, and transport to the gas stations where the oil was sold as gasoline. The Seven Sisters formed what economists call an oligopoly—a situation that exists when there are only a handful of suppliers that dominate the market. They were able to dictate prices independently of the forces of supply and demand. The Seven Sisters were primarily interested in securing long-term contracts at fixed prices. Such contracts allowed the oil oligopoly to control both oil prices and distribution more easily.

The Seven Sisters' dominance meant that the oil industry was under the tight control of American and European oil corporations. These companies controlled three-fourths of the oil that was not produced in the United States or in Communist countries.[3] Their profit margins were huge compared to those of other industries. It only cost 40¢ to produce a barrel (forty-two gallons) of oil and deliver it to the United States, but the Seven Sisters could demand prices of $2.50 a barrel or more of their buyers.[4]

The price for a barrel of oil remained more or less constant—$2.50 to $3 per barrel—from 1948 to 1970. It tended to rise slightly in times of crisis, such as during the 1950–53 Korean War or the 1967 Six-Day War. This situation must have been a great annoyance to the oil-producing nations, as the prices for industrial goods had increased considerably over the same period of time. Not only did the oil-producing nations receive a relatively low price for their oil, the money they received from their oil exports also declined in value when compared to their expenditure on imported goods. It was something of a paradox. The demand for oil had increased steadily since the Second World War, but when compared to the oil-producing nations' purchasing power, the price of oil from 1948 to 1970 actually sank by almost 40 percent. This meant the industrial nations were profiting from the low prices (or, in comparative terms, the falling prices) for oil and energy.

A Wave of Oil Nationalizations

The oil-producing nations attempted to break this trend and at the same time strengthen their hand against the oil companies. The countries of Iran, Iraq, Kuwait, Saudi Arabia, and Venezuela had already founded the Organization of the Petroleum Exporting Countries (OPEC) in 1960. They came together in order to counter the pressure exerted by the oil companies, who wanted to keep both the price of oil and the royalty payments as low as possible. In the early years, OPEC was committed to negotiating a larger share of the oil companies' profits for themselves as well as greater control over production quotas. In the 1960s OPEC called for wide-scale nationalization of the member states' oil fields, but the member states would do very little to realize these ideas over the next ten years. However, the situation suddenly exploded in the 1970s, and within a short period of time the entire oil trade had been shaken to its very foundation.

This radical break with the past had its roots in two important developments. In August 1971 President Richard Nixon abandoned the gold standard, whereupon the dollar immediately lost 20 to 40 percent of its value against most other currencies. As the global oil trade was based on dollars, this meant that the oil-producing nations were earning even less "real" income in terms of purchasing power. In effect, these countries had to spend more of the devalued dollars they had exchanged for oil to purchase goods on the international markets. Several important oil-producing countries now began nationalizing their domestic oil industries. The North African nation of Algeria was the first to do so, in 1971, and it was soon followed by neighboring Libya. The floodgates were opened when Iraq, one of the world's largest producers, nationalized the concessions belonging to British Petroleum, Royal Dutch Shell, the French Compagnie Française des Pétroles, Mobil, and Standard Oil of New Jersey (now Exxon) on June 1, 1972. Six months later OPEC pushed through a plan of gradual nationalization of all Western concessions in Kuwait, Qatar, Abu Dhabi, and Saudi Arabia, and in spring 1973 the Persian shah nationalized all of Iran's oil assets.[5]

Within only a few years the dynamics of power within the oil industry had been completely turned on their head—forever. Today, in 2009, the corporations that made up the Seven Sisters no longer control the global oil trade. There are now ten state oil companies that control three-fourths of global oil reserves.[6] The most important oil-producing companies are politically fragile states: Saudi Arabia (Saudi Aramco), Russia (Gazprom), and Iran (NIOC).

"I Was the Right Person at the Right Time"

In 1969 no one could have expected such a radical shakeup of the global oil trade, but the writing was on the wall for those who could read it. Developments in the oil market offered opportunities for those who were the first to recognize them and were willing to take the risks. As history has shown, times of upheaval and insecurity usually provide good pickings for commodities traders. An increase in insecurity and volatility within a commodities market goes hand in hand with an increasing demand for independent traders who can guarantee supplies for solid cash. These traders allow buyers to compensate for market fluctuations.

Alan Flacks was the first trader at Phillip Brothers to break into the oil trade, but he held back from taking these trades to the next step. He had no experience dealing with the particular problems inherent in the oil trade. The notion of taking risks was as foreign to him as it was for the entire company, and this idea was clearly reflected in the Philipp Brothers' German motto: *Besser gut schlafen, als gut essen.* It is better to sleep well than eat well. The principle was drummed into employees that it was better to avoid a lucrative deal if the risks involved were high enough that they might endanger the entire company.

In this respect, Marc Rich was more aggressive than his bosses, and it was this fear of risk, among other things, that would later lead Rich to leave Philipp Brothers in order to found his own company. "I was the right person in the right place at the right time," he told me, as if that were all there was to it. "I was working in a commodity trading house, and the oligopoly of the Seven Sisters was coming to a halt. Suddenly the world needed a new system of bringing the oil from the producing countries to the consuming countries, so that's exactly what I did."

Rich realized that if the oil-producing countries wished to break the dominance of the corporations, they would need independent traders like him. They simply did not have the means—the marketing know-how, the established distribution channels, contacts to the refineries— to market the oil themselves. Rich knew that he could offer all of these by utilizing Philipp Brothers' worldwide organization. He wanted to repeat the successes he had enjoyed trading mercury. He wanted to create a market.

Yet Rich had to deal with three important problems. First he had to get the oil. Then he had to find a buyer. The most difficult problem of them all was the delivery: How could he get the oil to the buyers? The handling and transportation of oil was much more complicated and expensive than transporting metals. Oil is a liquid with varying degrees of viscosity, and it can easily be lost as a result of evaporation or leakage. The physical characteristics of oil can change during transportation and according to temperature. Oil was also traded in huge quantities, and that meant one needed a lot of credit. Oil required special ships, and oil trades were conducted more quickly than other commodity trades. Whereas the time of delivery was not as crucial when it came to trading in baux-ite, manganese, or copper, time was of the essence when it came to the oil trade.

Every trader knows that the most important element of a deal is the execution of the trade. One of the world's most experienced traffic man-agers introduced me to the art of trade execution. Like many of my in-terviewees, he wished to remain anonymous. He even insisted that I leave the name of our meeting place out of this book. I wanted to know why he felt such an intense need for secrecy. "It's better for me and my business if no one knows who I am," he told me straight out.

"As a trader it is possible to close a fantastic deal," he said, "but it isn't worth anything if the execution goes wrong. Even worse: Every mistake can spell disaster. I've seen it all. For example, you might have a bad letter of credit that results in the cargo being delivered much later than planned or not at all. Or you might charter a ship and suddenly the ship is not allowed to enter the destination port. The deal would fall through, and you might lose millions or have to pay enormous demur-rage or storage fees, all because you didn't do your homework."

Pincus Green

If Rich wanted to get into the oil business with the goal of creating a free market, he would need an expert in trade execution. He knew he needed his own logistics system, and he knew immediately who was most qualified to set up such a system: Pincus "Pinky" Green. Green would soon become one of the most important people in Rich's life—his alter ego, so to speak. He had been working in the European headquarters of Philipp Brothers in Zug, Switzerland, since 1965. He was considered by many to be a logistical genius with a photographic memory. At any given moment, Green always knew who was offering the best shipping rates or where a shipment was currently located during transport.

Green is only a few months older than Rich, and the two have amaz-ingly similar family backgrounds. Green was born in the middle of the

Great Depression on March 11, 1934, in Brooklyn as the seventh of eight children. His parents, Sadie and Israel Green, fled from the Ukrainian part of the Soviet Union to the United States in the early twenties. The 1917 October Revolution had marked the beginning of a bloody civil war that would last until the winter of 1920–21. Several armies took part in the fighting—the Ukrainian army, peasant irregulars, the Red Army, and the counterrevolutionary White Guards. Terrible massacres were carried out against Ukraine's Jews. There were twelve hundred pogroms, 530 Jewish communities were attacked, and sixty thousand Jews were murdered.[7] Those Jews who were able to escape fled the country.

Israel Green ran a successful grocery store in Brooklyn that provided the family with a comfortable standard of living. Their success would not last long, however. Their bank collapsed on Black Tuesday, and the family lost everything in the 1929 economic crash. It was difficult enough to find a new job in those days of mass unemployment and mass poverty, but for Green, an Orthodox Jew who didn't work on Saturdays, it was virtually impossible. His four sons had to help the family make ends meet. On Sundays and after school, Pincus went from door to door selling candy from his little wagon. He attended a Jewish school in Brooklyn. At the age of sixteen he left high school and went to work as a stockboy stocking shelves in Manhattan's Garment District. He then got a job in the mailroom at Philipp Brothers and followed the same career path as all traders before him and Marc Rich after him. After serving in the army from 1955 to 1957, he married his lifelong love, Libby, in 1957. The two still live together and are the parents of four adult children.

The moment he heard of Rich's plans, Green was hooked on the idea of trading oil as if it were any other commodity. The two formed a disparate pair, for their characters could not have been more different. The cosmopolitan Rich did not believe in God, as he confided to me, favored a nice glass of wine, and wore tailor-made suits. Green, on the other hand, was deeply religious and would still live in a modest stucco house in Flatbush, a Brooklyn neighborhood inhabited mainly by Jewish immigrants, when he was a millionaire.

They were the perfect embodiment of the old saying about opposites attracting. Together they would revolutionize the global commodities trade.

6

ISRAEL *and the* SHAH

The traders who would soon shake the global oil market had a rather humble start. "We did one or two transactions with Tunis," Rich remembers. They made a profit of $60,000, which, although not exactly overwhelming, showed their bosses that there was money to be made in crude oil. Jesselson and Rothschild were open to the idea in principle, but they tended to be rather conservative and warned Rich of the potential dangers. They were aware of the inherent risks in the capital-intensive oil trade, as a failed deal could spell ruin for a company.

Rich had an idea that would later prove to be a stroke of genius. This idea would soon transform Philipp Brothers into a powerhouse of the international oil trade, and it speaks volumes about Rich and his successes. He suggested a deal between two parties who—at least officially—would have nothing to do with one another. It was a highly secretive and politically explosive deal, which remains shrouded in secrecy to this day.

I first heard of the deal when I interviewed Rich's former high-ranking employees in Madrid. I had wanted to know how Rich had managed to break into the oil-trading business so quickly. I got along quite well with one of these traders due to a shared passion for Africa. We were discussing whether Africa would one day be able to pull itself out of its poverty and misery, and we came to the conclusion that the continent could only do so on its own and not with the help of foreign aid. Suddenly he made a tapping gesture with his index finger and asked me to turn off my tape recorder.

Under the pledge of secrecy he proceeded to tell me an almost unbelievable tale. It was the story of an Iranian-Israeli oil pipeline that ran from Eilat—Israel's gateway to the Red Sea—to Ashkelon on the Mediterranean coast. It was thanks to this pipeline—and thanks to his cooperation with Iran and Israel—that Rich was able to get his foot in the door of the global oil trade.

Top-Secret Pipeline in Israel

To this day the Iranian connection to the oil pipeline is one of Israel's best-kept state secrets.[1] The pipeline was an attempt to solve one of the Jewish state's greatest strategic challenges, one that threatened the nation's very survival: access to a steady supply of oil. There's an old Israeli joke: Moses wandered the Middle East for forty years—and finally settled in the only place without any oil. Israel's oil-rich enemy neighbors were keen to keep the country from gaining access to this important raw material. Up to 90 percent of Israel's oil imports came from Iran. The Persian country, which is not Arab, had secretly supplied Israel with the black gold since the middle 1950s.[2]

In the summer of 1965, Golda Meir, then Israel's foreign minister, visited the shah in Tehran. She suggested the two nations cooperate in the construction and management of a pipeline. The meeting was top secret, as Iran did not officially recognize Israel. The shah had his own regional interests, and he had no desire to damage his relationship with the Arab world. The Arab nations considered Israel a pariah, and together they had organized a boycott of Israel. Nevertheless, the shah, whom the Israelis referred to by his cover name "Landlord," signaled that he was prepared to enter into secret negotiations. The Iranians were represented by the National Iranian Oil Company (NIOC), and the Israelis sent high-ranking government representatives as well as members of the Mossad to the talks—a fact that underscored the project's immense strategic importance.

Two years later the negotiations finally reached a turning point. President Nasser's closure of the Suez Canal in the wake of the Six-Day War convinced the shah that the pipeline was in Iran's strategic interest. Mohammad Reza Shah Pahlavi realized that the closure threatened Iran's main transport route, since Iran shipped three out of four barrels of its oil through the Suez Canal.[3] The closure threatened his plans to transform Iran into the region's dominant oil-producing nation. The shah, as the leader of the only non-Arab OPEC member nation in the region, also saw the presence of Egypt's Arab allies on Iran's doorstep as a hindrance to his desire to serve as a counterbalance to President Nasser. Thanks to the pipeline, Mohammad Reza Pahlavi could lessen his dependence on Egypt and the Suez Canal.

Israel and Iran agreed to set up a fifty-fifty joint venture, and together the two countries founded Trans-Asiatic Oil Ltd. in Switzerland. The shah demanded that Iran's participation in the company remain a secret. When asked, the official answer from Iran would always be the same: "We do not sell oil to Israel." Trans-Asiatic operated the pipeline, the oil terminals, and oil containers in Eilat and Ashkelon, and it even maintained a fleet of tankers to transport the oil.

The pipeline, 254 kilometers long and 106 centimeters in diameter, was completed in 1969, and in December of the same year the first Iranian oil began to flow. Ten million metric tons of oil were transported through the Israeli pipeline in the first year. Israel bought 3 million metric tons for its own supply. The Iranian navy accompanied the tankers from the ports of lading to the Strait of Hormuz, and the Israeli navy guarded the ships' entry into the Gulf of Aqaba at the Straits of Tiran.

The pipeline was what game theorists would call a "win-win situation"—a solution of equal benefit to both parties. "Thanks to the pipeline, the shah was able to gradually outrival the multinational oil companies and become a powerful force in the oil trade," a participant in the deal told me. NIOC was able to freely sell its oil on the open market for the first time ever. The shah made a lot of money and could continue to feed his extravagant lifestyle. Furthermore, the pipeline was a useful tool in his struggle to gain greater control over the oil companies. Israel, on the other side, earned good money on the transit fees for the pipeline and was at the same time able to secure a constant supply of oil.

Trading with the Shah of Persia

Rich wanted to go into business with the shah of Persia and find buyers for the Iranian oil that passed through Israel. It was the bold idea that would later become his great success. Rich's cometlike ascent could never have happened were it not for this deal, and, according to a well-informed insider, it was the true foundation of Rich's enterprise. Insiders also know that Rich could never have become the biggest independent oil trader in the world without the help of Pincus Green. "Marc is the visionary, Pinky makes things happen. It's impossible to think of one without the other," said a friend who has known both of them well for many years. This is primarily—but not solely—connected to Green's skills as a traffic manager. It was Pinky, as all his acquaintances call him, who was able to make the crucial contacts in Iran. These contacts formed the basis for the company that would become Marc Rich + Co. AG. Iran played such an important role in Green's career that he named the family office, i.e., a private company managing the family wealth, that he constructed after his retirement, Yeshil Management AG. *Yeshil* is the Farsi word for green.

Pinky Green was indicted in 1983 on exactly the same charges as Marc Rich, and he was pardoned in 2001 by President Bill Clinton at exactly the same time. Nevertheless, he has to a large extent managed to keep out of the headlines. Googling his name turns up a mere 6,710 hits, compared with a whopping 230,000 hits for Marc Rich.[4] Even his opponents can only find nice things to say about him. "If I wanted a neighbor, Pincus Green would be the perfect neighbor," U.S. Marshal Ken Hill told me.

In the 1960s Green traded mainly in chrome ore—which is used to make stainless steel—and copper for Philipp Brothers. Both metals were found in Persia, as Iran was more commonly called at the time. For this reason Green frequently traveled between New York and Iran, where he became friendly with Ali Rezai. The Rezai family were powerful and influential owner-operators of chrome and copper mines. Ali, who was known as "Mr. Steel" on account of his family's links to the industry, later became a member of the Majlis, the Iranian senate. More important, he was a friend of the shah, Mohammad Reza Pahlavi. "Pinky was very, very close to Ali Rezai," one Iran expert told me.

The connection to Rezai opened the doors to Iran's economic and political elite, and this access would prove to be of exceptional importance. It led Green right to the center of power in Persia, namely, the shah himself. "This relationship allowed Pinky to develop a relationship with the National Iranian Oil Company," Rich told me. Rich himself met the shah years later as a neighbor in St. Moritz.

The most important player in Rich's oil dealings was Parviz Mina. When Rich first met him, he was responsible for international relations on the administrative board of NIOC. Mina was reputedly exceptionally intelligent and highly competent in technical issues. Tony Benn, the British secretary of state for energy at the time, called him "brilliant."[5] Mina had earned a PhD in petroleum engineering at the University of Birmingham in Great Britain. He had been working in the Iranian oil industry since the fall of Mohammad Mossadegh, Iran's nationalist prime minister, in 1953. He had excellent contacts to the other oil-producing nations and was a member of the OPEC Long Term Strategy Committee for two years.

Crude Middleman

When I asked him about the pipeline business, Rich only stared at me for a wordless moment. It seemed he was considering whether or not he should admit to this secret. He then confessed to me that the pipeline was indeed a milestone of his career—"a very, very important business," as Rich put it. Thanks to the relationship with oil director Parviz Mina and "Mr. Steel" Ali Rezai, he started it in 1973. Rich can no longer say exactly how much oil he traded in the beginning. He still knows that he was able to expand the business with Iran over the years up to 8 to 10 million tons per year (approximately 60 to 75 million barrels). "People were reluctant to use the pipeline because the oil had passed through Israel," Rich told me. Whoever did official business with Israel ran the risk of being blacklisted by Arab nations. "Still, the pipeline was there. I decided that it was attractive and gradually introduced it." Rich secretly transported the politically controversial oil—some of it in Israeli tankers—across the Mediterranean to Spain, Rich's adopted country. In order to disguise the oil's origin, the tankers sometimes stopped in Romania. The Communist country, since 1965 ruled by the dictator Nicolae Ceauşescu, was the only Eastern Bloc nation that had not broken diplomatic relations with Israel in the wake of the Six-Day War.

There was a reason for such discretion. As mentioned earlier, Spain's fascist head of state, Generalissimo Francisco Franco, had consistently refused to officially recognize Israel, but he was very interested in obtaining oil. Spain had an incredible thirst for oil as a result of the nation's industrialization coupled with the economic boom of the "Spanish miracle" in the 1960s. As is often the case, pragmatism usually wins out over ideology in such situations. "Spain bought the oil—even though it had no diplomatic relations with Israel," an insider explained. "Politics," he said laughingly and shook his head.

As the oil was relatively cheap, Rich could offer it at prices that were lower than those of the competition. For customers who might have been concerned about the oil's Israeli connection, this was a decisive financial incentive. "There was a big price advantage," Rich explained. "The oil was cheaper because of the much cheaper freight. The transport of Iranian crude through the pipeline was much cheaper than going all the way around Africa." A metric ton of Iranian oil cost $21 in Eilat. The same oil cost $28 once it had been transported to Europe via the Cape of Good Hope.[6] At that time the usual route through the Suez Canal was not possible due to Egypt's closure of the canal from 1967 to 1975.

Rich gained access to Franco's government by means of his economist friend Alfredo Santos Blanco. "He was very helpful to me," Rich said. "He knew everybody and everybody knew him. Thanks to him we came into contact with the Spanish government and the Spanish refineries who eventually became our customers." Santos Blanco, who in 1974 would become Spain's minister of industry, even went on to join Rich's company as a public relations man after leaving office. Rich had won the privilege to supply Spain because he had been able to solve a problem between Spain and Egypt. Egypt owed Spain a substantial sum of money that it was unable to pay back. Rich arranged to buy Egyptian oil for Spain and used part of that credit for the purchase. "As compensation from Spain for this business, they gave me a part of the government quota to supply them," Rich explains. As is true of many countries, the Spanish government controlled a set percentage of all oil imports. Rich sold the "pipeline oil" for countless years to the Spanish government as part of this government quota of 30 percent.

"Yes, the pipeline was very important to me," Rich repeated and closed the door on the topic. The story is evidence of Rich's close cooperation with Iran, Israel, and Spain. It was a cooperation of great value to all involved, whose importance will be explained in the following chapters. It underscores Rich's contacts in Israel's intelligence service Mossad. There were very few deals that had as great an effect on Rich as the pipeline business. It proved to Rich that he could trust his instincts. Once again, Rich was at the right place at the right time and had made the right decision. It was no small risk given the political controversy surrounding Israel, but the risk proved to be manageable. Most important, however, the deal had paid off. In the early 1970s, Philipp Brothers became one of the world's largest oil-trading companies almost overnight, and Rich created the beginnings of a spot market for oil that he would later perfect in his own company. He sold most of the oil to Spain, but also to Italy and mid-sized oil companies in the United States. It was a novel development. Oil could now be bought "on the spot" on short notice with no need for long-term contracts or other obligations to the major companies or oil sheiks.

Rich's ability to bring together improbable business partners would soon become his trademark. He would repeatedly serve his clients as a discreet go-between—a kind of "crude oil middleman." It would prove again and again to be the most lucrative kind of deal. In times of crisis, governments were prepared to pay a premium for strategically important commodities such as oil. Rich carved out a niche for himself that would allow him to make contacts and gather experience in the oil trade on a grand scale. The contacts he made would soon allow him to leave Philipp Brothers and found his own company. Thanks to Israel and Spain—and Iran, of course—Rich would soon ascend the throne to become the undisputed King of Oil.

Yom Kippur War

Knowledge is power. This is probably more true of the commodities trade than of any other field—with the exception of the military. The difference between wealth and wreckage usually depends on access to superior information. The contacts that Rich and Green had made in Iran were worth their weight in (black) gold. Thanks to these excellent relations, Rich learned early in the 1970s that the oil-producing countries were incensed. The high inflation rates coupled with the massive devaluation of the dollar made their income from oil sales plummet. In spring 1973 Rich and Green heard of the "new structures" looming in the oil industry as well as of OPEC's desire to raise prices before the competition had gotten wind of it. "I wouldn't call it inside information, but direct information," one oil trader who was involved in the Iranian deals told me. "Contrary to the other companies, we were on the spot, we were there. Contrary to them, we got all the information available in the market."

Rich saw the opportunity that others had failed to see. "We felt the market was changing, the whole world was changing," he recalls. "We knew more than our competitors. Of course, I always develop relations with my customers." Green was once more in Iran in spring 1973 when he heard that NIOC wanted to sell oil on the free market. "We thought it would be a good idea to take a long position in crude." They bet on higher prices and signed a long-term contract with Iran without consulting their bosses at Philipp Brothers in New York. According to Rich, they committed themselves to purchasing a total of one million metric tons (approximately 7.5 million barrels) over a long period of time at a fixed price, namely $5 per barrel. The total value of the deal was $37.5 million.

Philipp Brothers president Ludwig Jesselson was shocked when he was informed of the deal. "How could you do that?" he yelled at Rich. Five dollars per barrel was at least $2 more than the oil's market price at the time. Worse still, it was not a back-to-back deal, for Rich and Green did not have a buyer for the huge quantity of oil. In other words, Philipp Brothers carried the entire risk at a price that was $15 million higher than the market price. This risk was intolerable for Jesselson, who still lived according to the company motto, "It is better to sleep well than eat well."

There followed a marathon series of telephone conferences, sometimes heated, at other times downright nasty, but the upshot was that Jesselson forced Rich and Green to get rid of the oil as quickly as possible. "It was very annoying," says Rich. They had no choice, but they obeyed their orders reluctantly. "Pinky sold the oil to Ashland Oil in Kentucky for a small profit. They took over the contract. Too bad," says Rich. He perceived Jesselson's behavior as a breach of trust and a rejection. It was a foreshadowing of the final split with Philipp Brothers that was soon to come.

It must have been one of the best deals in the history of Ashland Oil, for Rich and Green were proved right only months after the sale. On October 6, 1973, Yom Kippur, Egypt and Syria attacked Israel. The Arab nations brought Israel to the verge of military defeat for the first time in its history. The Soviet Union supported Egypt and Syria, whereas the United States weighed in on the side of the Israelis. The Jewish state only managed to drive its opponents back after conceding large areas of land. There was no victor in this three-week-long conflict, which was the fourth in a series of Israeli-Arab wars (after the Israeli war of independence in 1948, the Suez War of 1956–57, and the Six-Day War in 1967).

The oil-producing nations made a further attempt to use their oil as a weapon. This tactic may have failed miserably during the Six-Day War, but the political and economic situation was different this time. Libya and Saudi Arabia were the first to cease delivery to the United States and Western Europe. Six more important oil producers had joined the boycott by the end of 1973—the United Arab Emirates, Iran, Iraq, Kuwait, Algeria, and Qatar. At the same time, OPEC decided to cut oil production and raise prices. The "oil weapon," which had proved so lackluster only six years previously, now hit home with the force of a bomb. It was also around this time that President Nixon signed the Emergency Petroleum Allocation Act, which introduced controls on oil prices in the United States and would cause such enormous problems for Rich ten years later (see chapter 9).

The Breaking Off

By the end of the year, everyone realized how spot-on Marc Rich's instinct had been. The long-term contract with Iran had been a stroke of genius, the like of which has seldom been seen. The price per barrel rose from just under $3 before the war to an official $11.60. On the free market, however, oil could fetch anything up to the then record level of $13—over $8 more than Marc Rich had agreed with Iran. If the heads of Philipp Brothers had only trusted him, the company could have easily earned $60 million on this one deal. Nevertheless, Philipp Brothers profited from Rich's dealings with Israel, Spain, and Iran. The company, which by then was a division of Engelhard Mineral & Chemicals, posted record profits in 1973. This was mainly due to the trade in crude oil. Thanks to Marc Rich and Pinky Green, Philipp Brothers would soon be one of the largest oil traders in the world.

Never before in the company's history had only two men been responsible for so much profit. Rich and Green's trade in oil alone earned the company between $4 million and $5 million profit in 1973. Marc Rich did not earn much more than $70,000 per year at the time; with his bonus included he possibly made $100,000. After racking up such amazing trade successes, Rich came to the conclusion that $100,000 was nowhere near enough.

In February 1974 he flew from Madrid to Switzerland to negotiate with Jesselson, who was on a skiing holiday in the Swiss Alps. He demanded a bonus of $500,000 for himself and the same again for Green. "My request was influenced by what I knew the company was making," comments Rich. Jesselson, who was already sixty-three years old, offered Rich $150,000. He also tried to persuade Rich to return to New York, where he would become Jesselson's successor as president of Philipp Brothers. "I said yes, provided we come to an agreement on the remuneration," Rich told me. Jesselson refused on principle to pay more than $150,000. "So I had to leave," Rich says. "I didn't want to leave. I had been there for twenty years, I liked the company, I liked Jesselson, and I think he liked me. I always thought that the company would be my career for the rest of my life, but Jesselson got stuck on the principle."

As soon as the meeting was over Rich phoned Green, who was in

New York at the time. "I told him that I didn't reach an agreement with Jesselson." Pinky did not hesitate for a second. "So we're going," he said. That one telephone call would mark the beginning of the most successful commodities company the world had ever seen.

7

MARC RICH + COMPANY

Things now had to move quickly. After his unpleasant meeting with Jesselson, Rich immediately flew back to Madrid from Switzerland. He went straight from the airport to his office, where he informed his two most important employees what had happened. He intended to leave Philipp Brothers and set up his own company immediately together with Pinky Green. He also told them he was still looking for two or three more business partners. John Trafford, Rich's personal assistant, and Jacques Hachuel, an oil specialist in the regions of Africa and South America, accepted the offer without a moment's hesitation: "We're in," they said. Green was on the telephone shortly thereafter. He had wooed away Alexander "Alec" Hackel, who had worked with Green at Philipp Brothers' Swiss offices as an expert on alumina and Eastern Europe.

Not twenty-four hours had passed since Rich's split with Jesselson, yet Rich had already put together a core team for his new company—"the Founders" or "the Partners," as many former employees whom I interviewed for this book almost reverently called them. "We all liked each other, and they felt there was more opportunity to make money," Rich says. "To make money"—this was a phrase I heard time and again from Rich when he spoke of his own motivation or the motivation of others. Money was the prime mover. Senior executives at Philipp Brothers finally realized what had happened when they came together for the traditional group photograph for the 1974 annual report. Rich and Green were absent. "Before the rumors start," Jesselson began his speech, "I want to say that Rich and Green asked for bonuses so high they would break our rules and traditions. They have separated. It's time to close ranks."[1] Their departure was seen by many as an act of treachery. Philipp Brothers was a company where the employees began their careers at an early age and stayed on until they retired. The separation was like separations usually are: bitter. Rich and Jesselson never spoke another word to one another. "It's a sad chapter in my personal life," Jesselson said. "They were like my own sons. I brought them up from nothing, and they turned their backs on me."[2] "He forgot me in his will," Rich said sarcastically when I asked him about the split. He added, "Jesselson's wife called my mother and complained."

Though the skies were slightly overcast, April 3, 1974, was a warm day in the Swiss town of Zug. Marc Rich + Co. AG was founded that morning in a law firm's downtown office. The five partners brought a total of 2 million Swiss francs in seed capital to the table. Rich borrowed money from his father-in-law, Emil Eisenberg, as well as his own father. John Trafford sold his vintage car in order to contribute his share of the pot. Alec Hackel had no money at all, so Rich lent it to him. Altogether, 1,055,000 Swiss francs in common stock was deposited with Credit Suisse. Rich was the company's first president, and Green took up his position on the supervisory board together with three Swiss lawyers. Alec Hackel was chosen as the company's director.

Swiss Secrecy

Of course, it was no accident that Rich chose Switzerland as the location for the headquarters of Marc Rich + Co. AG. Philipp Brothers' European headquarters had been located in Zug since 1957. Situated on the banks of a lake and nestled between rolling hills, Zug is an idyllic small town in central Switzerland at the foot of the Alps. In addition to its natural beauty, Zug had three key advantages. First of all, Switzerland is politically neutral and in the mid-1970s was not even a member of the United Nations. Second, Zug is close to Zurich, one of the world's best and—thanks to strong banking secrecy regulations—most discreet financial centers, with access to an international airport and top-notch international schools. Finally, Zug is a tax paradise with comparatively low rates of income tax and corporate tax by international standards. In the mid-1970s, a midsized American company had to fork over nearly half of its profit to the IRS. In Zug a company only had to pay around 10 percent in taxes. "The only bad thing about Zug is the fog," Rich says.

With its policies of low taxes and simplified bureaucracy—both initiated after World War II—Zug managed to attract international companies and become an international center for trade and services. First came the American companies such as Philipp Brothers in the 1950s and 1960s. These were followed by German and British companies in the 1970s and 1980s, and since the 1990s Zug has attracted an increasing number of Russian companies. Zug seems to be the perfect example of supply-side economics in practice. The inhabitants of the canton of Zug had struggled for centuries to make a living from the dairy industry and livestock breeding, yet the canton is today one of the richest in Switzerland. In March 2009, it had an unemployment rate of only 2.5 percent.

The founding of Marc Rich + Co. AG was a heavy blow for Philipp Brothers, a trading giant that had survived two world wars. "Few events had as far-reaching consequences in the firm as Rich's departure," said Helmut Waszkis, an authority on the company who worked for the commodities giant for over half his life.[3] The commodities trade is a business without brands or trademarks. It is primarily based on personal relationships and trust. "You take your large customers and the little company secrets with you when you leave," one trader told me. Rich was considered a master of maintaining a network of connections. His black address book—in which every name, number, and date is meticulously written in tiny handwriting—is legendary among company employees. He never forgets a birthday, regularly sends flowers on holidays, and keeps in touch with his contacts. "Loyalty is a very important value to him," according to Ursula Santo Domingo. "He still calls me when he is in Madrid."

Vendetta

It was an unpretentious beginning. The handful of traders worked in a four-room apartment in Zug's less than glamorous Riedmatt quarter. The furnishings were simple. "At the beginning we had to use the local post office to send telexes," Rich remembers. Although the company soon had its own telex, veterans remember that the only space that could be found for it was in the restroom. With nothing but their know-how and their contacts, Rich and his partners set out to snatch deals from Rich's former employer and tear away Philipp Brothers' share of the market—a job that Philipp Brothers had trained them for.

Everyone was talking about a vendetta between Rich's company and Philipp Brothers (Phibro). Some of the stories sounded as if they had been taken from a spy film.[4] In Buenos Aires, Phibro employees caught one of Rich's employees paying large sums for Phibro company telexes. "They were beating our bids for metals by a fraction on every one," a Phibro representative complained. "They knew our bids before we did." A mole from Marc Rich + Co. was discovered in Phibro's Tokyo offices with the help of Phibro's own mole that they had infiltrated into Rich's company. Some believe that Rich knowingly lost money on deals in order to squeeze out Philipp Brothers. "Nonsense," says Rich. He attributes these stories to the emotions that accompanied his departure from the company. "No company is particularly pleased if its best people leave to start a competing operation."

Even if these reports of industrial espionage are mere cock-and-bull stories, they illustrate the fact that the commodities trade was a hard game—and the atmosphere became noticeably harder. The competitors gave each other a run for their money, and Philipp Brothers gave as good as they got. They even pressured Rich's banks not to extend him a line of credit, a financial expert involved in the affair told me. That would have meant an early death for Marc Rich + Co.

It is impossible to trade commodities quickly and on a global scale without credit. Credit is the lifeline of any commodities trading business. This was particularly true for the newly formed Marc Rich + Co., as it had practically no cash and no equity of its own. Therefore the company's most important goal was to obtain sufficient credit to allow it to trade oil. A bank extends credit (for which it charges a fee) up to an agreed-upon sum that the company can draw upon repeatedly when necessary. The commodities themselves serve as collateral. The letter of credit represents the bank's promise to pay for the commodities. It is a form of insurance for the seller as well as the buyer. The buyer only has to pay after the seller has delivered the agreed quantity and quality of raw materials. The seller has a guarantee that he will be paid after the goods have been delivered if he can present the required documents as evidence.

Thanks to Iranian Oil

Rich's decision to found his own company didn't come as a surprise. Jesselson had forced him to drop the long-term contract with Iran one year earlier, and since then Rich had known his time with Philipp Brothers was nearing its end. Rich began to see his departure from the company as a serious possibility, and like every other good trader, Rich wanted to be prepared for this eventuality should it indeed come to pass.

Rich's trump card was his continuing connection with the Iranian-Israeli oil pipeline. He managed to bring this business with him to his own company, thanks to his relationship to "Mr. Steel" Ali Rezai and to "Dr. Mina"—as Rich likes to call Parviz Mina, the NIOC director. "My knowledge of this contract allowed me to found the new company," Rich says. He had already found a long-term buyer for this oil: the Spanish government, which he had previously secretly supplied with oil. An additional purchaser of Iranian oil was the American oil firm Atlantic Richfield Company (ARCO), which would later become one of Rich's best customers. The contract with ARCO was of particular importance. He did not have to conduct this business secretly, as was the case in the Spanish deals. Instead, Rich was able to use this trade as a form of collateral in order to obtain his first, all-important line of credit.

John Trafford engineered the first new trade for the young company. Rich's former assistant had good contacts at the French oil company Elf, which was producing oil in the West African country of Nigeria. Rich in turn had a good relationship with Standard Oil of Ohio (Sohio, the company founded by John D. Rockefeller in 1870). "So we put Elf and Sohio together and made a profit: fifteen cents a barrel. That was a very good profit at the time," Rich remembers. A trade involving 150,000 metric tons of Nigerian Bony Light Crude (approx. 1.1 million barrels) brought the new company $165,000 in profit. Even more important, Sohio, too, agreed to pay with a letter of credit, which Rich could then use to purchase even more oil. "They were reluctant at first to pay by letter of credit, but they accepted because both the price and the supply were attractive to them. These letters of credit which came in we had transferred on to our suppliers," Rich explains.

Marc Rich + Co. was thus able to develop a long-term and stable network of suppliers and buyers within a very short period of time. The first trades were financed by Bankers Trust Company and, most important, by the French bank Paribas. "They liked the business. They opened letters of credit whenever and wherever we needed them," Rich explains. "To make money with other people's money, with the bank's money," as a former employee explained, was the company's financial philosophy. In these commodity trades, the risk was primarily carried by the bank that had extended the line of credit. Its collateral for the credit deal was the commodity at issue, in this case oil.

The Oil Shock of 1974

It was a good time for a commodities trader who wanted to go into business for himself. The world had been changed forever by the Arab oil embargo—imposed in the wake of the Yom Kippur War—and skyrocketing oil prices. These developments led to the world's first oil shock, a shock that would have serious economic consequences the world over. The price for a gallon of gasoline rose from 38.5¢ in May 1973 to 55.1¢ in June 1974.[5] It was the first time since the Second World War that the United States had seen gasoline shortages. Huge lines formed at the pumps throughout the country. It was a situation that had only been seen in poorer African or South American countries before then. Rapidly rising oil prices pushed the industrial nations into economic crisis.

It was a fabulous time for Rich and his partners. While the American oil companies and motorists were left high and dry, Marc Rich + Co. was simply swimming in oil—oil for which U.S. and European companies were willing to pay a very good price. "It was a good situation for us," Rich laughingly remembers. "It was a shortage of oil, and we had the oil." His company was able to gradually expand the contract with Iran to buy 8 million to 10 million metric tons per year (approximately 60 million to 75 million barrels).

"Then I learned that Ecuador was selling its share of oil. I sent Jacques Hachuel to Ecuador to buy it," Rich explains. A military coup had brought a sort of benevolent dictatorship to power in the South American country. Guillermo Rodríguez Lara, nicknamed "General Bombita" (General Balloon), invested massively in schools, hospitals, and the nation's infrastructure. These expenses could only be financed by a massive boost in oil production so that the *oro negro*—the black gold—could be sold for hard currency. This would prove a lucky break for Marc Rich + Co. Hachuel, a native-born Argentinean, came back with something worth much more than a tanker full of oil: a long-term contract with the state oil company of Ecuador, the Corporación Estatal Petrolera Ecuatoriana (CEPE). The biggest part was bought by ARCO.

From the company's very first days, Marc Rich + Co.'s financial success was nothing less than astounding. In 1974, the company's first fiscal year, it had a turnover of more than $1 billion while reaping a net profit of $28 million. The company's profit in 1975 was $50 million, and it went on to earn what was then an unbelievable $200 million in 1976.

Faster, Longer, More Aggressive

There were three main reasons for Rich's success—a success that took the industry completely by surprise. First of all, Rich's company was willing to take on a much higher level of risk than its competitors. Second, the best people in the business were working for the company. Finally, Marc Rich + Co. was the first company to develop a sophisticated system for trading oil independently. It is no exaggeration to state that Marc Rich and Pincus Green truly did invent the spot market for crude oil.

Marc Rich + Co. operated according to a completely different philosophy than did Philipp Brothers. It was more aggressive, faster, and more oriented toward long-term contracts. The partners recognized opportunities and followed up on them faster than the competition. They saw themselves as pioneers who were pushing forward into new territory, and they were interested in obtaining contracts that extended as far as possible into the future. Ecuador is selling oil? Fly over there immediately, and don't just buy the oil that is up for sale. Get the client to agree to a long-term contract. Turkey is looking for oil? Fly over there right away and sell it to them. "Pinky and I flew to Houston to discuss an oil deal," Rich recalls. "On the way there we learned that Turkey needed oil. Pinky, who once lived in Turkey, instantly interrupted his visit to Houston and flew to Istanbul. He concluded a very profitable transaction. We were faster than the others."

This willingness to take on risk was a big advantage in the years following the great oil shock. Rich won a lot of deals because he was ready to pay the oil-producing nations more for their oil than the competition. He enticed them with contracts that provided his company with stable supplies for several years into the future. Rich had analyzed the situation and had decided that the situation in the Middle East would remain insecure. According to Rich's theory, oil prices would continue to rise. "The world market was changing. The world was changing. The prices were going up," he explains. He was sure that these rising prices would more than compensate for the higher prices he was paying for the oil. "The most important thing as a trader," Rich says, "is to see the opportunity. The others didn't see what I saw."

In order to carry out his plans, Rich needed the right people. Rich knew exactly what he was looking for when he chose his four partners. Each was responsible for a different part of the world. Rich traded mainly in oil from Iran and selected the employees. Jacques Hachuel was responsible for the new markets in Africa and South America. John Trafford saw to North Africa and France. Finally, Alec Hackel was a specialist in metals and minerals who knew his way around Eastern Europe. Hackel would become one of the few people Rich would unquestioningly trust. "He is a wise man," Rich says, "and he always had the right answers—or questions."

The Invention of the Spot Market

Then there was the man without whom Rich could never have succeeded—Pinky Green, "the Admiral." Green was mainly responsible for transport and financing. "Each charter is a separate bargain," Rich explains. "He always knew everything—not only the prices but the technicalities, the condition of the charter, what is acceptable or unacceptable, and the best routes." One of the best-known experts in the field told me, "In the old days the traders looked down upon the charterers. Ever since Pincus Green came along they have enjoyed a much better reputation and are treated with a great deal of respect." A Swiss banker who regularly financed deals for Marc Rich + Co. told me, "Green was a logistics genius who could squeeze a profit from the smallest of price differences due to delays or distances."

The following is a poignant example from the company's later years that illustrates how Green was able to utilize such price differences. In the 1980s the Soviet Union supported Cuba, its "socialist brother nation," with cheap oil. Instead of transporting this oil over long distances from Russia to Cuba, the state trading company Cuba Metales traded a portion of this oil with Marc Rich + Co. Rich's company then delivered the same amount of oil to Cuba, obtained from nearby Venezuela. Rich was able to buy the Russian oil meant for Cuba at its reduced price and sell it for a profit on the global market.

Green developed the tanker trade, which had previously never existed outside of the Seven Sisters' supply network. Without this it would never have been possible to develop a competitive spot market for oil. Thanks to the spot market, consumers were no longer dependent on a single company controlling a value-creation chain that began at the oil wells and ended at the gas pump. Now buyers could purchase oil whenever and from whomever they wished. A large number of offers would soon develop, and a buyer could look for the cheapest barrel on the spot market. From an economic point of view, the spot market was much more efficient than the Seven Sisters' oligopoly. On the lookout for profit, companies attempted to find a niche at some stage of the process and remain as competitive as possible.

The development of freer markets was particularly advantageous for emerging African nations that possessed oil reserves but were unable to extract the oil and bring it to market themselves. "The spot oil market allowed and made it interesting for all the countries to explore, drill for, and export their own resources—their oil," an oil trader told me. The result was that from the mid-1970s onward, oil was traded more freely, more efficiently, and at more transparent prices than ever before. Tankers and refineries—the fixed costs—could be used more efficiently than under the multinational oil companies and governments thanks to independent oil traders like Marc Rich. Rich was able to achieve what the

Seven Sisters could not manage because of competitive pressures and cost structures. For example, Rich could sell one half of a tanker full of oil to a buyer in Spain and the other half to the same buyer's competitor in the United States. Both buyers enjoyed the benefits of cheaper bulk transport that they never could have afforded or utilized to full capacity on their own. Buyers for any possible surpluses could be found much more quickly, and supply gaps were easier to fill. In short, supply and demand could be balanced much more efficiently. The spot market brought with it an increase in productivity that helped to turn the entire industry inside out. Oil was now precisely what Rich had predicted only a few years before: just another commodity. "Marc Rich invented the concept of the independent oil trade. That's why he is such an important person in the history of trade," an expert who helped me understand the technical details of the oil trade told me.

Rich and his partners put the very same theory into practice that economists have expounded for years. Skillful traders do well when the risk is high and the supply is threatened by crisis. Only then can they use their competitive advantage to the best effect. "Trading companies reduce search, negotiation, and transaction costs and seem likely to be employed at least initially when the risks of international trade are high," says Geoffrey Jones, a professor of business history at Harvard Business School, who is a specialist in trading companies.[6] Traders can help their customers by compensating for a lack of information and trust.

Anyone who has ever haggled over the price of spices or carpets in an Arabian bazaar knows what it means to try to purchase goods without a reference price. To put it simply, experienced commodities traders know where and with whom they have to trade—particularly in areas where it is difficult to establish a contract. "We feel that the trader has a physical role to play: that of managing the flow of commodities both in time and in space in a universe characterized by instability. It is this very instability which in the final analysis provides the *raison d'être* of trade," says the French economics professor Philippe Chalmin, an expert in commodities markets with practical experience in the field.[7]

This ability to deal with instability and in turn secure a stable flow of oil was, ironically, also of use to the U.S. Department of Defense, which hired Marc Rich + Co. as a defense contractor. In July 1978 the DoD bought $45.6 million worth of oil from Marc Rich + Co. for the Strategic Petroleum Reserve, established after the oil shock of 1973, in order to guarantee the nation's energy security. That was followed by a further $46.7 million worth of oil in August. Altogether these purchases amounted to approximately 7.1 million barrels of oil (1 million metric tons).

The Secret of Trust

The employees at Marc Rich + Co. soon enjoyed a reputation as young, aggressive traders. Rich cultivated a distinct meritocracy. In this respect he stuck to the tried-and-true tradition he had learned at Philipp Brothers. Rich did not put much stock in university education but instead entrusted employees with as much freedom and responsibility as they could bear. "We throw young people into the swimming pool. Either they sink or they learn to swim," Rich once said. "Marc Rich bought me my freedom," a trader told me rather dramatically. "He allowed me to be what I am."

"When he trusts someone, he really trusts," says Avner Azulay, who has worked for Rich for over twenty-five years. "He lets you do it the way you see best. It allows you to put your whole heart into it without any limitations. He leaves you to decide using your best judgment." Trust is one of Rich's secrets of success, and trust also presents an economic advantage. In his acclaimed book *Trust,* the political economist Francis Fukuyama illustrates how the degree of trust in a society—and indeed in a company—can be decisive for both its prosperity and its ability to compete.[8] In "low-trust" societies such as China, France, or Italy, you cannot assume that everyone is following the rules. Members of these societies must always renegotiate these rules and often even have to go to court to do so. In "high-trust" societies such as Germany or Japan, however, businesspeople are more willing to trust that everyone holds to the same values, whereby deception is not accepted. A high degree of reciprocal trust substantially lowers the cost of business. It is much easier for large and successful private enterprises to blossom in societies with a high degree of social trust.

The distinguished economist and Nobel Prize winner Kenneth J. Arrow characterizes trust as "an important lubricant of a social system. It is extremely efficient; it saves a lot of trouble to have a fair degree of reliance on other people's word. . . . Trust and similar values, loyalty and truth-telling, are examples of what the economist would call 'externalities.' They are goods, they are commodities; they have real, practical, economic value; they increase the efficiency of the system."[9]

I experienced Rich's trust firsthand. It took several years before Rich agreed to meet with me. However, when he decided that he would make himself available for this book, he gave me free rein. I did not have to grapple with his lawyers as I had expected. He did not insist on the right to revise my manuscript. On the contrary, he accepted my desire to independently research and write the book. He guaranteed my complete control of its contents.

Dictum meum pactum—"My word is my bond." Traders have used this Latin phrase ever since the sixteenth century when carrying out business over long distances in situations where written contracts were impractical. *Dictum meum pactum* has been the motto of the London Stock Exchange since 1923. Rich identifies with this centuries-old merchant tradition. When I asked him about his most important leadership principle, Rich answered, "My principle is to perform what I say I'll do. Performance."

When I asked Robert Fink, who has served as Rich's lawyer for many years, about his client's strengths, he simply looked at me for some time without saying a word. It seemed as if he were contemplating whether I would believe his answer. He then said, "Rich is a man of his word. Being reliable, keeping your word, being honest—these are the reasons he is successful." Trust and dependability were decisive factors in the commodities trade in the 1970s. At that time the markets were much less transparent than they are today. There was no Internet, and there were no mobile phones; there was no constant flow of business data from news service agencies such as Bloomberg and Thomson Reuters. It was not as easy to compare prices as it is today. Whoever had access to trustworthy business contacts was at a great competitive advantage.

"Don't Let Them Eat Your Soul"

Rich's people repaid their employer with a high degree of loyalty and an above-average willingness to perform. They were "short on diplomas and long on work ethic."[10] It was not unusual for employees to work fifteen or sixteen hours a day. "I enjoyed my duty," a trader explained when talking about his work at the company. "I was in the office at a quarter to eight in the morning. I left at 1:00 A.M. I went Saturday and Sunday. I was in the office on December twenty-fifth or on January first. All the other traders were there as well." He then confided that he was later treated for work addiction.

One of the few women in the business admitted to me during a ride in a taxi, "We commodities traders are addicts." She gave up the job many years ago, but she still follows the daily price of bauxite and knows if workers are on strike in Guinea, one of the main producers of the ore. It seems that this addiction can be kept under control, but it can never be cured. I spoke with several traders who continued to carry a list of their most important contacts' telephone numbers or names of refineries and their production output in their wallets for years after they had gotten out of the business. A former Rich employee told me one of the wives of the five founders warned him, "Don't let them eat your soul."

Rich's traders could sometimes achieve celebrity status within their industry, and if they were successful they could earn even more money than an investment banker. The company is proud of the fact that it has created more millionaires than any other company in Switzerland. Rich's employees were encouraged to become shareholders in the company from its inception—quite a revolutionary step in those days. "I wanted my people to work for 'their' company and profit from its success," Rich explains. Even the secretaries received company stock.

"The person has to have a fire burning," Rich said when I asked him about his hiring criteria. "He or she has to have a passion for business. They have to be willing to work hard and long hours. They have to be able to insist and insist." One of his top managers says that the flat hierarchy and the open-door policy set the tone. "Marc's conduct toward his staff creates a family feeling, and people are proud to work for him," he says.

Pioneer of Globalization

"Marc Rich was a pioneer. He understood that globalization was going to arrive sooner or later. One of the keys to globalization was oil. It was a product that everyone needed." The trader who told me this had been a part of the oil trade from its very beginnings. I met him in Madrid, where he now runs his own trading company. His office consists of two small rooms. Three telephones, a secretary, a computer, and the contacts he has established over the years are all he needs to close solid business deals. He spoke with enthusiasm about the 1970s when he was still young and bold. "Oil was the glamour of the time. We, the oil traders, were the prima donnas, the stars of the time. This was completely new. It was a new commodity."

I have heard similar stories from various traders who have worked for Rich over the years. They all described discovering and developing new markets as the most fascinating and exciting times of their lives. "It's the most satisfactory thing when you arrive in a virgin country and you start investigating," said a trader who had sought out business op-portunities in those African countries that had achieved independence in the 1960s and 1970s. "Who are the key players? How do you get ac-cess to them? What business is there for you? And you have a company behind you like Marc Rich + Co. that does not tremble when you nego-tiate a trade worth a hundred million bucks. This feeling in your body is spectacular."

"We were discovering new worlds," an oil trader who was with the company at the beginning enthusiastically said. It really was a new world. The 1960s and 1970s marked the onset of a wave of globalization that had not been seen since the "First Era of Globalization"—a period of global trade spanning the nineteenth century that ended early in the twentieth with the outbreak of the First World War. This second era had a lasting effect on the global economy. At the end of the 1960s, only 5 percent of the world's crude oil was traded outside of the Seven Sisters oligopoly. A mere ten years later, more than half of all crude was sold on the spot market or traded at prices that were tied to the market price.[11]

No one knew how to profit more from these developments than Marc Rich, and within five years he had transformed his company into a trading empire. Marc Rich + Co. AG was the first newcomer in many years that had managed to establish itself in the industry—and not as a mere niche vendor but as a global powerhouse capable of pressuring the established powers. By the end of the 1970s, the company had thirty of-fices around the globe. The five partners divided themselves among New York (Rich and Green), London (John Trafford), Madrid (Jacques Hachuel), and Zug (Alec Hackel).

Then, suddenly, the international oil market was again struck by a wave of insecurity—the essential fuel of every commodities trader. On Tuesday, January 16, 1979, the 2,507-year-old reign of the Persian mon-archs came to an end. Mohammad Reza Shah Pahlavi and Empress Farah Diba left the country. The official explanation stated that the cou-ple was heading to Egypt on vacation, yet everyone knew that they would never return. The protests against the autocratic shah's absolute rule in the last months of his reign had brought Iran to the brink of civil war. An oil strike in the province of Khuzestan had lamed the nation's economy and significantly reduced the amount of oil the country could export. With the fall of the shah it seemed as if Rich had lost his most important trading partner: Iran.

8

TRADING *with the* AYATOLLAH KHOMEINI

The fall of the shah was undoubtedly the toughest business challenge Marc Rich faced in his career. Iran had been his most important supplier of crude oil ever since he had founded his own company. He was purchasing 8 million to 10 million metric tons of Iranian oil every year, 200,000 barrels every day. Without Iranian crude Marc Rich could never have become the King of Oil. Yet his best contacts were now forced into exile—along with their *Shah-en-Shah*, the "king of kings"—where substantial amounts were waiting for them in foreign bank accounts. "Dr." Parviz Mina, the director of the National Iranian Oil Company (NIOC), fled to Paris, where he would soon find work as an adviser to the oil industry. Ali Rezai, "Mr. Steel," the Iranian industrialist and senator, boarded a private plane for Los Angeles. It seemed as if Rich's Iranian adventure would soon come to a tragic end.

The traders saw that it was time to save what they could. Pinky Green, who spoke Farsi and was the company's expert on Iran, offered to travel to the country and seek out contacts in the new government. It was impossible to fly to Tehran during the first two weeks after the fall of the Persian monarchy, however, as one of the first acts of the new government led by the secular opposition politician Shahpur Bakhtiar was to close Mehrabad International Airport. On February 1, 1979—a day that would go down in history—Green arrived in Iran on one of the first flights to land at the newly reopened airport. This required no small amount of courage, as it was not exactly the most opportune of times for a Jewish American businessman to travel to Iran. A part of the Iranian population could not contain its hatred for the United States. Many thought the Americans had helped the unloved shah and his corrupt associates come to power and had served as their protector. Israel, which had maintained relatively good (and discreet) relations with Iran under the shah, was also a target of public scorn. One of Bakhtiar's first actions was to forbid the export of oil to Israel. He had hoped to placate public opinion and the religious opposition with this populist step.[1]

The troubles began the moment Green went through customs at Mehrabad airport. The Iranian immigration official immediately confiscated his American passport. Green politely yet firmly asked the official to return his passport, as he could not travel around the country without it. The official shook his head, and Green realized he would not return it. He was an experienced trader who was used to finding creative solutions to new problems. He needed a means of getting back his passport that would at the same time allow the immigration official to save face. Green asked him in Farsi for a receipt for his passport. His chutzpah was rewarded. The official wrote Green's name, date of birth, and passport number on the back of a piece of paper packaging and signed the unusual receipt.

Khomeini's Return

On that day, February 1, 1979, hundreds of thousands of people kept vigil at Mehrabad Airport. They were waiting for an aged man who finally arrived on an Air France Boeing 747: the seventy-six-year-old Ayatollah Ruhollah Khomeini, returning to Iran after fifteen years in exile in France. Four days later Khomeini appointed an "Islamic revolutionary government," and soon afterward Bakhtiar had to make way for Khomeini's appointed prime minister, Mehdi Bazargan.

All the while Green was stranded in Tehran without a passport. He was prohibited from working, and he was not allowed to travel. He was isolated. Employees back at company headquarters in Zug were beginning to worry about his safety. Green then proved what a savvy trader was capable of achieving. One week after he had arrived, he went to the customs office with the piece of paper upon which the customs official had written his name, date of birth, and passport number. Sure enough, Green managed to get back his passport and immediately leave the country at a time when Americans and Jews in Iran had to fear for their lives.

Two weeks after the Ayatollah Khomeini's return, Iran found itself in the iron grip of Islamic fundamentalists. In the wake of the takeover, dozens of ministers who had remained true to the shah were tried by "Islamic people's courts" in summary proceedings and sentenced to death. Thousands of army and police officers were arrested and shot. Prime Minister Bazargan broke off all relations with Israel, and the Israeli embassy was stormed and plundered by a rampaging mob. A few days later the Ayatollah Khomeini turned over the Israeli mission to the PLO; chairman Yasser Arafat flew to Iran to personally raise the Palestinian flag above the mission. The ayatollah set the tone for Iran's future stance on the Jewish state: Israel was a "cancer" that would destroy the Islamic religion and Muslims if it were not removed from the region.[2] Khomeini believed that according to the Koran Israel had no right to exist.

The United States and Israel evacuated all of their citizens then living in Iran. Nearly all international companies that were represented in the country withdrew their employees and closed their offices. However, one company kept its office open throughout the headiest days of the takeover: Marc Rich + Co. Rich had already gained experience in political instability and abrupt regime changes in the course of his dealings with Cuba and Bolivia. On no account did he want to give up the Iranian oil market that was so important to him, and he held out for as long as possible. His representative in Tehran was a French national who had worked in Iran for many years. During the takeover this representative was cut off from the outside world for days on end. At times he even had to barricade the office and take cover from ricocheting bullets. In the end, however, he managed to hold the fort, and, indeed, his perseverance would eventually pay off.

The Islamic revolution in Iran, one of the world's greatest oil producers, brought an unprecedented level of instability to the oil markets. Iranian oil production declined dramatically, and at times it was almost completely disrupted. In 1977 Iran had produced 7 million barrels of oil per day. In the early months of 1979, however, daily production levels dropped to just under half a million barrels. The laws of supply and demand dictated that a sharp drop in oil supplies would have an effect on oil prices, and soon enough the price for oil began to skyrocket. Following the end of the Arab oil embargo, prices had fluctuated little between 1974 and 1978 and remained relatively stable at $10.73 to $13.39 per barrel.[3] Shortly after the 1979 revolution, desperate American oil companies were suddenly willing to pay spot-market prices of up to $28 per barrel—more than twice the official OPEC price of $13.34.[4] The year 1979 was to be the craziest in the craziest decade in the oil industry's history. In two consecutive price hikes—each amounting to 15 percent—OPEC raised its official price to $16.75 per barrel.

Iran Hostage Crisis

Then came November 4, 1979—a day that would change the world, the United States, and the public's view of Marc Rich forever. On that Sunday five hundred Iranians calling themselves the Muslim Students of the Imam Khomeini Line stormed the American embassy in Tehran in the late morning and took ninety people hostage, including sixty-three U.S. citizens. The American chargé d'affaires, Bruce Laingen, and two other diplomats were seized at the Iranian foreign ministry. The Ayatollah Khomeini immediately lent his support to the hostage taking as the "natural reaction of the people" and characterized the embassy as an "American den of spies." Khomeini branded the United States "the Great Satan." (He would later call Israel "the Little Satan.")

In return for freeing the hostages, the alleged students demanded the United States return the ousted shah, Mohammad Reza Pahlavi, who had been undergoing treatment for lymphatic cancer at the Cornell Medical Center in New York for the previous two weeks. The mob chanted, "Khomeini struggles, Carter trembles. Give us the shah. America, America, death to your plots." By "plots" the hostage takers were referring to the coup against the former Iranian prime minister Mohammad Mossadegh. Mossadegh had nationalized the Iranian oil industry in 1951 and limited the shah's powers to such an extent that the ruler was ultimately forced to leave the country. In 1953 Mossadegh was deposed by Iranian army officers, supported by the CIA and the British Secret Intelligence Service.

The attack on the U.S. embassy and the taking of hostages was a violation of diplomatic immunity as laid out at the Vienna Congress of 1814–15, an agreement that even the Nazis had respected during World War II. Embassy grounds are considered extraterritorial areas that are beyond the legal reach of the host nation. President Jimmy Carter called the attack on the U.S. embassy what it was: a breach of international law and an act of terrorism. The hostages were humiliated and presented bound and blindfolded in front of international television cameras. The superpower could only watch powerlessly while the American flag was burned and Carter was hanged in effigy. Every evening the ABC television network broadcast a news program entitled *America Held Hostage* that kept viewers posted on the hostages' suffering. The Iranian hostage crisis was one of the worst humiliations ever suffered by the United States in its entire history, yet it was also an event that helped bring the nation closer together. Yellow ribbons were seen around trees and on house doors across the country as a symbol of solidarity with the hostages.

The Carter administration imposed an array of political and economic sanctions against Iran in mid-November 1979. The import of Iranian crude was prohibited, and approximately $8 billion of Iranian assets in the United States were frozen. Carter's order forbade the transfer of "all property and interests in property of the Government of Iran, its instrumentalities and controlled entities and the Central Bank of Iran which are or become subject to the jurisdiction of the United States."[5] The Iranians in turn canceled all contracts with American oil companies operating in Iran and forbade them from exporting crude oil out of the country.[6]

The United States broke off diplomatic relations with Iran on April 7, 1980. (Since then, U.S. interests in the country have been represented by the government of Switzerland as a protecting power.) President Carter forbade by executive order all financial transactions with Iran and banned "any person subject to the jurisdiction of the United States in connection with any transaction involving Iran, an Iranian governmental entity, an enterprise controlled by Iran or an Iranian governmental entity, or any person in Iran" from making "any payment, transfer of credit, or other transfer of funds or other property of interests therein, except for purposes of family remittances."[7] Only after 444 days were the hostages finally released on January 20, 1981.

The Iranian hostage crisis was a painful tragedy for the United States that seemed to offer proof of an even more painful truth: a miserable failure of U.S. foreign policy. In the wake of this failure, the center of power in the global oil market began to shift inexorably from the United States and other Western industrialized nations toward the oil-producing nations.[8]

The Second Oil Shock of 1979

The political escalation in Iran had three main effects on the oil market. The official OPEC price soared to $38 per barrel in 1980, and prices of up to $50 per barrel were paid for individual shipments—three to four times the price that had existed before the fall of the shah and the highest prices ever paid in the history of the oil business. The price of gasoline doubled within the same time period from 63¢ to $1.30 per gallon. Second, the supply of oil to the United States was endangered—at least temporarily. Finally, the mullahs had broken off contact with American and European companies. If they wanted to continue selling oil, they were in desperate need of a new intermediary.

The decision to locate the headquarters of Marc Rich + Co. in Switzerland, a neutral nation, finally paid off. Rich bought and sold most of the oil he traded through his company in Zug. He did so primarily for tax reasons, but in the case of Iran (and later South Africa) Rich was aware of the political advantages of using a Swiss company to complete his trades. President Carter's executive order excluded "any person subject to the jurisdiction of the United States which is a non-banking association, corporation, or other organization *organized and doing business under the laws of any foreign country* [emphasis added]."⁹ Rich believed that his Swiss company was exempt from the order according to this definition.

The spring of 1979 saw the beginning of one of the twentieth century's most astounding business partnerships. Shortly after the revolution, the anti-Semitic, anticapitalist, and anti-American regime of the Ayatollah Khomeini decided to do business with none other than the Jewish American businessman Marc Rich. In the end, the new government, which had canceled most of the contracts signed during the shah's reign, decided to trade with one of his most important partners.

"They respected the contracts," Rich tells me over lunch. NIOC continued to sell Marc Rich + Co. 8 million to 10 million metric tons of oil per year (approximately 60 million to 75 million barrels) as stipulated by the contract Rich had signed with the shah's government. "They didn't have any objections," he says, as if there were nothing at all unusual about the situation. I had asked him how he had managed to gain the trust of the new Khomeini regime, even though he had worked closely with the shah's government. His laconic answer helps to explain why traders such as Rich exist in the first place and why they are in such great demand. "We performed a service for them," Rich explains. "We bought the oil, we handled the transport, and we sold it. They couldn't do it themselves, so we were able to do it."

The more experienced and successful managers at NIOC during the reign of the shah fled the country when he did, and all other foreign experts had already left. The new executives had no experience whatsoever in running an oil company. They were appointed to head the company for ideological and theological reasons, not for their expertise. They were completely illiterate in even the most basic fundamentals of the commodities trade such as financing, insurance, lading, transport, and unlading. "They were certainly not trained," Rich remembers. I ask Rich if the new directors at NIOC had depended on his company's know-how. Would the Iranians have been helpless without him? Rich laughs. "They didn't behave that way, but in a way it's true."

Rich maintained a much more intensive and much longer business relationship with Iran than was previously known. It is a relationship that extended far beyond the five transactions later listed in prosecutor Rudolph W. Giuliani's indictment. The contract with Iran, which was renewed yearly, remained valid throughout the hostage crisis. "It was a political development which did not affect the business," Rich says. "It was very unpleasant and tragic for the hostages and humiliating for America, but it didn't affect the business. We sold oil because a) it was available and b) the price was right. That's why we did business. We didn't force anyone to either buy from us or sell it to us. In both cases the seller sold it to us because it suited him and the buyer bought it because it suited him. It was a service." I ask him how long he did business with Iran. "Forever," he explains, "until I sold my company to the management" in 1994.[10]

"We Had Oil Available, and Our Competitors Did Not"

The second global oil crisis of 1979 would prove to be—like the first crisis sparked by the Arab oil embargo in 1973—a boon to Marc Rich. Using the information provided by his contacts in the oil-producing nations, Rich had gambled that the political situation in the Middle East would remain unstable. He was convinced that the oil price would continue to rise over the medium term. He therefore continued to seek out new suppliers and was ready to pay good prices for long-term supply guarantees. Iran was by far the most important country—but not the only one—from which Rich purchased his oil.

Jacques Hachuel had, as explained in the previous chapter, already signed a contract of this kind with Ecuador for Marc Rich + Co. before the crisis. The company's partnerships with two African nations were also of great importance. Nigeria, the most populous nation on the continent, had risen to become Africa's largest oil exporter by the 1970s. The West African nation provides a stunning example of the sad phenomenon known as the "resource curse." The nation's immense oil riches never trickled down to benefit the wider population. The country has a history of coups after which the new ruling elite would pillage the treasury and fill their coffers with the nation's wealth. Rich, who has had years of experience with Nigeria, describes the country as "the global capital of corruption." "It is a very unpleasant situation for the people," he says and shakes his head. "Such a rich country, and the people see nothing of it." None of this prevented Rich from signing long-term contracts with the state-owned Nigerian National Petroleum Corporation in November 1976 and September 1978 for the delivery of over fifty thousand barrels per day. In 1976 he also concluded long-term contracts with the Marxist regime in southwestern Angola for large amounts of oil (see chapter 14).

Rich himself describes his long-term way of thinking as one of the most important secrets of his success. "It was always clear to me. We need to have a long-term relationship with our customers. This was our big advantage, the fact that we had a long-term supply. We had oil available, and our competitors did not." He could thus supply the American (and European) oil companies with the oil they so dearly needed. "He was one of the most reliable traders in the sense that if he [said he] had some crude, he really had it," one of his former American buyers said.[11] According to Richard Perkins, then director of global oil trading at

Chevron, "Marc Rich has always performed on his contracts and has good standing with the majors."[12]

The sudden ebb in the flow of Iranian oil posed a serious problem to the United States, which had imported approximately 1 million barrels of oil per day from Iran—around 6 percent of total U.S. consumption. However, this seemingly small percentage caused dramatic supply gaps, and long lines of cars again began to form at the filling stations. In his "Crisis of Confidence" speech, President Carter described the energy crisis as "the moral equivalent of war."[13] Particularly hard hit were the smaller American companies in the "Iranian consortium." This consortium, made up of the state-owned National Iranian Oil Company and American, British, Dutch, and French firms, was founded in the early 1950s after the nationalization of the Iranian oil industry and later dissolved in the wake of the Iranian revolution.[14] While the larger American companies such as Exxon, Gulf Oil, or Mobil could meet demand to some extent with oil from other countries, smaller companies such as Atlantic Richfield were faced with collapse.

ARCO, then the seventh-largest oil company in the United States, exemplified the problems of smaller oil companies in those turbulent times. The company was suddenly short the 125,000 barrels of oil per day that Khomeini's government was no longer willing to deliver. It soon looked as if ARCO would no longer be able to fulfill its contracts, a fact that would have surely spelled ruin for the company. As we have seen (chapter 7), it was thanks to his contract with ARCO that Rich had received his first line of credit in 1974. William F. Ariano, a senior trader at ARCO, had remained Rich's close friend—and steady customer—ever since. When Ariano found he could no longer purchase Iranian oil after the Islamic revolution, he turned in desperation to Rich in August 1979. Marc Rich + Co. became ARCO's largest supplier throughout the crisis. In 1979 and 1980, Rich's company delivered tens of thousands of barrels of mainly Nigerian oil per day. In total, ARCO purchased nearly 27 million barrels from Marc Rich + Co. According to the contract, it

ALAMEDA FREE LIBRARY

had to pay between $2.50 and $8 more per barrel than Rich paid his suppliers. "Try to buy the crude at the lowest price you can, but get the crude. Those were the orders to the crude people," an ARCO representative summed up the sentiment of those years.[15] In his dealings with ARCO alone, Rich made a profit of approximately $120 million within eighteen months. ARCO was pleased to pay the prices Rich asked for, as it was still getting a very good deal. The spot price for crude was much higher than the price Rich asked of his steady clients.

He did not want to ask for the highest possible price, as that would have contradicted his long-term strategy. "To sell a product at the highest possible price to a client in need is like taking candy from a baby," one of Rich's experienced traders explained the company's philosophy. "We just wanted to make something on top of it all. We knew the customers would be grateful and would someday make it up to us. We were investing in the future. The highest price was not the most important factor. What was important was to build up a stable position and a stable business relationship."

This did not mean the company had to go without making a tidy profit, however. A former employee told me that in the wake of the Iranian revolution, Marc Rich + Co. was at times making a profit of up to $14 per barrel.

Israel's Salvation

Rich's most important client in these years was one that would remain forever grateful to him and would later come to his aid: Israel. "The Little Satan" and "the enemy of Islam," as Khomeini referred to the Jewish state, was hit harder by the fall of the shah than any other country— except perhaps for South Africa. The new regime added a clause to all contracts that explicitly prohibited the further sale of Iranian oil to Israel or South Africa. During the reign of Mohammad Reza Pahlavi, Israel imported between 60 and 90 percent of its oil from the shah, making the country almost completely dependent on Iran for its energy needs.[16]

ALAMEDA FREE LIBRARY

The Iranian revolution thus placed Israel in an extremely precarious situation.

Israel's salvation came from none other than Marc Rich—a fact that has remained largely unknown to this day. "Israel owes a great debt to Marc. He provided Israel with all its energy needs in its most difficult times," Avner Azulay told me. Azulay, a former colonel in the Israeli Defense Forces and a high-ranking Mossad agent with a solid network of political contacts, today directs Rich's philanthropic foundation.

Beginning in 1973, Rich would serve as Israel's most important supplier of oil for twenty years. Israel's very survival was dependent on the trader. Rich remembers selling Israel 1 million to 2 million metric tons per year, approximately 7 million to 15 million barrels. The country's oil needs were between 100,000 and 200,000 barrels a day in the 1970s.[17] In other words, Rich provided at least one out of every five barrels.

It was perhaps the ideal trade for Rich. He earned a lot of money while at the same time helping guarantee Israel's survival. "Being Jewish, I didn't mind helping Israel. On the contrary," Rich told me with just the right amount of understatement. "It was a business, but he felt that Israel needed his help," one of Rich's few close friends told me. The Iranian government's official line was that Israel had no right to exist, but Iranian inner circles were well aware of Rich's dealings with Israel. They knew exactly where their oil was flowing, yet no one at NIOC seemed to mind. "They didn't care," Rich told me. "The professionals in the oil business in Iran didn't care. They just wanted to sell oil." This business relationship, which continued up until the mid-1990s, exposed the hypocrisy of the Iranian fundamentalists. When it came to money, profit seemed to be of more importance than radical rhetoric. It was proof of the triumph of the free market over ideology. Moreover, the deal was further proof of Rich's ability to retain his contracts despite radical regime change and against all odds.

Rich's services to Israel granted him access to the highest levels of the Israeli government. He was personally acquainted with Prime Ministers Yitzhak Rabin, Menachem Begin, Yitzhak Shamir, and Shimon

Peres. "I met them particularly because of the business, and also because of Israel in general," Rich explains. His dealings with Israel also strengthened his contacts to the Mossad. The Israeli foreign intelligence service always had a role to play when it came to strategically important energy matters. It took great interest in Rich's many business contacts, as will be shown in chapter 12.

By the beginning of the 1980s, Rich had reached his zenith in terms of power and influence. He was the world's largest independent oil trader and bought and sold more oil every day than Kuwait. "In 1979 you had to know Marc Rich to be able to figure out if you could or couldn't get oil on the spot market," according to Amy Myers Jaffe from the James Baker Institute.[18] "Rich became so big in oil that he seemed to appear like a Saudi sheik wherever there was an oil deal to be made—often to the embarrassment of the American oil companies," wrote A. Craig Copetas.[19]

In 1980 Rich's company had a turnover of $15 billion—more than the gross domestic product of many of the countries with which Rich traded.[20] A look at the tax records in Zug shows that Rich declared a fortune worth 292,784,000 Swiss francs (then around $175 million) in Switzerland alone. His company in Switzerland declared a net profit of 406,400,000 Swiss francs (then approximately $260 million) in the same year.[21] The period between 1974 and 1983, a period that spans the founding of the company and the Iranian revolution, was referred to by Rich's employees as "the golden age." "It was a wonderful feeling," a trader who was with the company at the time enthusiastically explained. "We can take on everybody. We can win the world."

At the high point of Rich's career came the fall from grace. It began one day with a telephone call to a Manhattan office at 1 St. Andrews Plaza.

9

The CASE

One morning in the late fall of 1981, the phone rang in Morris "Sandy" Weinberg's office at 1 St. Andrews Plaza. Weinberg was an ambitious young assistant U.S. attorney for the Southern District of New York. On the other end of the line was a staffer at the Fraud Section of the Department of Justice's Criminal Division. The Justice Department had received a lead involving a crude oil trader named Marc Rich, who maintained an office on New York's Park Avenue. "Marc who?" Weinberg asked. "I've never heard of a Marc Rich."

The former assistant U.S. attorney—today partner in a successful law firm—looks a lot younger than his fifty-seven years of age. He is wearing a blue shirt and a yellow tie and is sipping at a bottle of Perrier. We are sitting at a huge oval table in soft office chairs of artificial leather. On this cool spring morning the visitor can see all the way to St. Petersburg from Weinberg's office on the twelfth floor of the Bank of America Building in downtown Tampa. A pelican flies past the window.[1]

We break the ice by chatting a bit about Roger Federer, the Swiss tennis player who is undisputedly the world's number one player at the time. Weinberg, a fervid wrestler in his youth who once won the Mid-South

Championships, considers Federer to be the best tennis player the world has ever seen.

Weinberg speaks with the singing drawl of a Tennessean born in Chattanooga. He is a classic southern liberal who was heavily influenced by the civil rights movement. His mother was a Southern Baptist, his father a Jew from Brooklyn who knew about discrimination from personal experience. Speaking of himself, Weinberg claims he had a "very progressive upbringing." Like both his brothers, he studied at Princeton, where he graduated magna cum laude. He then attended Vanderbilt University Law School. Weinberg became a federal prosecutor at the age of twenty-nine. At the age of thirty he got the phone call from the Justice Department and was assigned to the Marc Rich case.

Marc Who?

In the late fall of 1981, Rich was almost completely unknown to the public at large, although he was already the world's largest independent oil trader and one of the richest men in America. Outside the close-knit community of commodity traders, almost no one knew his name. Up until 1981 not a single article on either Rich or his company had ever been published outside of the trade journals. He had never given an interview, and Rich was quite happy with the fact that the press did not have a single photograph of him. "We are happiest when nothing is written about us," a Jewish trader in Zurich once told me. "If I was Catholic I would say commodity traders fear publicity like the devil fears holy water."

After the call from the Justice Department, it would not be long until the whole world knew the name Marc Rich. The FBI had already begun looking into deals made by Marc Rich International, a subsidiary of Marc Rich + Co. AG that had a New York office.[2] The Feds had received tips from two Texas oil traders who accused Rich of hiding profits from the Internal Revenue Service by funneling the money to offshore companies and foreign bank accounts. In December 1981, just a few weeks after the call from the Justice Department, Weinberg and an FBI agent flew to Texas to meet with these oil traders.

The tip came from David Ratliff and John Troland, who together had directed West Texas Marketing (WTM) in Abilene. They were serving fourteen months in a federal penitentiary in Big Spring, Texas, at the time, having been convicted in an unrelated case concerning illegal oil transactions, and were hoping to cut a deal with the government in order to avoid serving their entire sentence.[3] Weinberg immediately got them out of prison on furlough, whereupon the two took Weinberg to their office in Abilene. "So there I was in Abilene on a weekend in a godforsaken place," Weinberg told me, "and they pulled out what they called the 'pot file' and explained the scheme. They showed me that over seventy million dollars were in this 'pot.' Marc Rich had in 1980 and 1981 earned more than seventy million in illegal reseller profits and funneled those funds offshore to his Swiss company in order to evade federal income tax and federal energy oil control regulations."

Weinberg realized immediately that he was dealing with a very big case. "It was a big deal. I was very fortunate. It defined me as a young lawyer." What is more, it was the case that put Weinberg's name in the headlines and lent him the national stardom that ultimately launched him on his lucrative career as a lawyer in Tampa. Upon reviewing Troland and Ratliff's dealings with Marc Rich, Weinberg came to the personal conclusion that he had uncovered "the biggest tax fraud of all times," as he proudly tells me. "The case was simple," he says while sizing me up with his glacial blue eyes. "The man made a whole bunch of money that was illegal. He couldn't recognize it. He didn't want to give it up, so he had to get it out of the country some way. He devised a scheme to launder the money outside of the United States by creating these phony oil transactions."

On the flight back to New York, Weinberg began putting his prosecution team together in his mind—the FBI had to be a part of it, the Treasury Department, the Internal Revenue Service, the Customs Service, the State Department. Weinberg was thrilled. "I felt passionately about the case," he says. This was no run-of-the-mill case. This case would set a precedent.

"With Our Shotguns Blazing"

Edward Bennett Williams had seen it all. Nothing could shake the legendary Washington trial lawyer, who had defended high-profile clients such as the singer Frank Sinatra, U.S. Senator Joseph McCarthy, *Playboy* owner Hugh Hefner, financier Robert Vesco, Soviet spy Igor Melekh, and reputed Mafioso Frank Costello. He was a "superlawyer," considered "the ultimate insider," the man to see if you had really big legal trouble. He had a stellar reputation as a "miracle worker who could make the guilty go free."[4]

Marc Rich knew Williams. The lawyer sat on the board of the film studio 20th Century Fox, half of which Rich secretly owned. When it soon became apparent that the Southern District of New York meant business, Rich hired Williams to represent him. Williams had comforting words for Rich. The matter at hand appeared to be an ordinary energy case parading as a tax case—the type of proceedings the government routinely settled without pressing criminal charges. He assured Rich that he could settle the case without an indictment if Rich agreed to pay a fine and a portion of the taxes he allegedly owed. He gave the same advice to Rich that he gave to all of his clients: Keep quiet and stonewall. "The worst you can do is talk to the prosecutors. I can get rid of it for thirty million," he told Rich and then offered him the following words of encouragement: "We shall go to the U.S. Attorney with our shotguns blazing."[5]

Williams adopted this attitude when he visited Assistant U.S. Attorney Sandy Weinberg in his office in New York in May 1983. He threw himself onto a chair, leaned back, put his feet on the table, and asked Weinberg how much money the government wanted to settle the case. "You don't have to worry," Williams added patronizingly, "my clients don't flee."⁶ He proposed to dispose of the case by having Rich pay the taxes owed plus a substantial fine.

Was Williams putting too much stock in his reputation? Did he think he could easily put one over on the young assistant U.S. attorney? Whatever the case, this tactic did not work on Sandy Weinberg.

Weinberg looked the celebrity superlawyer straight in the eye, shook his head, and said with no more respect than necessary that he was not interested in a plea deal. Puzzled, Williams asked Weinberg what he had in mind. Weinberg spelled it out for him: "J-A-I-L."⁷ The government, he continued, would not accept a plea agreement unless it included both "a huge fine and substantial jail time." Weinberg would not change his mind, even after Williams raised his offer to $100 million (see chapter 13). According to Rich's Swiss lawyer André A. Wicki, Weinberg was seeking a twenty-five-year prison sentence. He threatened to indict Rich, his partner Pinky Green, and the Rich companies on racketeering charges if no such settlement could be reached.

Weinberg clearly looks back on his former brazenness with delight. "I took Ed Williams's breath away a bit," he says. The attorney, who—ironically—now defends white-collar criminals, believes his refusal to deal with Williams was a matter of principle. "If we allowed people to buy their way out of it, if you don't go to jail for [what in his mind was] the biggest tax fraud, we could never bring another tax case."

Rich's Flight to Switzerland

The Rich family was then staying at their weekend house on Long Island's Lido Beach, as was usually the case at that time of year. "We were at the beach for the weekend, and Marc said we may have to leave the country," Denise Rich remembers with a shudder. We are sitting in her penthouse at 785 Fifth Avenue. Above the photographs of her daughters' weddings hangs a still life of flowers by Marc Chagall.

Denise Rich knows how to give a convincing performance. She shakes her head in wide-eyed disbelief as if Rich himself had just given her the devastating news. "I had no clue, believe me. I didn't know anything about what was going on. 'Why?' I asked Marc. 'There may be a few problems,' he answered. 'Why?' 'The lawyer will talk to you.' The lawyer, Bob Thomajan, walked me around the block three times in New York and I still didn't know why. If we were going to have to leave, what was I going to do? As a wife, you know, I love my husband. I love my children. I consulted my father, who was a very smart man; he was my rock. What should I do? Papa said, 'You go with your husband, of course.' "

Denise did just as her father, Emil Eisenberg, advised. In the first week of June 1983, the Rich family hastily relocated to Switzerland, where Rich had based his company nine years earlier. Rich was rattled by the fact that Williams had lost control of the case—and with that lost the opportunity to settle the case out of court. Rich, who stresses his innocence to this day, was alarmed by the prosecutor's aggressive posture. The threat of racketeering charges was a dramatic escalation. A RICO indictment, Williams explained, would mean all of Rich's assets could be frozen before the case even came to trial. The statute, about which I will write more later in the chapter, also provided for draconian jail sentences.

Rich was deeply shocked. The man who was used to settling so much with money had simply not expected events to turn against him. He took it as a sign that he should flee the country, but the few weeks of absence that Denise Rich had initially expected soon became an eternity. In Rich's mind, his flight to Switzerland represented a second escape (the first being from Antwerp) and a journey of no return. Rich had renounced his U.S. citizenship and became a naturalized Spaniard in September 1982. "I was naturalized under the laws of Spain, swore an oath of allegiance to the King of Spain, and formally stated that I thereby renounced U.S. nationality," he claims.[8] However, the State Department takes the view that it never approved Rich's Certificate of Loss of Nationality and thus he had failed to renounce his U.S. citizenship.[9] Rich also took on Israeli citizenship in July 1983.

Ed Williams's biographer describes how the lawyer was standing in

Marvin Davis's office in Los Angeles when he heard the news that his client was on the lam. Williams screamed into the telephone, "You know something, Marc? You spit on the American flag. You spit on the jury system. Whatever you get, you deserve. We could have gotten the minimum. Now you're going to sink."[10] Rich claims there is not a shred of truth in this version of events. On the contrary, Rich maintains that neither Williams nor any of his other lawyers had ever asked him to return to the United States.

Regardless, Williams's overconfident performance caused quite a bit of damage. His misinterpretation of the situation led his client down a dead-end street—and into the headlines. "It was a scorched earth policy," said Michael Green, who joined Rich's legal team in 1985. "Ed was known as a tough litigator. Sometimes it works. In Rich's case it did not."

Rudolph W. Giuliani Takes Over

The case was exactly the type the media loves. It was a case of "historic" significance, as the prosecuting attorneys never tired of stating: a virtually unknown millionaire with a beautiful wife who lived in a Park Avenue penthouse. Journalists soon discovered that Rich owned half of 20th Century Fox, as a silent partner. His name had not surfaced publicly when Denver oilman Marvin Davis negotiated the $722 million purchase in June 1981.[11] The film studio was riding on a wave of success at the time. George Lucas's *Return of the Jedi*, the third part of the Star Wars saga, had just opened; at the time it was the greatest box-office success in cinematic history. Several prominent Americans sat on 20th Century Fox's board of directors, including former president Gerald R. Ford and former secretary of state Henry A. Kissinger.

When Rudolph W. Giuliani was appointed U.S. attorney for the Southern District of New York in the spring of 1983, the case, which had been slowly simmering over a relatively small flame for a year, suddenly became a raging wildfire. Giuliani pressed his subordinates to prosecute cases more quickly; happy to see himself in the role of an anti-Mafia crusader willing to take on Wall Street and white-collar criminals, he did not doubt in the least that he was born for a greater purpose. "Aggressive" was the label that was most often used to describe Giuliani. His tactics, as the former mayor of New York David Dinkins once said, were "dangerously close" to a "philosophy that the ends justify the means."[12] Ed Williams's biographer described the prosecutor and later mayor of New York City as "zealous and politically ambitious."[13] According to Leonard Garment, the former special counsel to President Richard Nixon and former U.S. delegate to the United Nations who began to represent Marc Rich in 1985, Giuliani quickly realized that he had a "blockbuster case" on his hands.[14]

The result was a calamitous breakdown in communications between the government and Rich's lawyers. The situation was worsened by the fact that Rich's then legal team had attempted all sorts of dubious maneuvers in order to have the case deferred. Sandy Weinberg still has trouble understanding Rich's behavior. "It was just stupid," he tells me, shaking his head. "It was self-destructive. He underestimated us. He played games with the documents. He made the case ten times bigger than it ever would have been. If he had stayed here and addressed it, it would have been manageable. He would have done some jail time, you know, but it would have been manageable."

The spark in the powder keg was a dispute over business documents belonging to Rich's companies. After the Southern District had begun its examination of the case, it convened a grand jury that soon began subpoenaing millions of documents from Marc Rich International, Marc Rich + Co. AG, and oil companies and resellers in the United States that had done business with Rich. Marc Rich International—a Swiss subsidiary with a branch office in New York that paid taxes in the United States—complied with the subpoenas. However, Marc Rich + Co. AG, as a Swiss company operating in Switzerland under Swiss law, refused to obey the order. The company argued that Swiss secrecy law prohibited the company from producing documents without the express permission of the Swiss government.[15]

Draconian Fine

Nevertheless, District Judge Leonard Sand denied Rich's lawyers' motion to dismiss the subpoenas and ordered Marc Rich + Co. AG to produce the documents located at the company's headquarters in Zug. When the company continued to refuse, Judge Sand ordered a draconian contempt fine of $50,000 per day until the documents were delivered. The fine was applied beginning in late June 1983, even though the Swiss government protested the decision with unusual vigor as an unacceptable violation of Swiss sovereignty.

Rich refused to pay the fine. He secretly sold Marc Rich International to Alec Hackel, his close friend and one of the founders of the company, who then ran the company under the name Clarendon Ltd. in Zug. Judge Sand labeled the sale a "ploy to frustrate the implementation of the court's order" and threatened to freeze up to $55 million of Marc Rich + Co. AG's assets in twenty American and European banks and other companies that owed Rich's company money.[16]

Rich's business was soon suffering under Judge Sand's record contempt fine and the drastic threat to freeze the company's accounts. Several business partners and banks pressured Rich to find a solution to the problem. Faced with increasing difficulties in obtaining credit, Rich's lawyers began to negotiate a resolution. On August 5, 1983, lawyers for both sides met in Judge Sand's Manhattan apartment and discussed the case until late into the night. They finally reached a deal just before midnight: Rich agreed to pay the New York court $1.35 million toward the accumulated fine, to produce the court-ordered documents in Switzerland, and to pay off the remaining fines at a future date. The agreement appeared to smooth all the ruffled feathers, and it seemed as if the case would finally take on a semblance of normality.

Four days later, however, on August 9, 1983, Weinberg received a telephone call. "A guy said, 'This is Deep Throat,' no kidding," Weinberg recounts. "He called out of Milgrim, Thomajan & Lee, Marc Rich's law firm, and warned us that subpoenaed documents were being shipped out of the United States on a Swissair flight. He even called back to give us the correct flight number, SR 111 to Geneva and Zurich." Weinberg could not believe his ears. He cursed so loudly that his colleagues came into his office to see what was wrong. After he cooled down, he immediately sent a few agents to John F. Kennedy International Airport.

At 7:00 P.M. the Swissair Boeing 747 was already on the runway and ready for takeoff; the police were able to stop the plane only minutes before its departure. Thanks to the tip-off from Rich's own law firm, agents recovered two steamer trunks full of business documents. Shortly afterward, the media-savvy Giuliani had the trunks brought to Judge Sand's courtroom as physical evidence of Rich's brazen behavior and immediately held a press conference to publicize the seizure. The episode was soon referred to as the "steamer trunk affair." "By this time Marc Rich had lost all credibility; he was down the toilet. After that affair he was viewed as a scoundrel," says Weinberg, who felt that Rich's actions strengthened the prosecution's hand. "It prejudiced him in court and in the public opinion. When people obstruct justice and try to interfere with your investigation, that indicates that you're right." Rich's lawyers maintained they were only shipping the papers to Switzerland to let them be viewed by an attorney in order to make sure they contained no confidential information. As a result of the incident, a furious Judge Sand ordered that all of Rich's companies produce the subpoenaed documents by the following Friday. "By Friday?" Rich's flabbergasted attorney asked. "We have forty-eight offices worldwide." "By Friday!" Judge Sand ordered.

Caught in the Crossfire

August of 1983 was one of the hottest that Switzerland had ever seen. It seemed even hotter in Rich's headquarters in Zug. A dozen people sorted through the documents they needed to send to the United States in a jet that Rich had chartered especially for the purpose. "We worked day and night," one of them told me, "fourteen, fifteen hours per day." Four of the five founding partners were present—Marc Rich, Pinky Green, Alec Hackel, and John Trafford—as well as two lawyers and a handful of young employees. Within three days the group handed over two hundred thousand documents to officials in the United States, and that was just the beginning.

Then, on August 13, officers from the Office of the Attorney General of Switzerland knocked on the door of Marc Rich + Co. AG in Zug. They had come to seize any remaining documents that had been subpoenaed by the U.S. government. They cited article 273 of the Swiss Penal Code, which deals with the disclosure of information to foreign countries and economic espionage. The Swiss government wrote a letter to the State Department and the district court stating that it was "legally and physically impossible for Marc Rich + Co AG to provide the U.S. Attorney with any single document located in Switzerland."[17] Now Rich not only had the government of the United States to worry about; the Swiss government was after him as well. "He was caught in the crossfire," remembers one of the participants, who is still in the commodities business.

The Swiss government's actions did nothing to dampen Judge Sand's resolve. He continued to demand all of the subpoenaed documents and ruled that the contempt fine of $50,000 per day should continue. For the next year one of Marc Rich's messengers would deliver a check for $200,000 to the federal courthouse each Friday and a check for $150,000 each Monday—all in all, more than $21 million. The Swiss repeated their protest in an official note describing the "violation of generally recognized principles of international law. The imposition by a foreign authority of acts aimed at having effects on Swiss territory violates the sovereignty of Switzerland and is therefore unacceptable."[18]

Rich, who one year earlier had been one of the great unknowns of the international oil trade, was now recognized by over half of the entire world—a fact that certainly seemed to boost the reputations of Rudy Giuliani and Sandy Weinberg. The American and international media reported regularly on the Rich affair and its international implications, and thus made the two prosecutors national celebrities.

Giuliani, who pushed his attorneys to produce indictments, had a few more aces up his sleeve. In mid-September 1983 he invited journalists to a press conference the likes of which they had never before seen. In Giuliani's view, this press conference was a historic event.

"The Largest Tax Evasion Indictment Ever"

Journalists called to the law library on the eighth floor of the U.S. attorney's office, where Rudolph W. Giuliani was waiting on Monday, September 19, 1983, witnessed a rarity: a prosecutor reading aloud from a bill of indictment. When Giuliani began performing *United States of America v. Marc Rich, Pincus Green, et. al.,* he evoked an atmosphere of Chicago in the old days. Fifty-one counts of fraud, racketeering, tax evasion, and other charges were contained in the indictment.[19]

It was "the largest tax evasion indictment ever," Giuliani said.[20] He continued to read from the indictment. "The defendants engaged in this scheme as a part of a pattern of racketeering activity in which they concealed in excess of $100 million in taxable income of the defendant *Marc Rich International*, most of which income was illegally generated through the defendants' violations of federal energy laws and regulations. This scheme, and pattern of racketeering activity, enabled the defendant *Marc Rich International* to evade in excess of $48 million in United States taxes for the 1980 and 1981 tax years."[21]

Giuliani, however, held back the most serious charge until the end of the press conference. It was a charge that would follow Rich for the rest of his life. "On November 4, 1979, Iranian nationals invaded the U.S. Embassy in Teheran, Iran. Thereafter, 53 American citizens were held hostage for over 14 months until their release on January 19, 1981." Despite the trade embargo and further regulations that President Jimmy Carter imposed after the hostage-taking incident, the indictment stated, Marc Rich + Co. AG "entered into contracts with the National Iranian Oil Company (NIOC) to purchase Iranian crude and fuel oil." Marc Rich and Pincus Green had personally "negotiated from the offices of *Marc Rich International* in New York . . . the sale of approximately 6,250,000 barrels of Iranian crude oil for approximately $202,806,291.00."[22]

Trading with the enemy—the gravest of accusations. Congressman Chris Shays (R–Connecticut) summarized the public mood toward Marc Rich and Pincus Green, "saying they were two traitors to their country and our country."[23] Sandy Weinberg told me it was an accidental discovery, as they had only come across the dealings with Iran in the course of the investigation. "These Iranian transactions were outrageous," he told me.

The Oil Price Control

To fully understand the criminal case against Rich, we must begin with a highly simplified explanation of the extraordinary complex federal price control regulations that governed the sale of crude oil in the United States after the first oil crisis in 1973. As we've seen, the Arab oil embargo of October 1973 that followed in the aftermath of the Yom Kippur War unleashed an oil shock throughout the United States. President Richard Nixon signed the Emergency Petroleum Allocation Act only a few weeks after the embargo had gone into effect.[24]

From November 1973 to February 1981, the United States regulated the price of American crude oil to encourage domestic production. Different prices were allowed for three categories of oil. These three types of oil were chemically indistinguishable but were categorized on the basis of their source. Crude oil from a well operating at or below its 1972 production levels was known as "old oil," the cheapest of the three. Then came "new oil," which included oil discovered after 1973 or oil obtained from existing wells in excess of 1972 production levels. The most expensive category of oil was known as "stripper oil," oil obtained by squeezing the last drops of oil from wells that were nearly exhausted and whose average daily production was less than ten barrels.

Only American stripper oil could be sold openly for whatever price the world market would bear—a price that far exceeded the regulated prices for old and new oil. In 1980 a barrel of stripper oil could generally be sold for over $20 more than a barrel of old oil and $15 more than a barrel of new oil.[25] These regulations had no effect on the price of oil in other parts of the world.

This Byzantine pricing system was in fact a regulatory nightmare that completely flouted free-market principles. Different regulations applied to different types of oil producers, oil refiners, and resellers, as well as to oil produced from different types of wells according to the amount of oil these wells had produced in the past. It was a political farce that distorted the international and domestic crude oil markets. President Ronald Reagan abolished the act by executive order on his first day in office in January 1981.

Although the regulations were complicated, the reality in the market was even more so. The system of price controls only applied to the first sale of regulated oil in the United States. Upon subsequent sales of the same oil, further regulations limited an increase in price by restricting the amount of profit that a reseller was allowed to make by trading in or speculating on crude oil. This "permissible average markup" (PAM) was calculated by the Department of Energy based on a given company's past profit margins. Newer companies with little or no trading history, such as Marc Rich International, were not allocated a PAM until September 1980. Beginning on September 1, 1980—only months before Reagan abolished the act and paved the way for deregulation—these resellers were permitted a fixed maximum profit of twenty cents per barrel.

It was against this backdrop of regulation and price controls that Rich sought to run his business and turn a profit. Where others saw only obstacles and difficulties, Rich saw business opportunities. He attempted to use the regulations to his advantage and earn the maximum possible return. The oil markets adapted to the regulations very quickly, while dealers tried to avoid the price caps wherever possible. One way of doing this was by combining a deal involving price-controlled domestic oil with a deal involving nonregulated foreign oil. Companies began to swap oil from different categories in order to allow one party to obtain unregulated oil that could be sold at the full market price. Discounts and additional advantages were made available for this purpose. For these types of deals, U.S. companies needed an experienced international reseller with good contacts in the global market. Marc Rich was the perfect candidate. In 1979 and 1980 he was *the* international oil trader. No one else had better business relations with partners in the Middle East, Africa, and Europe. His two companies—Marc Rich International (MRI), with a branch office in New York, and Marc Rich + Co. AG in Switzerland—were perfectly positioned to profit from this trade.

John Troland, co-owner of West Texas Marketing, was aware of this fact, and in the fall of 1979 he suggested a deal to Rich. According to Troland, WTM could legally "tier trade" regulated oil obtained at the lower regulated prices for uncontrolled domestic oil that could then be sold at the unregulated free market price. However, WTM had difficulty obtaining regulated oil. Many producers were willing to sell their regulated oil at the controlled price only in combination with an additional transaction that they themselves would benefit from. These transactions involved unregulated foreign oil sold at a discounted price. WTM, Troland explained, did not have the necessary access to the foreign oil market to engage in this additional transaction. Troland knew that Rich had the knowledge, the connections, and the capacity to trade in the global oil market.

In a typical example of this process, Marc Rich + Co. made discounted offshore sales of unregulated foreign oil to Charter Crude Oil Company, an American oil producer from Texas. Charter then agreed to sell cheap price-controlled domestic oil to MRI that MRI would then resell to WTM. WTM swapped this cheap oil for higher-value unregulated oil and sold it back to MRI at a discount. MRI subsequently sold the oil at market prices on the global market. After the transaction was completed, MRI compensated Marc Rich + Co. for the discount it had given to Charter in order to obtain the regulated oil. Without this discount, Charter would never have been able to sell cheap domestic oil.

This form of transaction continued after the twenty-cent permissible average markup was imposed on MRI in September 1980, but the transactions were restructured to greatly reduce MRI's role. MRI no longer acquired the tier-traded domestic oil at a discount and no longer reimbursed Marc Rich + Co. for its losses on the offshore trades at the beginning of the transactions. Instead, WTM and another reseller, Listo Petroleum, sold the tier-traded domestic oil at the higher unregulated price and paid Marc Rich + Co. for its contribution to the entire transaction. The U.S. oil producers involved in these restructured transactions were Charter and Atlantic Richfield—the longtime trading partner of Marc Rich International.

The purpose of these complicated transactions was always the same. One of the traders in the chain gained access to unregulated oil that could later be sold for the highest price that could be obtained on the global market. In return the business partners involved in these linked transactions were compensated for their costs and troubles.

"Sham Transactions"

These tier trades were considered legal and were practiced by all of the established oil companies. However, the payments that had been transferred back and forth between Marc Rich International and Marc Rich + Co. were a point of contention. Rich's lawyers emphasize the fact that these payments were "entirely proper" under the tax treaty between the United States and Switzerland. According to his Washington attorney Michael Green, the Swiss tax treaty "was the beginning and the end of the linkage." Prosecutors Weinberg and Giuliani were of a completely different opinion. The Southern District alleged that Marc Rich International had evaded paying taxes by diverting income taxable in the United States to its Swiss parent company, Marc Rich + Co. AG, which did not pay taxes in the United States. They did not even address the issue of the Swiss tax treaty. The prosecutors viewed the various transactions that constituted these trades and exchanges with a high degree of suspicion. They did not believe that offshore foreign oil transactions, which initiated the later movements of oil, justified the amounts of money that were transferred offshore. The prosecutors referred to such moves as "sham transactions" and "fraudulent deductions" that were covered up by "false and fraudulent invoices." They believed Rich channeled the illicit profits abroad by means of further such "sham transactions."[26]

According to the indictment, Rich and WTM had agreed that these huge profits, which they referred to as the "pot," would be retained by WTM so that they would not be reflected in MRI's books. "To further conceal the scheme [Rich and Green] did cause WTM to prepare and mail invoices . . . which falsely indicated that WTM had sold the stripper barrels to the defendant [Marc Rich] International at the high world market price, when in truth and in fact the defendant [Marc Rich] International was paying a far lower price upon WTM's agreement secretly to kickback to the defendants the huge profits held by WTM for the defendant International in the 'pot.' "[27]

According to the prosecutors, Marc Rich had sold regulated oil at profits exceeding the permitted maximum level and had evaded reporting the excess profits by secretly funneling them offshore. They accused the Swiss company Marc Rich + Co. of covering up the profits by selling oil to its U.S. subsidiary Marc Rich International at an artificially high rate. When the subsidiary then resold the oil at lower market rates, it incurred a sizable loss in the United States, thus allowing the company to avoid income taxes.[28] "Instead of the allowed twenty cents per barrel, Marc Rich made five dollars per barrel," Weinberg explained. "We found two sets of handwritten ledgers that showed both sides of the phony transactions—shipments that don't exist. You tell me, that's legal? Bunch of nonsense!" The prosecutors definitely did not view these transactions as a legal form of tax optimization. To them it was more, much more: organized crime.

Prosecutors Go Nuclear

The law designed to combat organized crime was intentionally named the Racketeer Influenced and Corrupt Organizations Act in order to obtain the acronym RICO, after the ambitious gangster played by Edward G. Robinson in the 1931 film *Little Caesar*. The act was intended to make it easier to prosecute organized crime figures and strike a devastating blow against their economic structures. Under RICO the defendant's assets can be seized before the case comes to trial or even before an indictment. It is the heaviest piece of artillery in a federal prosecutor's arsenal. John W. Dean, former counsel to President Richard Nixon, dubbed RICO "the prosecutor's equivalent of nuclear weaponry."[29] It is considered to be one of the most controversial statutes in the federal criminal code.[30]

In Marc Rich's case, Giuliani used RICO for the first time ever in a case that did not explicitly deal with more archetypal examples of organized crime, such as the Mafia or drug trafficking. After Rich's indictment, U.S. authorities blocked all of the bank accounts belonging either to Rich personally or to his companies on American soil. These included Rich's stock interests in Marc Rich + Co. and 20th Century Fox. Shortly after the indictment, the IRS issued a jeopardy assessment of more than $91 million against Marc Rich International. The assets, "subject to forfeiture to the United States," included everything from bank accounts, securities, and real estate to office equipment, furniture, and fixtures. The list of seized assets amounted to six pages of the indictment.[31] Rich's Fifth Avenue apartment was considered blocked, as were his weekend condominium on Long Island, his interest in Steinhardt Investments (the early hedge fund run by Michael Steinhardt), and the interest in his retirement account. Furthermore, the IRS served levy notices on banks and companies doing business with Rich. These companies were advised that money they received from Rich could be seized.

They were also prohibited from paying back any money they might have owed Rich.

"It was phenomenal," Sandy Weinberg told me with glee. "We tied up all U.S. assets, including 20th Century Fox. We shut 'em down completely. We shut the company down for a year. They couldn't operate in the U.S. It cost them dearly. I assume it cost them probably a billion dollars."

Unconditional Surrender

The company's credit lifeline was practically severed. Many trading houses were trying to reduce their exposure to the company and were cutting their trading limit with Rich. "Our companies were collapsing," Rich himself summed it up when we talked about the consequences of the freeze. The RICO strategy, with which Giuliani and Weinberg intended to force Rich into capitulation, worked. It pressured him into plea negotiations. "The alternatives were to plead guilty and pay—or to die," Rich's Swiss attorney André A. Wicki told me. "RICO was the death sentence against the companies," said attorney Michael Green. "Giuliani wanted victory at all costs, another feather in his cap. He wanted to polish his image as a crime fighter." The result was total and unconditional surrender.

On October 10, 1984, in a plea bargain Marc Rich + Co. AG and Marc Rich International pleaded guilty to making false statements as part of a scheme to circumvent profit controls and thus evade $48 million in taxes. The companies agreed to pay a settlement of $150 million and $813,000 in fines and court costs, to forfeit $21 million in contempt fines, and to forgo income tax deductions on the settlement worth up to an additional $40 million. Altogether the settlement was worth more than $200 million. In return the government lifted the yearlong freeze on Rich's U.S. assets. In order to pay the settlement, Rich had to sell his 50 percent share in 20th Century Fox, for which he received $116 million from Marvin Davis. He also sold an oil refinery in Guam.

One day later, on October 11, 1984, a memorable meeting took place in the federal courthouse at Foley Square. Rich's lawyer handed a check for $130 million to a lawyer from Chase Manhattan Bank for money owed to fourteen U.S. and European banks. Chase Manhattan's lawyer simultaneously handed Sandy Weinberg a check for $113,018,306.71. The lawyer from Marc Rich International announced the company would abandon rights to the $36,981,693.29 that the IRS had seized a year earlier. Giuliani immediately held a press conference at which he proudly waved the check in his outstretched hand. Once again he stressed the historic importance of his success. The total settlement of roughly $200 million, Giuliani said, "represents the largest amount of money ever recovered by the United States in a criminal tax-evasion case."[32]

While their companies were back in business, Rich and Green themselves were not included in the settlement. Prosecutor Giuliani repeated what Weinberg had said to Ed Williams more than a year earlier: He would accept no plea bargain from the traders unless it would "expose them to substantial prison terms."[33] "Rudy wasn't very secure, you know," remembers Sandy Weinberg, and it is easy to believe him when he says he would never vote for Giuliani in an election. "He's so political. He was concerned that he'd be criticized by the *New York Times* if he did a deal with a fugitive." All of the charges against Rich and Green remained outstanding for the next seventeen years. Under U.S. law the accused could not be tried in their absence.

What Giuliani failed to mention to reporters at the press conference was that he had had a first-class opportunity the previous year to have Marc Rich arrested, and didn't.

10

RUDY GIULIANI'S FAILURES

It was a rainy summer's day on June 28, 1983, when Jürg Leutert, the Swiss government's lawyer, visited the U.S. attorney in his Manhattan office. It was nearly three months before the September press conference when Giuliani would read out the indictment against Marc Rich. Both Rich and Green had fled to Switzerland with their families only a short time ago. It was a very low-key face-to-face meeting, the existence of which has remained unknown until now. Leutert was on an official visit in the name of the Swiss government, which considered the entire Rich affair something of an inopportune embarrassment. In recent years, the United States and Switzerland had fought out several legal disputes involving insider trading, which, as was the case in many other countries, was not illegal in Switzerland at that time. The tone between the two countries had hardened.

Switzerland's economic ties with the United States were of the utmost importance. In 1983, Swiss participation in the U.S. equity market alone accounted for almost one sixth of all foreign trading and amounted to over $20 billion.[1] The United States was Switzerland's second-largest export market after Germany. The hype surrounding the Rich case was not at all in the interest of the Swiss government, and this led Switzerland to seek out a more pragmatic solution that would allow both countries to save face.

When he walked into the prosecutor's office on that day in late June 1983, Jürg Leutert was prepared to make Giuliani just such an offer. Leutert first explained that the Swiss government had no interest in defending the interests of an alleged tax criminal. He also made it clear, however, that Switzerland would defend its sovereignty and would never allow foreign law enforcement agencies to operate on Swiss soil in any way or form without the government's explicit approval. "Swiss companies are subject to Swiss law," Leutert stated. Leutert then asked Giuliani what he had on Marc Rich. "For the longest time we did not know what the charges against Rich actually were. Was it tax evasion? In that case Swiss law would have prevented us from offering legal assistance. I told Giuliani if it was tax fraud, however, we might be able to help," Leutert told me during a telephone interview from Brazil, where he served as the Swiss ambassador for several years and now runs a management consultancy firm. Switzerland is unique when it comes to differentiating between tax *evasion* and tax *fraud*.[2] In Switzerland the intentional failure to report income or assets on a tax return is not considered a crime but a case of tax evasion, which is dealt with using only administrative sanctions. Tax fraud, involving criminal sanctions, takes place when income is fraudulently identified using a falsified document, such as a bank statement, an invoice, or a balance sheet.

In 1983 there were basically two legal instruments available to foreign prosecutors asking for Swiss help: an extradition treaty signed in 1900 and the new Swiss Federal Act on International Mutual Assistance in Criminal Matters (IMAC), which had come into effect on January 1. Leutert provided Giuliani with a detailed explanation of how he should proceed. IMAC allowed the exchange of information, documents, details from witness interrogations, and the confiscation of assets in the case of tax fraud. Even more interesting, according to the 1900 agreement extradition was possible for persons charged with "counterfeiting or forgery of public or private documents; the fraudulent use of counterfeited or forged instruments . . . [; or] obtaining money or other property by false pretences." This was almost the exact wording that Giluliani would later use in the indictment against Rich.[3]

A Mysterious Lapse

"Within the framework of this agreement, a telephone call would have been enough," recounted Leutert. "The Americans only needed to tell us that they had a huge case of fraud or forgery on their hands, involving a certain Marc Rich living in Switzerland. They only needed to ask us: Could you please arrest him pending receipt of an extradition request? It all would have happened fairly quickly after that, and Swiss police would have taken Marc Rich into provisional custody. This was exactly the course of action that I presented to Giuliani. It was a very good conversation lasting two hours—very open, very friendly, and very cooperative. Giuliani told me that it was indeed a case of fraud and that he could use the information I had given him, but nothing happened. Giuliani's reasons for failing to use the agreement remain a mystery for me to this day."

Under the terms of IMAC, Giuliani could have written a letter of request asking the Swiss government to hand over business documents belonging to Marc Rich + Co., as IMAC takes precedence over Swiss bank secrecy provisions. The established channels of mutual assistance, Leutert reminded Giuliani, had proven extremely successful. Of the 250 requests that the U.S. government had sent to Switzerland over the previous six years, the Swiss government had granted 248, and the Alpine nation had never rejected a single U.S. extradition request.

Viewed objectively, this would have been a course of action that would have allowed prosecutors to arrest Rich and gain access to his covert business activities. Giuliani knew this, of course, and at the September 1983 press conference where he read aloud from the bill of indictment, he announced that U.S. authorities would file a request for extradition. In fact, the U.S. attorney later chose a different strategy—a strategy that was much more likely to get the case in the headlines. Giuliani did not file a letter of request but instead chose to let the case escalate. He wanted to prove that he was tough on white-collar criminals by making an example of Rich. He wanted to play hardball.

The affair soon erupted into the worst diplomatic conflict of all time between Switzerland and the United States, culminating in an open diplomatic clash, and it poisoned relations between the two countries for years to come. Even the conservative *Neue Zürcher Zeitung*, a rather staid Swiss daily, expressed its confusion over Giuliani's mistakes: "The reason behind the United States' decision not to request [Swiss] legal assistance at the very beginning of the affair, as is usually the case in such instances and given that such assistance can normally be administered without difficulty, largely remains a mystery even to local [American] observers."[4] The internationally respected weekly *Die Weltwoche*, which is usually rather pro-American in tone, commented, "It is not entirely clear why the United States is balking at the due process of law. It is possible that the New York prosecutor Giuliani is seeking the loudest possible fanfare for his dream trial that involves 'the biggest tax fraud in the history of the United States.' "[5]

The Stubborn Swiss

The U.S. Department of Justice finally applied for Swiss legal assistance in the case in July 1984, a year after the conversation between Giuliani and Leutert and ten months after the indictment was issued. A short time later the United States demanded Rich's extradition. However, the daily fines of $50,000 were not withdrawn despite Swiss protests. The Swiss authorities reacted with stubbornness. Although they had promised a speedy handling of the request "in as little as three weeks," they refused to extradite Rich and held back from delivering the requested documents. The Swiss Office for Police Matters issued an official explanation stating that it denied the requests because under Swiss law Rich's actions "qualified as fiscal violations" and violations of "provisions concerning currency, trade policy and economic policy."[6]

This was only half true, however. The Swiss government had long ceased to be concerned with this one particular case against Rich. Now the authorities were more concerned with issues of Swiss sovereignty, which they believed was being abused by U.S. actions. "Legal assistance and sanctions issued by a foreign government are mutually exclusive," stated the Swiss government clearly.[7] A confidential paper issued by the Swiss embassy in Washington on July 13, 1984, warned that the "unilateral acts of coercion carried out by U.S. authorities on Swiss soil" should not be rewarded with legal assistance. The Swiss thus made their promise of legal assistance dependent on American respect for Swiss sovereignty.

A senior top Swiss official involved in the case told me, "Whoever wants Swiss cooperation cannot simultaneously ignore Swiss law by employing compulsory measures. A year earlier we would have regarded an arrest request with great favor." Jürg Leutert, for his part, remembers a walk he took with Minister of Justice Kurt Furgler at the beginning of the affair, during which the minister told him point-blank, "So just give the Americans what they want." That is exactly what Rich's lawyers had feared most, as they were well aware that the Swiss government was anxious to maintain good relations with the United States. "The extradition request was the worst," André Wicki told me. "At least we could avoid Marc Rich and Pincus Green being arrested pending extradition."

What would have happened if Giuliani had already made an extradition request in 1983? Statements made by Swiss diplomats and Rich's lawyer make it clear that Rich would have at the very least been taken into provisional custody pending extradition. Whether the charges would have been sufficient to allow for extradition remains open for debate. However, the whole story—and Rich's willingness to cooperate—would certainly have taken a much different course. In the event, Giuliani, the canny attorney who always knew what was best for his own career, let this unique opportunity to have Rich arrested slip through his fingers.

American Legal Isolationism

The American authorities were aware of the importance of a provisional arrest. "Usually, the key to a successful extradition is the provisional arrest of the fugitive," Alvin D. Lodish later explained in this matter. Lodish served as a senior trial attorney with the Office of International Affairs at the U.S. Department of Justice. "Many cases are quickly resolved after the provisional arrest has been perfected. The requirements for provisional arrest are significantly less burdensome than the requirements for the full extradition."[8]

Giuliani's tough-guy bearing got in the way of all this. It was one of the early cases of American legal (and political) isolationism—the tendency of the American government to ignore other jurisdictions. It was a strategy that led the United States into a blind alley. In retrospect, it is striking how the most powerful nation on earth proceeded: without forging alliances, without having a comprehensive strategy, without taking into account the political realities—at the risk of alienating friends and allies.

Giuliani's "shoot first, ask questions later mentality" led to a "fruitless stalemate," according to a diplomat in the Swiss capital who was assigned to the case. Thus the window of opportunity that had been wide open in the summer of 1983 was bolted and barred a year later. According to Leutert, Assistant U.S. Attorney Weinberg "was very aggressive with me personally and very impolite. He treated me as if I were a representative of a banana republic or a criminal government." That is hardly the best way to treat someone you are asking for cooperation and information. It is therefore not surprising that Leutert soon came to the conclusion that prosecutors were "not at all interested in finding a solution." The commentary in the British *Economist* magazine was brief and to the point: "[The Americans] have antagonized the understandably furious Swiss at the wrong moment."[9]

The Swiss, whose stubbornness toward larger countries helped them to win and helps them to retain their independence, were not about to bow to pressure. They felt U.S. actions were a particularly grave affront because Switzerland has represented U.S. interests in Havana and Tehran since the severing of diplomatic ties with Cuba in January 1961 and Iran after the 1979 Iranian hostage crisis.

Independent observers have also been critical of U.S. legal actions in the case of Marc Rich. "The Marc Rich litigation . . . has been a case study in how not to achieve successful intergovernmental cooperation," criticized J. Ross MacDonald, one of the leading tax experts in the United States.[10] The American authorities "ignored interest balancing entirely" in this case, admonished Harold G. Maier, who served as counselor on international law to the U.S. State Department at the time. "The sharpest confrontations and the ones with the greatest potential for disrupting amicable political and economic relations . . . occur when the United States seeks to use its power over persons or entities before its courts or agencies to enforce its policies by requiring or prohibiting acts or omissions abroad that are contrary to the laws or policies of the foreign territorial sovereign."[11]

Maier's opinion, which asserts that such actions only serve to harm the United States, leaves no room for doubt. "Protection of sovereign rights is not solely, or even primarily, for the benefit of individual nations. It is in the interest of the general community as well . . . In those instances where a direct clash of sovereign policies and assertion of United States enforcement jurisdiction will inevitably lead to requiring acts contrary to the legitimate wishes of a foreign sovereign in its own territory, United States courts should indulge the strong presumption that international law and, thus, the law of the United States does not permit such interference."[12]

The damage caused by American legal isolationism in the case of Marc Rich was also highlighted by the British economist Alan Neale, a world authority on international law. "It is hard to avoid the conclusion that . . . claims to U.S. jurisdiction which have encroached on the sovereign rights of other countries have largely been a disaster for the United States. . . . In the *Marc Rich* case, the insistence of the U.S. Department of Justice on enforcing U.S. court subpoenas against the Swiss-incorporated company (combined with a curiously negligent approach to obtaining the documents held by the associated U.S. company) was wholly ineffective."[13]

Why were Giuliani and Weinberg so uncooperative in their dealings with Swiss authorities? Why did they fail to take advantage of so many opportunities? Why did they choose to allow the case to escalate? Giuliani refused several times to be interviewed or answer written questions even though I took great pains to schedule an interview that would fit in with his schedule. Weinberg was visibly annoyed when I brought up the inconsistencies surrounding the matter of Rich's extradition during our interview in his office. "We don't do the extraditions," he finally said. "The extradition is handled through the Department of Justice, through the Office of International Affairs in Washington." When I provoked him by suggesting that he must have been pleased with the case's escalation, Weinberg answered after a brief pause, "The Swiss actions helped me."

Too Many Mistakes

The prosecution's lapses in the case certainly played no small role in Rich remaining at large. Even Wicki, Rich's Swiss lawyer, was surprised— and relieved—by the prosecution's behavior. "The U.S. government never challenged the decision of the Swiss government not to extradite Marc Rich. Neither did it renew its extradition request." Both of these steps could have been taken without difficulty. The second extradition request would have only needed to list the charges that were punishable in both countries, such as fraud or forgery, as Leutert had suggested to Giuliani.

Years later, in 1992, the high-powered House Committee on Government Operations set up an investigation to determine why Marc Rich and Pinky Green had never been apprehended. The committee came to the same conclusions—and raised serious allegations concerning the authorities' actions. "It appears that no effort was made to charge additional crimes that might be extraditable or to extradite on fewer offenses. There is also a possibility that the U.S. Government may have missed opportunities to investigate potential additional violations of the law which would be more easily extraditable."[14] U.S. authorities also never sent an extradition request to Spain and Israel, where Rich traveled frequently. He often spent summer holidays in the south of Spain with his family in his villa in Marbella, and while he may initially have pursued only business interests in Israel, he more and more often visited for the purpose of furthering his philanthropic activities there.

As evidence of the investigators' halfhearted, almost naive approach to Rich's extradition, the Department of Justice in the early 1990s was not even sure whether Rich actually held Israeli citizenship. It had simply neglected to address the issue.[15] Back in 1984, the department had asked Israel to arrest Rich the next time he visited the country, but it was ten years before the answer came: No. The demand, Michael Ben-Yair, then Israel's attorney general, explained, "was not followed by an extradition request or a copy of the charges and affidavits. We considered the issue and found it had no legal validity. The charges against Mr. Rich were fiscal and not fraud-related, and, therefore, the extradition treaty between the two countries did not cover his case."[16]

U.S. authorities did not even attempt to have Rich extradited from Spain, as they simply assumed that the country did not allow the extradition of its own citizens. The fact that U.S. authorities were satisfied with this assumption was harshly criticized by the House committee: "These citizenships were acquired after the date in which the crimes were alleged to have been committed, thus, their nationality should not be a bar to extradition."[17] Furthermore, the U.S. National Central Bureau of Interpol did not issue an International Red Notice (File No. 5031/87,

Control No. A–147/4/1987) until three years after the indictment. An Interpol Red Notice requests the provisional arrest of a subject with a view toward extradition. Red Notices have traditionally played a very important role in apprehending international fugitives, and all law enforcement experts know that the sooner a Red Notice is issued, the greater the chance that the suspect will be detained. The sheer number of mistakes and delayed actions on the behalf of the prosecution would appear to indicate that Giuliani, Weinberg, and their successors were in no way inconvenienced by the fact that Rich and Green were never apprehended. The situation was quite clear to the House committee: "The United States lacked the political will to effect the return of these fugitives."[18]

Not Presumed Innocent

Marc Rich was never convicted. The case never had the opportunity to go to trial, as Rich never returned to the United States. No court ever issued a ruling on the validity of the government's charges against him. If we are to follow the time-honored American tradition of "innocent until proven guilty," then Rich must be considered innocent.[19]

The reality is something entirely different. Rich was judged both before the media and in the court of public opinion, and many journalists and politicians have made statements that violated Rich's right to be presumed innocent. Over the course of time, Rich has been transformed from a suspect and defendant into a fraudster and an enemy of the state—and none of these accusations has ever been proven in court. Even prosecutor Sandy Weinberg found that Rich "had been tarnished and tainted and represented basically as one of the world's greatest criminals."[20]

It is the purpose of this book not to prove Rich's guilt or innocence but to pose questions and to point out the mistakes made throughout the entire affair by all sides. The legal situation is not as clear as the prosecution's case described in the previous chapter of this book. In fact, some of the United States' top legal experts have come to the conclusion that the investigation and the indictment were flawed. These experts include the former White House counsels Leonard Garment and Jack Quinn; I. Lewis "Scooter" Libby, former assistant to the president and chief of staff to the vice president; Professor Martin Ginsburg of Georgetown University Law Center; Bernard Wolfman from the Harvard School of Law; and Laurence Urgenson, former deputy assistant attorney general and chief of the Fraud Section of the Department of Justice. All are convinced that Marc Rich is innocent of the charges brought against him.

Over the years, Rich has hired all of these lawyers to scrutinize his case and, in some cases, to defend him in court. Nonetheless, their arguments must be taken seriously.

Five Flaws

Their conclusion is based on the following five points, which do indeed raise serious doubts about the charges presented in the indictment. Years later, Jack Quinn would list some of these arguments in the petition made to President Clinton for Rich's pardon (see chapter 18).

1. *RICO.* Rich's was the first case in which RICO—the Racketeer Influenced and Corrupt Organizations Act—and RICO forfeiture statutes were employed in a case of white-collar crime that had nothing to do with the Mafia, the drug trade, kidnapping, or murder. Rich's lawyers were critical of the fact that Rudy Giuliani and Sandy Weinberg had transformed a relatively straightforward tax evasion case into a draconian RICO prosecution. "RICO was misused as a sledgehammer to attack Rich," Jack Quinn told me during a long telephone interview. He was chief of staff for Vice President Al Gore before becoming White House counsel for President Bill Clinton. Quinn was keen to point out that after Rich's indictment, the Justice Department determined that Congress had not intended RICO

statutes or mail and wire fraud charges to be applied in cases of tax evasion.[21] Even more important, the Justice Department recognized the coercive effect of overdrawn RICO forfeitures and in 1989 consequently prohibited prosecutors from seeking forfeitures or pretrial restraints that are disproportionate or disrupt normal and legitimate activities.[22]

2. *Civil, not criminal.* Rich's lawyers stress that this case was unique in that the charges against Rich's companies were criminal rather than civil in nature. In all other comparable actions, they say, the cases were tried by civil courts. According to Rich's legal team, the case was in essence a regulatory dispute concerning price control and taxes. None of the U.S. oil producers, who were the ones who insisted on linking their domestic oil sales with offshore foreign oil transactions, was ever criminally prosecuted.

3. *Department of Energy.* In a related 1985 case, Rich's lawyers argue, the U.S. Department of Energy had recognized that Rich's companies had properly linked the domestic and foreign transactions for accounting purposes. Prosecutors took the exact opposite position and attacked some of the same transactions in their indictment.

4. *The tax professors' analysis.* Leonard Garment commissioned the eminent tax professors Martin Ginsburg of Georgetown Law and Bernard Wolfman of Harvard Law School to provide an independent analysis of the transactions upon which the indictment was based. Furthermore, they expressed their opinions regarding consequences of these transactions as they relate to federal income taxes. For their efforts, Ginsburg—the husband of Supreme Court Justice Ruth Bader Ginsburg—and Wolfman received $66,199 and $30,745, respectively. The analysis came to a remarkable conclusion: "MRI and AG [Marc Rich + Co. AG] were correct in their U.S. income tax treatment of all the items in question, and there was no unreported federal income

or additional tax liability attributable to any of the transactions described in the superseding indictment."[23] The report also stated that the income from the two Swiss companies was accurately treated as "foreign source income" and was thus "exempt from U.S. tax under the U.S.-Swiss tax treaty." What the prosecutors saw as "false deductions" were actually the "costs of goods sold." According to the two tax professors' findings, Rich's companies did not owe any taxes whatsoever.

5. *Iran.* To this day, Rich is haunted by the accusations that he personally traded with the enemy. It was, according to *Time* magazine, "one of the most serious charges."[24] What many often forget is the fact that MRI and Marc Rich + Co. were both Swiss companies. MRI was "duly organized" under the laws of Switzerland in 1978 as a wholly owned subsidiary of Marc Rich + Co., which was a Swiss company duly organized in 1974. At all times relevant to the case, MRI and Marc Rich + Co. both conducted their substantial business in Zug, Switzerland, where both companies were headquartered. Such companies, Rich's lawyers argue, and even foreign subsidiaries owned and controlled by American companies, were expressly exempted from the embargo and thus were guilty of no crimes as a result of their dealings with the Iranians. As we've seen, this exemption is clearly stated in the executive order issued by President Carter.[25] Several companies allowed their foreign subsidiaries to trade with Iran during the hostage crisis, and two defense contractors can even be found among the list of firms that legally ignored the embargo against Iran.[26]

"I believe that the Southern District of New York misconstrued the facts and the law," Scooter Libby testified before the House Committee on Government Reform. "I do not believe that these two gentlemen [Marc Rich and Pincus Green], based on all of the evidence available to me, were guilty of the charges for which they were indicted."[27] Libby, later assistant to President George W. Bush and chief of staff to Vice President Dick Cheney, represented Rich in the middle and late 1980s (but did not work on the pardon). "I remain to this day absolutely and unshakably convinced that the prosecutors constructed a legal house of cards in this indictment," Jack Quinn told the House committee. "The case was fundamentally flawed."[28] Quinn still is convinced, as he wrote to President Clinton, "of both Marc's innocence and the outrageously prejudicial and unfair treatment of him by the then-new U.S. Attorney in New York, Mr. Guiliani [sic]."[29]

Of course, it is the lawyers' task to present their client in the best possible manner, and whoever intends to weigh up such arguments must take this fact into consideration. It is striking, however, that these arguments have generally been ignored in the years since the indictment—by the press and even more so by the judiciary (see chapter 13). The reason for this lack of discussion is probably that opinions had already been formed. Rich was described as the greatest tax fraudster in the history of the United States, and any other description would have been seen as politically incorrect. For whatever reason, journalists and commentators usually left out the adjective "alleged" or "accused."

Those who fought against white-collar criminals and organized crime were the heroes of the 1970s and 1980s. Rudy Giuliani was celebrated in the tabloids as the modern incarnation of Eliot Ness, the legendary Chicago crime fighter who went up against Al Capone. Rich, on the other hand, was the bad guy who made huge profits on oil at a time when drivers were stuck in long lines at the pump. Consumers were faced with record inflation as a result of soaring oil prices, and American citizens were being held hostage by Rich's most important business partner, Iran. To put it mildly, Rich was not exactly going to win the hearts and minds of the American public. As a longtime oil trader prosaically put it, "When the markets turn sour, many people look for someone to blame."

An additional problem was the fact that Rich was a tangible individual who the public could easily comprehend. His companies carried his name, whereas most other oil companies were publicly traded companies with countless anonymous stockholders. Furthermore, the public was suspicious of commodities traders in general, if only because they were capable of moving billions of dollars' worth of goods and earning millions of dollars for themselves armed with nothing but an address book, a telephone, and a plane ticket.

Rich's Obstruction

At the time, no one in the media was interested in telling the story from Rich's perspective. This is in part due to Rich's catastrophic communication strategy, which was completely unable to gauge the media reality of the day. Rich's relationship to the media could at times only be described as paranoid. For years Rich gave hardly any interviews, and he was not in the habit of returning journalists' phone calls. This, of course, meant that Rich could neither dispute nor comment on anything that had been written about him. For the most part, Rich failed even to communicate his belief in his own innocence. This cemented Rich's image in the eyes of the public—a secretive trader with something to hide, a man who will not defend himself because there must be something behind all the allegations. His PR advisers had not kept up with the times, and in the end they did him more harm than good.

The legal team's incomprehensible obstructive strategy—particularly early on—helped to blow the case completely out of proportion. The stonewalling, the steamer trunk affair, and the apparent sale and subsequent renaming of MRI as Clarendon all did nothing to convince either the prosecution or the public. Jack Quinn later summed up the situation. "Mr. Rich's defense followed a most unfortunate no-communication, no-cooperation, no-negotiation strategy," he wrote in a letter to one of Giuliani's successors. It was "an expensive but ill-advised strategy."[30]

There were very few dissident voices among those members of the media who refused to go along with the herd. One of the most prominent journalists who was not afraid to express his opinion was Gordon Crovitz, a graduate of Yale Law School and former publisher of the *Wall*

Street Journal. "It's worth taking a second look at Mr. Giuliani's first big RICO case," Crovitz wrote. "This was the much-celebrated 1984 case against Marc Rich, the wealthy oil trader. A close reading of the allegations shows that these effectively reduce to tax charges. The core of the case is that Mr. Rich wrongly attributed domestic income to a foreign subsidiary. Again, this sounds like a standard civil tax case, not RICO. Mr. Rich has stayed in Switzerland rather than go to court on RICO charges."[31]

"Rudy Giuliani is a public relations genius," Laurence Urgenson told me. Without RICO and Iran, the case would have ostensibly remained a case of tax fraud that would have disappeared relatively quickly from the newspaper headlines. "These charges were highlighted in the press release announcing the indictment, and the press connected the charges to the 1980 hostage crisis," wrote Leonard Garment.[32] The charges surrounding Rich's dealings with Iran "had only one effect: to whip up the fury of the press and public against the 'traitor' Marc Rich," according to André Wicki. "Iran was added at the last minute, and it became a big deal," says Robert Fink, who has served as Rich's lawyer in New York since 1979. "It was so inflammatory," Fink says over his Caesar salad while waving his hands in the air. "The case went away, you know, totally disproportionate. RICO and Iran were so emotionally charged. The government intended to paint Rich into the corner."

It would be easy to simply discount such statements as lawyers lobbying on their client's behalf, but public reaction to the charges against Rich proved the validity of their statements. The charge of trading with the enemy changed everything. All of the anger and sadness unleashed by the Iranian hostage crisis rained down upon Rich. After these accusations had been made, it would no longer be possible to consider the case solely from a legal point of view. It was no longer a matter of legality and illegality. It was now an issue of morality. "The courts of morality know no rules of procedure," my political philosophy professor liked to warn.[33] They don't pursue exonerating evidence. The verdict of the public is definite. There is no appeal.

"He fled to Zug to live in luxury, and he dealt with the Iranians while they were torturing and holding our people hostage. This is not a good guy," said Howard Safir, the associate director of operations for the U.S. Marshals Service who pursued Rich to no avail for seventeen years and who later served as Mayor Giuliani's police commissioner (see chapter 12).[34] "One case that stands out glaringly is Iran," House Government Reform Committee chairman Dan Burton said. "We had hostages over there at the time that Mr. Rich was trading with them. He violated the embargo. He was working with the Iranians selling their oil, and our hostages—American citizens—were languishing under very difficult circumstances for a long, long time at that time."[35] It is one of the ironies of the case against Marc Rich that at about the same time, the Reagan administration secretly sold weapons to Iran and used the funds to support the anti-Communist Contra rebels in Nicaragua. President George H. W. Bush later pardoned several people involved in the Iran-Contra affair, among them Secretary of Defense Caspar W. Weinberger.

A Political Case

Rich and his companies sometimes pushed up against the boundaries of what is allowed in order to carry out their business. They used every tax loophole that they could find. He sometimes operated in the darker parts of capitalism's gray areas. Rich lived according to the motto he quoted to one of his earliest employees the day he was hired: "As a trader you often walk on the blade. Be careful and don't step off." Yet I am not convinced that Rich would actually have been found guilty in court. There is simply too much reasonable doubt surrounding his guilt. I have come to this decision after my conversations with members of the judiciary, diplomats, and other individuals directly involved in the case and after having viewed countless documents, some of which were confidential.

As my research has clearly illustrated, there was a political aspect to the case. U.S. Attorney Giuliani knew that the case would serve as a springboard for his political career—a career that would lead him to become the mayor of New York and later to make an unsuccessful bid for the U.S. presidency. One could go as far as to say that Giuliani's political and very public career actually began with this case. As history has shown, the fact that the case escalated rapidly before virtually exploding as a media event was not exactly to Giuliani's disadvantage. In all likelihood, this escalation was even desired.

Cardiff University's Michael Levi, a noted expert on white-collar crime, also sees political motivations in the case against Rich. "Political reasons may underline the decision to prosecute. For example, U.S. commodities trader Marc Rich was prosecuted in 1983–84 for tax evasion and other frauds . . . plus secretly buying Iranian oil after the U.S. trade ban. He did, in the end, plead guilty to some charges, but skeptics might ask themselves whether the prosecution would have occurred had he not traded with the enemy."[36]

The temperature in Sandy Weinberg's Tampa office suddenly seems to fall by a couple of degrees when I want to discuss these issues with him. It is one of the few moments in which the attorney has to struggle with his composure while remaining polite to his guest. This comes as no surprise. The question gets straight to the heart of the fundamental criticism surrounding the case.

"We did this investigation in a very professional way," Weinberg says with a studied calmness. "We've been fair. We didn't have a good case, we had an overwhelming case. Believe me, I know how to make a case. If Jack Quinn says that we had a legal house of cards, well, it was all aces. Why did the lawyers wait until I was gone? None of these arguments were raised in 1983 or 1984. The lawyers never came in and said: There was no crime, this is just a civil case." What does Weinberg have to say about the tax analysis carried out by Bernard Wolfman and Martin Ginsburg, considered by many to be two of the nation's best tax professors? "It's ridiculous, it's poppycock, it's garbage," Weinberg replies before pausing as if he were completely taken aback by his own rude emotional explosion. He then looks me directly in the eyes and seems to consider which argument would have the greatest effect on me. "And don't forget," he says, "don't forget: Rich's companies pled guilty; he was a fugitive. If this case was so flawed, why didn't he come back and face the charges?"

An excellent question—a question that only Rich himself can, and indeed will, answer in the next chapter.

11

"I NEVER BROKE *the* LAW"

Rich's voice is even quieter than usual. "I don't think he's straight," he says and throws me a stern look. He is dressed in his usual attire for our meetings—dark suit, white shirt, red tie, and a gold Rolex sparkling on his left wrist. At seventy-four, Rich still exhibits the handsome features that made him such a good-looking man in his younger years. One can see a strong resemblance to Rudolph Valentino, the tragic star of the silent film era, in Rich's earlier photographs. Rich is an acute observer and a man of few words with a soft voice and a barely noticeable lisp. He is always precise and to the point. There is something catlike about him, beyond his apparent nine lives. He cautiously keeps his distance and waits, ready to jump. He might be ready to flee—or attack. I had asked him his opinion of Rudolph W. Giuliani, his nemesis. "I don't think he's straight. I think he's only interested in himself. That's it," Rich says. It is the first time the commodities trader has spoken openly about his case. Rich does not attempt to outmaneuver or avoid my questions. On the contrary—and rather surprisingly for someone who for the last twenty-five years has been labeled one of the greatest tax fraudsters—Rich maintains his innocence. Of course he tried to minimize his taxes, he admits. Of course he funneled his profits to Switzerland, where the tax burden is substantially lower than in the United States. Of course his companies practiced "transfer pricing." Every international company does. Rich makes an effort not to sound too apologetic when stressing his innocence. "I never crossed the border of legality. Everything I did was perfectly in order. I never broke the law. I did nothing wrong."

"A Scapegoat Was Needed"

For the first time ever, Marc Rich is willing to discuss his international trading activities. "The trading with the enemy charge was clearly the most inflammatory part of the indictment. The truth is far different," Rich explains. "I was doing business with Iran for a Swiss company, and it was completely legal. Marc Rich + Co., a Swiss corporation, had historically purchased oil from the National Iranian Oil Company before the overthrow of the shah and the seizure of American hostages. We then resold the oil on the world market. Like all other foreign-based oil companies, including those which were subsidiaries of U.S. companies, Marc Rich + Co. continued to do oil business with the National Iranian Oil Company after the Iranian revolution took place."

If he was indeed innocent, as he claims, I interject, why was he branded the greatest tax fraudster and an enemy of the state? Rich tilts his head to one side, and the red birthmark on his left cheek seems to glow brighter than usual. "I believe it was a combination of political problems and that a scapegoat was needed at the time," Rich says. "I was an easy target, one individual, very successful, making a lot of money, and Jewish. I stood outside of the establishment."

He is convinced that he was "singled out" for precisely these reasons. It was easier for prosecutors, he thinks, to go after him rather than to sift through the hundreds of public companies with their anonymous stockholders that often employed similar practices. After Richard Nixon introduced price regulations for crude oil in 1973, oil resellers seemed to sprout up everywhere. Prior to the Arab oil embargo, there were only twelve oil resellers in the United States. By 1978 there were five hundred companies in the business. "I was singled out by individuals. Individuals with a clear personal interest in self-promotion," Rich believes. "Mr. Giuliani escalated the case because he saw a chance to achieve more publicity for himself," he maintains. "Personal interests and feelings on their side got into the way of a fair solution."

Marc Rich seems almost bashful as he tells me this. I am reminded of how one of his friends once explained that Rich was actually a very reserved person—a virtual introvert—who preferred to sit quietly in the corner at social events. He would just smoke his cigar and observe other people. In all truth, Rich—contrary to his public image as an ice-cold, unscrupulous businessman—is the personification of understatement.

Gross Overreaction

Our discussion of Rich's own case developed into a conversation on the tendency of the United States to put its own laws above the laws of other nations. Europeans have a humorous expression: The United States has three main exports—rock 'n' roll, blue jeans, and its view of the world. "The United States wants to apply its own peculiar laws to the whole world," Rich claims. "I was and am satisfied that Switzerland lived up to its historic image and did not allow itself to be bullied by a big nation." He adds in German, *"Die Schweiz verbeugte sich nicht."* Switzerland did not bow.

"The U.S. political and legal system has a long and very well known history of grossly overreacting," Rich continues. "They often shoot with big cannons at small birds. Well-known recent examples include the cases against Martha Stewart or Arthur Andersen, [the latter of] which was one of the five biggest auditing companies before the U.S. destroyed it. It was destroyed because of the actions of a handful of its executives, and all eighty-five thousand innocent employees had to bear the dire consequences along with the shareholders."

When I ask him if he doubts the American justice system, Rich answers, "I do believe in the rule of law. Unfortunately, like everything created and applied by man, it is not always perfect. Winston Churchill once said, 'You can always count on the Americans to do the right thing—after they have tried everything else.'"

Rich's Biggest Mistake

"My biggest mistake?" Rich repeats my question. "I clearly underestimated the zealots on the U.S. side, and I chose the wrong lawyers. In the past, whenever I had an issue with the police, I talked to them and settled it. I even proposed to do the same thing with the prosecutors, but my lawyer at that time, Ed Williams, said, 'The worst you could do is to talk to them. We will confront them head-on.' That was a huge mistake that greatly aggravated the problem. I regret it."

Rich suddenly switches languages in order to use a very German word: *die Ohnmacht*, which translates as "powerlessness" or "impotence." I had asked him what he felt was the worst aspect of the entire affair. For a man who had pulled himself up by his own bootstraps, the fact that he was powerless despite all of his money, his contacts, and his iron will must have been unbearable. "He likes to be in control," Denise Rich told me when we spoke of the effect the case had had on the family. "At that time he was out of control because he couldn't do what he wanted to do. He couldn't travel. He was depressed." In my career as an investigative journalist, I have often spoken with people who were utterly convinced that they had been the victim of an overly zealous media and judiciary. Each and every one of them was deeply affected by the feeling of helplessness, the inability to make themselves heard, and a public perception of the events that was the complete opposite of their own views. Rich is no different. "I always had a good reputation. This case unjustifiably harmed my reputation," he says.

"Die Ohnmacht," Rich repeats before continuing again in English, "and the feeling of not getting a fair trial. We had the experience of how [the prosecutors] proceeded in the past, how they blocked all our accounts,

and how they blocked all our relationships. It was, you know, a total at-tack. It had a very negative effect. Our companies were collapsing." His trading empire would have been much larger had it not been for the case, he claims. According to Rich, persecution by U.S. authorities was one of the primary factors that forced him to sell his company years later (see chapter 17).

After the indictment in September 1983, Rich's competitors were sure that his companies were dead in the water. The racketeering charge combined with the freezing of millions of dollars in assets would have ruined most companies, but Rich's managed to carry on. They may have been severely crippled, but they had survived. "My family, my friends, and my business partners always supported me because they knew better. Our business partners knew us as an honest, reliable, and competitive company, so they continued to do business with us," Rich explains.

Why He Didn't Come Back

There was one decisive question that Sandy Weinberg did not hesitate to ask me: "If the case was so flawed, why didn't he come back and face the charges?" On hearing the question, Rich looks at me as if he has trouble believing that I still do not understand. He continues in a low voice, "I saw no hope of getting a fair trial because of the unstable and inflamed environment. My case was very bad—unjustifiably so." He once more points out his belief that this was a case in which the pros-ecution had overstepped the limits of acceptable conduct. "The situa-tion was so negative, I didn't trust the situation, it wasn't a normal situation."

In this, Rich receives support from unexpected quarters. The former Swiss minister of justice Elisabeth Kopp-Iklé is of a similar opinion. She is a highly intelligent, reserved, and serious woman who harbors great sympathy for the United States, stemming from the years she spent in there in her youth. "Marc Rich was prejudged by the media. The public was agitated and Rudolph Giuliani was pursuing his own goals," Kopp-Iklé said. "I realized that Rich had no chance of receiving justice in the United States. He could not be sure of a fair trial," she told me.

"Everybody was inflamed," Rich's longtime lawyer Robert Fink confirmed. He made a gesture with the flat of his hand as if he were running it over a wooden slat. "It was a train on a track that could not be stopped. The atmosphere was very polluted. There was so much anger, pressure, and threats. Marc was thoroughly demonized."

"Marc was characterized as a villain," Wall Street financier Michael Steinhardt told me. "We all got the impression that if he came back, they would lock him up and throw away the key."

"Nonsense," Sandy Weinberg said when I confronted him with this criticism. "Rich would have gotten a fair trial. He created the publicity, not us. It was self-inflicted." However, the prosecution's threat of 325 years in prison was "shocking to the entire defense team," Laurence Urgenson told me. Urgenson has served as Rich's lawyer since 1994 and also represented him during the postpardon hearings. He offered a piece of wisdom in parting, gained from his thirty years' experience as a lawyer, prosecutor, and deputy assistant attorney general in the Reagan and George H. W. Bush administrations. "When cases become symbols, the defendant is in trouble," Urgenson said at the end of our discussion. "For the Southern District of New York, Marc Rich had become a symbol. For them he was a wealthy guy—the rogue billionaire who thinks he's above the law. They thought, 'We don't let this rich guy get away with it.' "

This was certainly the case with the U.S. Marshals Service, which is responsible for conveying international fugitives to U.S. courts. Many of their cases involve fugitives on the lam, their whereabouts unknown, but the U.S. marshals knew exactly where Rich was to be found. They even had his address: Himmelrichstrasse 28. He lived in a large house at the edge of the woods in Baar, a rural village with a wonderful view of Lake Zug. The very fact that Rich was living so openly infuriated the agents, and they swore they would get him. Howard Safir, the associate director of operations for the U.S. Marshals Service, knew that special problems required special solutions. He was prepared to do everything possible to bring Rich before an American court, "as long as it doesn't involve a violation of the fugitive's human rights."[1] In October 1985, Safir packed his bags and headed to Switzerland. He did not intend to return empty-handed. "This time," he told his colleagues, "this time we'll get him."

12

The HUNT for MARC RICH

A s befitted a man regarded by the United States as a traitor and fugitive, American officials made strenuous and sometimes almost comical efforts over the years to apprehend Marc Rich, ranging from psychological pressure to tricks to lure him away from Switzerland to spying to outright kidnapping. Many of these efforts have never before been revealed.

A shroud of fog covered Lake Zug against the backdrop of beautiful central Switzerland on an October morning in 1985. As is often the case in the fall, the fog would dissolve in the course of the afternoon. Howard Safir traveled to Zug that morning disguised as a tourist. He was accompanied by Chief Inspector Don Ferrarone, a legendary former DEA agent with vast international experience who was involved in the famous "French Connection" heroin case. The two U.S. marshals brought with them detailed maps of Rich's mansion and business offices as part of the ingenious plan they had devised to capture Rich. They even knew the gradient of the street in Baar. Their reconnaissance had discovered that a helicopter could land on the street, if necessary.

Safir's plan was to overpower Rich and secretly smuggle him out of the country. It was all to take place without the knowledge of the Swiss authorities and was thoroughly illegal. He wanted to ferry the oil trader to either Germany or France over Switzerland's "green border"—the national boundary characterized by numerous border crossings that are not subject to constant to constant surveillance by Swiss customs officers. Safir left nothing to chance. Before traveling onward to Switzerland, the U.S. marshal had met with local police in Germany in order to discuss the case. Shortly before departing on his delicate mission, Safir had made sure that the U.S. office of Interpol had sent an arrest warrant for Rich "with a view to extradition" to the Interpol headquarters in Saint-Cloud on the outskirts of Paris.

"WANTED INTERNATIONAL CRIMINAL" served as a title for the arrest warrant that had been signed on October 9, 1985, by Richard C. Stiener, then the director of the U.S. office of Interpol. Marc Rich, it said, was "a commodities trader/businessman" who was wanted on charges including "Income Tax Evasion, Racketeering, Trading with the Enemy." The maximum possible penalty for these charges amounted to "325 years' imprisonment and/or $100 million forfeiture and/or fines." Rich's physical description on the warrant—177.8 cm, 81 kg, black hair, brown eyes—was accompanied by a photograph. It was the only recent photograph of Rich; prosecutors had taken it from a 1984 *Forbes* article. The warrant described a "slight red mark on left cheek" as one of Rich's "distinguishing marks."

The marshals had covered every angle. As soon as Safir crossed the Swiss border with Rich, he could drop his tourist disguise. Rich would have immediately been arrested by any French or German police officer. However, Safir knew that his activities as a U.S. marshal in Switzerland were illegal. Article 271 of the Swiss Penal Code prohibits anyone from undertaking action for a foreign country without Swiss approval. Punishment for violating this law would be nothing less than a prison term. Safir and Ferrarone were well aware that kidnapping Rich was a serious offense. They were prepared to take the risk, however, as Rich's arrest was of the utmost importance.

The two undercover marshals tried to keep a low profile while waiting for an opportune moment in front of Rich's office building in Zug—with limited success. Two men approached them after a while and identified themselves as police officers. They wanted to see Safir and Ferrarone's identification. Safir knew immediately that his cover was blown. In the most courteous of tones, the Swiss police threatened the two U.S. marshals: "If you take any more action in Switzerland, you will be arrested."

The U.S. marshals called this type of secret operation "extraordinary rendition," a form of state-sanctioned kidnapping. It was a term that would become widely known in George W. Bush's "War on Terror." Such methods have their origins in nineteenth-century bounty hunting. One of the most prominent examples is the case of the former CIA agent Edwin Wilson, who was involved in the illegal export of arms and explosives. In 1982 an undercover U.S. marshal tricked Wilson into leaving his Libyan safe haven. Wilson flew to a meeting in the Dominican Republic, where he was seized and put on a plane to the United States.[1] The U.S. Supreme Court later explicitly legitimized such abductions in the now famous case of Humberto Álvarez Machaín.[2] This Mexican physician, who was allegedly involved in the killing of a U.S. drug agent, was abducted from Mexico by bounty hunters and brought to trial in the United States. (He was acquitted.)

A Leak in the U.S. Administration

On that foggy day on Lake Zug in October 1985, Howard Safir was suddenly struck by a terrible thought—there was a leak somewhere in the U.S. administration or in the international law enforcement establishment. Safir was by no means wrong. Although the authorities still cannot officially confirm it was the case, a Swiss official who was involved in the affair admits that the Swiss had received a quiet tip-off concerning Safir's activities. Whether this tip came from the U.S. Department of Justice or the U.S. State Department remains a subject of debate. A classified report from the Swiss embassy in Washington dated from the time of the case provides a telling hint: "Top [U.S.] officials are slowly becoming aware of the fact that agencies and courts have gone too far in recent years. They are beginning to realize that the most wonderful precedents blessed by the highest courts are of absolutely no use in cases where the foreign country opposes the decision. In fact, as in the Marc Rich case, they appear almost ludicrous to their foreign partners." It is an open secret that the State Department and the Department of Justice often opposed one another in the Rich case. The State Department had actually wanted to seek out Swiss cooperation, whereas the Department of Justice had wanted to go it alone.

Safir's failed mission was a small part of a huge, top-secret project known as the Otford Project, the goal of which was to apprehend Marc Rich and Pinky Green at almost any price. A multiagency team was put together consisting of personnel from the FBI, the IRS, the Office of International Affairs at the Department of Justice, the U.S. attorney for the Southern District of New York, Interpol, and the U.S. Marshals Service. The Otford Project was directed by the U.S. Marshals Service, which as of 1979 was responsible for apprehending federal fugitives (previously the responsibility of the FBI).

The U.S. marshal who was assigned by Safir to hunt down Rich was Ken Hill. Ever since Rich had fled to Switzerland in 1983, Hill had been devoted "solely and exclusively" to the case—and remained so in the role of case agent for fourteen years.[3] The former New York policeman probably knew more about the wanted commodities trader than Rich's own family did. From his Manhattan office in a faded brick building near the Brooklyn Bridge, Hill kept on the trail of Rich and Green. The task would soon become his entire life.

I spoke to Ken Hill in Florida.[4] He retired in 1997 and became a diving instructor after thirty years of service to the United States. Secrecy is still of the utmost importance to the sixty-two-year-old former marshal. Only a single photograph of Hill is officially known to exist, in which he appears—unrecognizable—in a wet suit and diving mask. Hill called me shortly before 9:00 A.M. in my Tampa hotel room.

Code Name: The Riddler

"It's all about money," Hill told me right after the initial greetings. "If Marc Rich calls you he asks himself a) can I make money with you today, b) can I make money with you tomorrow? If not, good-bye." Hill's code name was "the Riddler." He was on Rich's heels for fourteen years. During this time Hill spoke with countless people who had had some form of contact with Marc Rich, whether as frustrated employees or tough competitors. Hill had a fixed picture of Rich in his mind. "Do you have children?" he suddenly asked me on the telephone. "He was like a child, you know, who thinks, 'The rules don't apply to me. I can get away with it.' The man is a genius, no doubt, but he thought his entire life, 'The rules don't apply to me.' He had no respect for no country, no people, no law. He screwed a lot of people."

I could sense that the Rich case had been no routine job for Hill. The hunt soon became an obsession. "He worked an incredible amount of time on the case," a former official at the U.S. Department of Justice said. Hill was so frustrated toward the end that his colleagues feared he might be suffering from burnout. This would come as no surprise. The average tax evasion suspect, the U.S. government once calculated, remains at large for three years and eight months. Rich and Green, however, were at large for more than seventeen years before they were pardoned by Bill President Clinton in January 2001.

One can feel the deep resentment in Hill's account of the events. During the 1991 Gulf War, for example, as Hill explains, "I phoned Pinky in his hotel in Jerusalem when the Iraqis were firing the Scuds on the city and asked him if he still didn't want to come back." Another time he sent Rich a bottle of scotch while the trader was on a ski holiday in St. Moritz. Hill wanted to prove to him that he always knew exactly where he was. He wanted to remind Rich of his favorite maxim: "I can make a million mistakes, you can make none."

The U.S. marshals called this form of psychological warfare "mistake-provoking strategy." The Riddler was driven by the hope that Rich would eventually make some kind of mistake—sometime, somewhere, somehow—but Rich never did slip up. "Marc Rich is described as a man of stealth," Hill says. "In reality, he paid very well for security. His infrastructure was so wide, he knew everybody, he knew everything. He was so rich, he had so much power. He had security everywhere. People were on the lookout for suspicious signs. He had the money to buy what he needed. It was like tackling a country." Seldom had U.S. investigators proved themselves as creative as in the case of Rich and Green. They masqueraded as commodities traders in order to keep their most important business contacts in dozens of countries under surveillance. They were in regular contact with local flight regulatory authorities in order to determine if Rich had booked a ticket on a scheduled flight. They sought information from customs authorities all over the world to determine if their targets were currently visiting the country in question. They even sought the assistance of the cartographic company Jeppesen Sanderson, which had a near global monopoly on map and navigational material, asking to be notified whenever Rich's pilots ordered new map material for exotic destinations.[5] They kept in contact with Swiss police, who unofficially assisted the marshals, although officially they were prohibited from doing so. "We had a cordial relationship with the Swiss police," Hill added. The marshals were hoping for a decisive tip-off about Rich's travel plans.

London Fog Saved Rich

In November 1987, two years after Howard Safir's failed mission in Switzerland, it finally seemed as if the authorities were presented with an opportunity to catch Rich. Hill's efforts to find regular contacts among Rich's business partners had finally paid off. One of these business partners had betrayed Rich and informed the authorities that Rich intended to fly to London the following weekend. The trader would be on board a private Gulfstream IV that would take off from Zürich-Kloten Airport and land at London Biggin Hill Airport in Kent.

Ken Hill, alias the Riddler, immediately set off for London, where he liaised with the Fraud Unit as well as the Extradition Unit of London's Metropolitan Police. On a cool fall morning, the U.S. marshal and his British colleagues waited for Rich in a comfortable lounge at Biggin Hill while keeping an eye on the airstrip. The airport, which was the principal fighter station for the British Royal Air Force during World War II, was now a civilian airport for affluent business travelers who appreciated its convenient access to the city of London. The U.S. marshal had known for quite some time what he would say when he finally had the opportunity to arrest Marc Rich: *You made the one mistake.* Hill even had one of the first-ever satellite telephones in order to report the arrest as soon as he had Rich in his custody.

It was another foggy day at Biggin Hill. The fog grew thicker and thicker as Hill sat waiting for Rich, and soon he could just make out the faint outlines of the airstrip. At 8:00 A.M. the weather service reported that the fog now covered half of mainland Britain. Hundreds of flights would have to be redirected or canceled.

Rich was sitting in the Gulfstream on the way to a party in London when his flight, too, was canceled. The fog proved to be a stroke of luck for the wanted trader. The airplane was forced to turn around while still above the European continent and fly back to Zürich-Kloten in Switzerland. Hill woke his superior, Assistant U.S. Attorney James Comey (who would later serve as deputy attorney general under George W. Bush), in New York at 4:00 A.M. local time to give him the bad news. "Damned fog," Hill cursed quietly into his satellite phone.[6]

"I Was Very Careful"

Was Rich aware of the U.S. authorities' attempt to arrest him? "In general, yes," Rich tells me and takes a bite of his *Tafelspitz*, an Austrian specialty consisting of boiled beef. We are having lunch at the Glashof, Rich's favorite restaurant in Zug. Although the restaurant is just across the street from the office, both of Rich's bodyguards accompany us to lunch. One of them walks ahead of us while the other brings up the rear. The commodities trader still takes security very seriously. We enter the Glashof—which Rich's company once bought in order to provide Pincus Green and other observant employees with kosher meals—by means of a side entrance and are seated in a private room. We are greeted personally and served by the restaurant's manager. We drink Rich's favorite wine, the one he served in his chalet in St. Moritz: a 2000 CVNE Rioja Imperial Reserva. "I was careful," he says, "and while being careful I learned they tried to make certain attempts."

He then tells me a story that sounds as if it could have been taken directly from the pages of a spy novel. In the late summer of 1992, Rich received a visitor from Israel whom he had known for quite some time. He introduced a Russian who was interested in doing business with Rich involving a big oil deal. "It seemed very attractive," Rich explains. Mikhail Gorbachev had just resigned from office in December 1991, and the Soviet Union was officially dissolved on December 25 of the same year. The Communist "Evil Empire," as Ronald Reagan once described it, had simply ceased to exist. Boris Yeltsin, the new Russian president, immediately introduced a program of economic reform. He put an end to the Soviet-era price controls, cut state spending, and introduced an open foreign trade regime early in 1992. Russia embarked on the largest privatization program that the world had ever seen. If that was not a gigantic business opportunity, what else is?

"The Russian businessman told me that I had to come to Moscow in order to sign the deal," Rich says. Nothing spoke against the trip, and Rich trusted the Israeli acquaintance who had arranged the contact. He was a former agent of Shin Bet, Israel's domestic intelligence service, and now worked in London for Kroll, the global risk consulting company. "If you don't have the time, we can send you a private aircraft. The new Russian government is interested in you," the Russian casually mentioned. They discussed the possibility of meeting in the second week of September 1992.

On September 1 at 8:56 P.M. EDT, the FBI sent a confidential fax to the Russian bureau of Interpol marked FOR POLICE USE ONLY: "The FBI has received reliable information that Rich will travel to Moscow on or about September 6, 1992, for meetings in Moscow on September 7, 1992, possibly until September 11, 1992. He will reportedly stay at the Metropol Hotel in Moscow." The FBI asked the local Russian police to determine if Rich would indeed be staying at the Hotel Metropol during these dates. The Office of International Affairs at the Department of Justice issued a provisional arrest warrant. The Russian police were informed that Rich might register at the hotel under a different name, and the "use of his photograph left with Interpol will be essential." The FBI thought of everything and warned their colleagues in Russia that "Rich should be considered armed and dangerous because he allegedly travels with armed bodyguards and may utilize, in addition to his own personal staff, hired uniformed private armed security guards who reportedly travel with Rich in a motorcade through the streets."

Avner Azulay

"They offered to send him an aircraft?" Avner Azulay pricked up his ears when Rich told him of his plans to fly to Moscow. "This didn't sound kosher to me." We were drinking coffee in a stylish hotel in the center of Lucerne in the heart of Switzerland. "I only trust once," he warned me before our interview began. He wanted to know everything about me before I was allowed to ask him any questions. Azulay, a good-looking man in his early seventies with warm eyes and silver hair, was responsible for Rich's security for many years. He was paid to be suspicious and ask the right questions. "Who is going to protect you in Russia?" he asked Rich and raised a cause for concern. "They don't have any laws there just after the fall of the Soviet Empire. And don't forget, they would do anything to please the Americans."

Rich grudgingly canceled his trip to Moscow—which turned out to have been a wise decision. Azulay's instincts had once again proven accurate, and he later found out that the entire affair had been a clever plan to lure Rich to Russia. Of all people, the Israeli acquaintance—a former intelligence agent—had unknowingly been used by American agents. They had successfully smuggled a mole into Rich's network. Rich had almost made the one mistake that Ken Hill was hoping for. "We tried luring him to countries where he could have been extradited," the former U.S. marshal confided. "Did Rich have close calls? We certainly think so."

Rich's ability to evade the agents of the most powerful nation in the world for nearly twenty years was largely due to Azulay's good instincts and experience. Azulay was the perfect candidate, a former colonel in the Israeli Defense Forces and a high-ranking Mossad agent who had worked undercover in Spain during the 1970s, a time when Spain had no diplomatic ties with Israel. He was later assigned to one of the most difficult regions in the intelligence world: Lebanon. He had a top-secret base in Beirut, and he was smuggled in and out of the country by sea. It was during this time that Azulay met Ehud Barak, who was the head of Israeli military intelligence and would later become the prime minister of Israel.[7]

In 1983–84, after having resigned from the Mossad, Azulay was advising a Spanish bank on how to deal with Basque terrorists when he was introduced to Marc Rich. Rich engaged his services during the time of Giuliani's indictment against him. "He had security problems. He had business intelligence problems," Azulay remembers and explains how he went about determining Rich's security vulnerabilities. "It's not magic. It's about accurately evaluating each situation. For example, when Marc was invited to somewhere, I used to ask, 'How did the invitation come about? Who made the invitation? Who is behind the invitation? What is the reason for the invitation? Does it make sense to you?' It's all about assessing what is plausible." Azulay had access to the best of security and intelligence networks. He personally knew many European intelligence officials, as he had cooperated with them in the past.

Rich was well aware that he could be arrested in many of the countries he visited and extradited to the United States. He therefore was very careful when planning his travels. He avoided taking regular scheduled flights where possible. He preferred to fly by private jet—but never his own plane, as this would have been much too dangerous. The registration number would have served as a flashing red beacon to the world's police authorities. If Rich flew to South America or the Caribbean, he had to be extremely careful that his plane avoided U.S. airspace. He always registered in hotels under an assumed name. For a time, Rich rode in a bulletproof Mercedes in Switzerland. A small team of bodyguards—battle-hardened Israelis at first, and later a group of specially trained Swiss—accompanied him everywhere. A sophisticated surveillance system allowed the driver and license plate of every car that approached Rich's residence to be recorded and registered. The local police were notified for the slightest of reasons. The system even prevented a mentally ill Canadian, who was obsessed by the media reports on Marc Rich and who had killed his own parents, from penetrating the private Rich residence.

Pitiful Attempts

Rich's private security team simply had an edge on the U.S. government's multiagency task force. In the fall of 1987 a U.S. marshal assigned to the project barely missed apprehending Rich in France after Rich canceled a meeting with an African oil minister.[8] Agents apparently tried to trick Rich into flying to Düsseldorf, Germany, for a business meeting, but his private plane never arrived, "leaving U.S. authorities stewing at the airport."[9] In September 1991 the FBI and Interpol attempted to arrest Rich in Finland. Pertti Ruoho, a Finnish manager of the oil concern Neste, had told agents that Rich was flying to Helsinki in order to purchase large amounts of his company's stock.[10] Ruoho promised to provide Rich's itinerary. Finnish police spent the whole weekend feverishly checking passenger lists and passports, but Rich's name could not be found. The U.S. Marshals Service believes to this day that Rich's plane diverted to Sweden at the very last minute after he had somehow received a warning.

Another hot tip had Rich traveling to Jamaica, where he had extensive business dealings, but "we missed him by a day or two," said Howard Safir.[11] Rich laughs and shakes his head when I mention this story to him in the Glashof restaurant: "I don't believe it. I was in Jamaica in 1966 during my first honeymoon. It was raining all the time, and I stepped on a sea urchin. I've never been there again."

In the face of their obvious failure to capture Rich and Green, prosecutors desperately followed every lead that came their way. The hunt for Marc Rich at times seemed almost pitiful, as classified police documents show. On May 5, 1992, a U.S. citizen thought he saw a sign welcoming "Mr. Rich" at Moscow's Sheremetyevo II International Airport. He dutifully reported what he had seen to the police. A welcome sign for a Mr. Rich? Reason enough for Mary Jo Grotenrath, associate director of the Office of International Affairs, to phone Boris Senchukov at the Russian bureau of Interpol the following day. According to police logs marked CRITICAL URGENT and FOR POLICE/COURT USE ONLY, Grotenrath requested Senchukov's assistance in determining whether Rich was actually in Moscow, saying, "Your assistance in this most urgent matter is greatly appreciated." Nothing came of this.

A fax dated February 21, 1992, and marked URGENT also casts a rather poor light on the U.S. investigation. Donald S. Donovan, assistant director at the U.S. National Central Bureau of Interpol, sent the fax to Don Ward, the deputy director of the U.S. Marshals. "Our criminal police have found out the above subject [Marc Rich] set up a branch of the 'Marc Rich' Company at address as follows: Stepanska 34, Prague 1, Czechoslovakia," it said. This explosive piece of information, apparently of the utmost urgency, had already been officially published in Prague's commercial register six months previously.

In their desperation, federal agents even sought out the assistance of Josef Lang. Lang, a former Trotskyist and ultra-left member of the Swiss parliament, was a well-known local critic of Rich. Lang once described the United States as a "warmonger" and its presidents as "death-penalty barbarians." True to the Arabic proverb "The enemy of my enemy is my friend," the FBI approached Lang in 1992. Lang was invited to the four-teenth floor of 26 Federal Plaza in Manhattan, the headquarters of the FBI's New York field office. There two agents tried to persuade him to recruit informants working among the mechanics at Zurich's airport. They hoped he could tip them off when Rich was due to leave the coun-try. "I had to say, 'Sorry, I am a politician, not a private eye.' Besides, it was against Swiss law," recounts Lang.[12] The fact that the FBI agents repeatedly referred to the $750,000 reward on Rich's head did nothing to sway the Swiss politician.

Although the exact amount of the reward was never officially men-tioned, the fact that it existed was known the world over. The U.S. gov-ernment broadcast an International Crime Alert over the entire globe on the Voice of America. The alert promised, "The U.S. will pay a reward for information that leads to the arrest of Marc David Rich. The U.S. guarantees that all reports will be investigated and all information will be kept confidential. If appropriate, the U.S. is prepared to protect infor-mants by relocating them." This made Rich a target for bounty hunters, kidnappers, and envious competitors. There were even rumors that Eu-ropean terrorists had offered to catch Rich for money and deliver him to U.S. authorities.[13]

The U.S. government expended 19.2 man-years at a level of "GS/GM 13 or higher" (more than 1.5 years of experience) between the years of 1984 and 1990 in order to apprehend Rich. In other words, the equiva-lent of three people worked full-time on the hunt for the fugitive trader. In this same period, $55,000 was spent on travel expenses alone.[14]

Yet it was all for nothing. Rich was always just a step or two ahead of his pursuers. Rich did nothing to hide his business successes, his riches, or even his ridicule of the authorities. He celebrated his fiftieth birthday at the Grand Hotel National in Lucerne, where two of Switzer-land's most famous clowns appeared onstage for a rather special boxing match. The clown wearing a Marc Rich logo on his back went after the other clown, dressed as a member of the NYPD, with an oversized rubber hammer. The three hundred guests, who had traveled from every corner of the globe to attend the party, loved this bit of slapstick.

Secret Protection?

It must have infuriated Rich's pursuers. Rich was listed on the FBI's Most Wanted list between Victor Gerena, wanted for armed robbery, and Eric Rudolph, the abortion clinic and Atlanta Olympic Park bomber, but Rich could nevertheless continue to do business all over the world. He traveled "extensively," as the police documents stated—Spain, Portugal, Belgium, Bolivia, Great Britain, Eastern Europe, Israel, Scandinavia, and the former Soviet Union.

"What are the reasons that the most powerful government in the world cannot apprehend some of its most notorious fugitives?" asked an exasperated Rep. Robert E. Wise (D–West Virginia).[15] "This isn't your miscreant who has fled the country for knocking over fifteen 7-Elevens and is kicking around the dock at Marseilles. This is Marc Rich operating with total impunity out of a tall office building in Switzerland. And why hasn't this been made a high priority?"[16] Such questions led to hearings by the House Committee on Government Operations, then led by Michigan Democrat John Conyers, in spring 1992.[17]

Rich's lasting ability to escape from his pursuers led to the suspicion that someone was protecting him. The best proof was that Howard Safir's plans to snatch Rich in Switzerland were betrayed to Swiss police. One can assume that Rich (or those surrounding him) regularly received information that enabled him to avoid arrest, although this is officially denied by all sides. "I'm very sure the Mossad helped him," Ken Hill told me in Florida. Jean Ziegler, a former UN special envoy and member of the Swiss parliament, stated that Rich enjoyed "secret protection in the Swiss Administration, particularly in the Federal Department of Justice and Police."[18]

Ken Hill, the man who was on Rich's trail for fourteen years, sees no more room for doubt. The former U.S. marshal understands that Rich was a valuable business partner for a number of countries. He was much too important for them to forgo his services and turn him over to the Americans. "I mean, he was a key element in providing commodities to many nations in Europe and Asia," Hill told me. "Don't forget, there are only a few people that can loan one billion dollars to each other. This is a very exclusive club, a very strong network. This privilege turned out to be a safety net for him. He must have got the protection of [intelligence] services." Such statements help explain the fact that the United States did not receive the cooperation it had hoped for from a number of countries. The prosecutors submitted requests for provisional arrests to several countries, all of them members of Interpol, but none of these requests was successful. "He was hard to get because he had a great deal of influence in a lot of countries," Howard Safir confirmed.[19]

"Crusade Against Me"

"Other nations did not share the U.S. view and consequently refused to be instrumentalized for their crusade against me," Rich says calmly. When I ask if he had been tipped off and protected, Rich's answer is as short as it is telling. "Maybe," he says, smiling, before taking another sip of wine.

Even today, hardly anyone realizes that employees at the U.S. State Department, who naturally were aware of the government's international activities, were in direct personal contact with Rich, as I will show later, even though he was considered a fugitive and was at the same time being pursued by other government agencies. In the powder keg of the Middle East, of particular strategic importance to the United States, Rich was actually considered an active diplomatic asset.

The gumshoes in the field were also aware of this. Howard Safir proved particularly outspoken and blunt. "I have found that the biggest impediment to operational law enforcement is having to deal through the bureaucracy of the State Department," he stated in his testimony before the Committee on Government Operations. He criticized certain "policy restraints" and stated that in his opinion the failures to apprehend the fugitives were due to the lack of support at the highest levels of government: "I believe that if a political decision was made at the highest levels of this government that we were going to apprehend Marc Rich and Pincus Green and use all of the available tools, that we would have Marc Rich and Pincus Green very quickly." The Committee on Government Reform came to the same conclusion: "The United States lacked the political will to effect the return of these fugitives."[20] At the same time, it lacked the political will to settle the case.

13

CLANDESTINE TALKS

The group that came together on July 28, 1992, in Zurich was an illustrious one. Fittingly, they chose to meet in the best hotel in town, the luxurious Grand Hotel Dolder perched high above summery Lake Zurich and set against the backdrop of the perpetual snow of the Swiss Alps. Leonard Garment, Marc Rich's well-connected Washington lawyer, believed the time had come to have another go at persuading the prosecutors to discuss a settlement in the Rich affair.

Eleven years had passed since Sandy Weinberg had been put on the Marc Rich case. In the meantime, both the U.S. attorney and the assistant U.S. attorney responsible for the case had changed. Weinberg had left the post in 1985 to work as a lawyer in Florida. The Rich case had been a first-class springboard into an extremely lucrative career in corporate law. Weinberg, by the way, still refers to it in his own publicity material: "As a 32-year-old prosecutor, he led the prosecution against international financier Marc Rich and his network of commodity trading companies in one of the most celebrated tax fraud cases in U.S. history. Mr. Weinberg was able to unravel Rich's complicated fraud scheme and successfully battle against his team of veteran lawyers from the best firms in the country."[1] Giuliani, for his part, had left public office and become a partner in a law firm after failing to be elected mayor of New York in 1989. He would win four years later.

Leonard Garment, the former White House counsel for Richard Nixon, was hoping that their successors would see the case less emotionally. He was hoping they would be more prepared to concede what he regarded as fundamental weaknesses in the case against Rich. In November 1990 Garment contacted Giuliani's successor, Otto G. Obermaier. "The dispute and the accompanying threats and publicity ballooned beyond all legitimate proportion," Garment wrote in a twenty-page memo to Obermaier. "The case involves many disturbing features, but at its core are transactions which were not criminal. It employed an unprecedented use of RICO that resulted in the defendant's capitulation, without trial, to the government's charges. . . . The circumstances of the case, the consequences of its outcome, and the extraordinarily important questions of criminal law enforcement it poses, justify considering such a review."[2]

Secret Meeting with Marc Rich

Obermaier actually agreed to discuss the case with Garment, and he was even willing to travel to Switzerland to meet Marc Rich in person. Traveling to a foreign country to negotiate with a defendant was a highly unusual step for a U.S. attorney to take. It awakened Rich's hopes that Obermaier was amenable to negotiations. These expectations were reinforced by the fact that Obermaier was being accompanied by Assistant U.S. Attorney James Comey.

That is how Obermaier and Comey came to be sitting around a table with Marc Rich, Leonard Garment, and André A. Wicki, Rich's Swiss attorney, in the Grand Hotel Dolder in Zurich at lunchtime on Tuesday, July 28, 1992. Before getting down to business, the adversaries ate *Zürcher Geschnetzeltes mit Rösti,* a local specialty consisting of a ragout of veal and mushrooms in a cream sauce served with hash browns. After lunch, Garment and Wicki set out their client's position (see chapter 10).

"Because the case was billed as the 'biggest tax fraud case' in history, we asked the prosecutors to review the Wolfman-Ginsburg tax analysis. We once more offered to make the [tax] professors available to address any flaws the Southern District might find in their analysis," Wicki recounted to me. "It was easy to talk to them," Rich recalls. His side presented their four most important arguments: the tax professors' conclusion that Rich's firms had correctly declared all of their earnings and deducted the right amount of taxes; the lawyers' view that the "draconian" racketeering statute was a "sledgehammer," inappropriate in the circumstances; the fact that all comparable cases had been pursued in the civil rather than the criminal courts; and the Department of Energy's conclusion in a related case that the transactions being objected to by the prosecution had been correctly accounted for by Rich's firms.

"Obermaier and Comey listened patiently," says Rich. "At first I thought the meeting was positive." The atmosphere may not have been exactly friendly, but relations were characterized by mutual respect for the first time in eleven years. The parties even arranged to meet for a second time the next day. Then Obermaier said, "Our hands are tied." The government, the prosecutor said, had a rigid policy against negotiating with fugitives. They would not be able to review the validity of the underlying tax charges unless Rich first returned to the United States and faced trial. Like Weinberg and Giuliani before him, U.S. Attorney Obermaier took the position that Rich would have to face jail before any other terms and conditions could be discussed, and the government would not provide any guarantees as to the sentences the defendants would receive.

"Not One Day in Jail"

Garment tried to cheer Rich up after the meeting even though he was deeply disappointed by the prosecution's refusal to negotiate. His client only had two options. Rich could either take his chance on a trial or plead guilty to some charge, which might involve a short prison term. "It's a few months," Garment told Rich. "You'll lose weight. It'll be easy. No manacles. You'll come back."[3] Rich shot back immediately, "Not one day. I will not spend one day in jail, because I did not commit a crime." As a child, Rich had been held in an internment camp in Morocco with his parents. Close friends say that was one of his most traumatic experiences, and he never wanted to face imprisonment again. "It goes against my nature," he says when asked why he did not agree to go back. "I'm innocent. I like to be free."

Rich nevertheless refused to quit. After all, he had become one of the most successful traders of all time because he never gave up. For him, a no was never final. Rich always thought long term in business, and his approach to his case was no different: "Let it sit for a while and try it again." Every time a new U.S. attorney or assistant U.S. attorney was appointed, his lawyers tried to make contact. Their names read like a who's who of the American justice system.

When Obermaier left office in 1993, Mary Jo White became the first woman to be appointed U.S. attorney in the Southern District of New York. Later in the same year, she was to preside over the successful prosecutions in the World Trade Center bombing cases. She was also ultimately to become the prosecutor in charge of the investigation surrounding President Clinton's decision to pardon Rich. "We are hopeful you will agree that the time for a constructive dialogue with the Government is now," Jack Quinn wrote in a letter requesting a meeting.[4] The hope was dashed.

When Gerard E. Lynch, who played an important role in the Iran-Contra investigation, was named head of the Criminal Division of the Southern District of New York, he received a letter from Professor Bernard Wolfman, one of the coauthors of the tax analysis. "Professor Ginsburg and I would be happy to discuss our views with you at your convenience and hope you will afford us the opportunity to do so," Wolfman wrote.[5] Lynch didn't afford the opportunity.

Patrick Fitzgerald also received a letter when he was assistant U.S.

attorney; he would later become famous for his role as special counsel in charge of the Department of Justice's investigation into the Valerie Plame Wilson affair. "The discussions we seek," Rich's lawyer Laurence A. Urgenson wrote to Fitzgerald, "concern clear and important issues which we assure you can be determined with a modest investment of time and without running afoul of your office policies."[6] Fitzgerald turned down the request.

No Negotiations with Fugitives

Just as Rich's lawyers trotted out the same arguments over and over again, the prosecutors rejected them with the same arguments. "There is every reason to believe that if a full discussion of the evidence took place and convinced you that the Government could prove your clients' guilt, little would change," Fitzgerald wrote to Urgenson.[7] "Your clients would continue their life on the lam—with, perhaps, another change of lawyers. It is for that reason that the Government views discussions as to the merits of the case as inappropriate and pointless."

"It is our firm policy not to negotiate dispositions of criminal charges with fugitives," Mary Jo White told Jack Quinn.[8] "Such negotiations would give defendants an incentive to flee, and from the Government's perspective, would provide defendants with the inappropriate leverage and luxury of remaining absent unless and until the Government agrees to their terms." André Wicki, a thoughtful, humorous man, is annoyed by White's response to this day. "There is no such policy. On the contrary. Federal prosecutors in the Southern District and elsewhere have entered into negotiation and settlement of criminal cases against indicted individuals who did not return to face trial," he says.

It is surprising the amount of time and the enormous quantity of money that Rich was prepared to invest trying his luck with the Southern District of New York only to be disappointed time and time again. He spent millions in lawyers' fees. It was not unusual for one of his lawyers to receive a retainer of $55,000—per month.

"Personal interests and feelings on their side got into the way of a fair solution. I kept trying and nothing succeeded," Rich says matter-of-factly, as if he were talking about the lottery. So why on earth did he make the effort? "It's normal," he says. "I'm innocent." "You could have said to yourself," I interject, " 'I'm safe in Switzerland, business is going well, let's forget about this case in the United States and move on.' " "I did pretty much that, but I was always interested to settle it if possible," Rich answers. I ask him what the advantage of a settlement would have been. "To be completely free," he says, "which is what I am now." Why were the prosecutors of the Southern District of New York so dogged? "I guess they had nothing to gain by settling," Rich says quietly, not betraying any sign of how angry he was at the behavior of the prosecutors back then. "Marc was genuinely completely confounded as to why he was so vilified and unable to present, you know, his side of the story and put it into context," Laurence Urgenson revealed.

"Vindictive Time"

Marc Rich's lawyers do not try to conceal their dissatisfaction with U.S. justice, as it was practiced in the Southern District of New York. "The fact that this truth mattered not one whit to the U.S. Attorney's office, and the fact that the political system as a whole allowed the prosecutors to behave with such willfulness, was one of the chief examples of the dangerous state into which our politics had fallen after Watergate," wrote Leonard Garment, referring to a "vindictive time." "[Marc Rich] had the bad luck to be pulled into the vortex of post-Vietnam, post-Watergate American politics, in which every policy problem was labeled a scandal and each dispute with the government was considered a criminal matter."[9] The U.S. attorneys, Bob Fink said, "were much more interested in maintaining the credibility of the U.S. Attorney's Office than in reviewing if mistakes had been made. If they were wrong in such an important case it would damage their reputation and influence."

Marc Rich spent almost two decades on the FBI's Most Wanted list.

His name was only removed from it on January 21, 2001—the day after Bill Clinton pardoned him. This fact made Rich's business transactions rather more difficult, but it did not put a stop to them. "Contrary to the myth, I was able to travel to a number of other countries, so I did not feel too restricted," he told me. He seemed to take great satisfaction from that.

14

The SECRETS of SUCCESS

From Angola to South Africa

It came as a surprise to all, and for some it was nothing less than "one of the wonders of the business world."[1] Even though he was pursued by the most powerful nation on earth, which did everything possible to thwart his business dealings, Marc Rich was able to continually expand his company, until it became the world's largest and most successful independent oil and metals trading company. In 1990, seven years after he was indicted in New York, he was active in 128 countries, had forty-eight offices around the globe, and employed twelve hundred people. He bought and sold 1.5 million barrels of oil each day—more than the daily average output of Kuwait. He ruled over a trading empire with an annual turnover of $30 billion. The company earned anywhere from $200 million to $400 million in profits each year. Rich's personal fortune was an estimated $1 billion. As the *Financial Times* stated in almost reverential terms, Rich was "one of the wealthiest and most powerful commodities traders ever to have lived."[2]

Not even the wildest optimists at Marc Rich + Co. had expected that the company would enjoy such success. Five years previously, Rich's legal difficulties and the fact that he was living in exile had led commentators and businesspeople alike to practically write Rich off. One of his partners from the very beginning, Jacques Hachuel, was convinced that the end was nigh and decided to leave the company. The two traders have not spoken a word since. All told, Rich's unlikely comeback made a huge impact on the world of commodities trading.

How did he do it? How was he able to beat the competition? What did he do differently? Why was he better? These are the most important questions when it comes to unveiling the secrets of Rich's success. To get to the bottom of this untold story of success, I interviewed dozens of commodities traders from five continents over the past three years. In these three years (2006–2008) the world—and particularly the United States—experienced the kind of dramatic changes that have not been seen in decades. The financial crisis that began in 2008 led to developments that only the gloomiest of pessimists previously believed possible. Lehman Brothers, a traditional banking powerhouse founded in 1850, collapsed, making for the largest bankruptcy in the history of the United States. Goldman Sachs and Morgan Stanley gave up their status as investment banks. It was the end of an era.

It's the Long Term, Stupid

When we look back at these crazy times in search of the deep-rooted causes of the worst financial crisis in generations, one answer will most certainly stand out: the short-term thinking that has held sway among the managers of listed companies since the 1980s. Nothing seemed more important than quarterly profits. The economic common sense that had developed over the course of decades was no longer viewed as important. Equity returns of 20 to 30 percent? Double-digit profit growth? Quick profits from risky leveraged investments? Extravagant salaries? All that was once considered extraordinary seemed routine. It was, as history has shown time and again, too good to be true. What does this have to do with Marc Rich? More than one might believe at first glance.

As we have seen, his company is in many ways the antithesis of the fallen business elite that does not seem capable of looking past the next quarter. An era in which oil prices reached new records saw the reemergence of the myth of the commodities trader as a man who could make millions of dollars in seconds with a single telephone call. The reality is something entirely different. The commodities trade is a hard, capital-intensive business with tight margins. Profits of 2 to 3 percent are considered quite satisfactory in normal times. It is only during unsteady times, such as the oil crises of 1973–74 and 1979–80, that profits are significantly higher.

In the cyclical business of the commodities trade, successful traders always have to look far ahead into the future. "The key to success—and to real wealth—is long-term thinking," Rich says. Six months in South Africa in order to negotiate the purchase of a mine? Six months in Cuba in order to ensure a loan is paid back? Advance financing of a smelter that will not be completed for years to come? Such actions are nearly unthinkable for listed companies obsessed with quarterly returns. In some businesses, long-term thinking has been virtually forgotten. On the other hand, it is the traditional virtue of family businesses in which one generation always has its children in mind. It is my belief that this long-term way of thinking is the most important secret of Rich's success and can explain many of the strategies and courses of action he has followed over the years.

Rich was always interested in obtaining long-term contracts with his clients. In economic terms, the development of new markets, making business contacts, and negotiating contracts cost a lot of money. Once a business relationship has been established, many of the so-called transaction costs no longer apply. The longer the relationship, the lower the marginal costs and the higher the potential profits. "We didn't get into a new country to make a million dollars and then go home. We went to stay there," said a trader who had opened African markets while working for Rich in the 1970s. "We wanted to convince them we were there to stay. This was a very important basis for our success."

The Bribes

The House Committee on Government Reform has a completely different opinion of Rich's success. The committee accused Rich, as described in chapter 2, of developing a trading empire that "was based largely on systematic bribes and kickbacks to corrupt local officials." The committee also claimed Rich made his fortune "doing business without legal, ethical, or even moral constraints."[3] "He is only interested in making money, and for that he is prepared to stop at nothing," a Swiss trader who had worked for Rich once told me. "Rich is without scruples," a competitor in the aluminum industry said. "He does not owe his fortune to brilliance alone. People in the trade knew that I, on the other hand, was not for sale."

"I don't agree," Rich says with little indignation when asked about these accusations. In truth, Marc Rich + Co. would never have been able to make the trades it actually completed if it had not paid bribes—really big bribes. Whoever has worked in the Middle East or Africa knows that it is impossible to do business without paying *"un petit cadeau"* (a little present), a "sweetener," or baksheesh—regardless of the company code of conduct. According to anonymous traders quoted in A. Craig Copetas's book *Metal Men*, Rich's company paid a bribe of $125,000 to the director of the National Iranian Oil Company. The book also states that the Nigerian minister of transportation received a bribe of $1 million in order to ensure the Nigerian government continued to work with Rich.[4] Although he does not go into the details of these (or any other) bribes, Rich does not deny that he had authorized them in the past. "The bribes were paid in order to be able to do the business at the same price as other people were willing to do the business," Rich claims. "It's not a price which is disadvantageous for the government involved in the selling or buying country."

Depending on a person's ethical standards, the bribing of officials or politicians in order to do business in the third world could well be regarded as morally questionable, if not outright unethical and reprehensible. Still, bribery was certainly common practice, and by no means only for commodities traders. The bribing of foreign officials was legal in the United States until the passing of the Foreign Corrupt Practices Act of 1977. In Switzerland it remained legal until 2000. Companies in Switzerland and in many other countries could deduct bribes as "commercially justified expenses" from their taxes. When asked about corruption, Rich's lawyers maintain that he never broke Swiss law. A trader who was active in African nations such as Nigeria and Zaire—two notoriously corrupt countries—told me, "The law is the benchmark, not your morality. As a trader you should abstract yourself from your personal morality. If you don't agree, you can leave the company."

In some cases, Rich may have been able to close a deal more quickly than the competition thanks to corrupt officials. Bribery may have allowed him to trump his competitors, but it is not realistic to attribute Rich's success to such activities alone. The fact that Rich was able to dominate the commodities trade for decades is not the result of mere corruption. "The successful traders are not the bribers. They don't last too long," said the director of one of the world's largest trading companies, who did not wish to be quoted by name. "[Rich] has survived because he has the most talent," according to Slimane Bouguerra, the director of the Algerian state oil company, Sonatrach.[5]

The Talented Mr. Rich

A few of Rich's talents have already been described in this book. Rich was faster and more aggressive than his competitors. He was able to recognize trends before other traders, and he successfully created new markets. Rich himself describes this as his most important skill: the ability to see opportunity. His stroke of genius was the fact that in the middle and late 1970s he had been willing to enter into long-term contracts with Iran, Nigeria, Angola, and Ecuador based on his prediction that the price of oil would continue to rise.

LEFT: Saved from the Holocaust: Marc Rich flees war-torn Europe with his parents David and Paula on the freighter *Monviso* in 1940. The family slept on improvised hammocks strung between pipes below deck. "We lost everything," says Rich, "but we survived."

BELOW: Seven-year-old Marc Rich in 1942 in New York with his mother Paula *(right)*, his grandmother *(middle)*, and her twin sister *(left)*: "I was always very pro-American. It's a generous country that accepted my parents and me."

ABOVE LEFT: Sixteen-year-old Marc in 1951 in Kansas City, Missouri: "He was small, he was different, he had an accent, and he was Jewish," recalled a classmate. He attended twelve different schools in twelve years. The Rich family became American citizens on St. Valentine's Day 1947.

ABOVE RIGHT: Marc Rich in his early twenties as a junior trader at Philipp Brothers, then the world's largest trader in raw materials: "I was fascinated by the size of the market. Take oil or aluminum. You can find those materials in almost any product you touch. The whole world needs them, from east to west and north to south."

A visit to the lost past: Marc with his parents in Scheveningen near The Hague, the Netherlands, 1962. He was born as Marcell David Reich in Antwerp, Belgium. "My father is definitely the person who influenced me most. We fled from Belgium and he managed to build up an important business from zero," Rich said.

A glass of champagne with the future Mrs. Rich: Marc Rich and Denise Eisenberg in 1966. They met on a blind date organized by their parents. "Marc proposed to me after two weeks of touring in the north of Spain. It was very romantic," said Denise.

Denise Eisenberg Rich would become an acclaimed songwriter in the 1980s and 1990s after moving to Switzerland with her husband. "I started writing songs at that point also because I was alone so much of the time."

Marc Rich with his parents in Bolivia: Rich spent six months there in the late 1950s and not only learned Spanish, but he also picked up the essentials of doing business in politically volatile countries. Bolivian tin was the first commodity he traded.

The founders: Rich *(right)* with his partners Alexander "Alec" Hackel *(left)* and Pincus "Pinky" Green *(middle)* in the 1980s. Together they revolutionized the global oil and commodities trade. In 1983 Rudy Giuliani indicted Rich and Green for what he claimed was "the biggest tax fraud in history," racketeering, and trading with the enemy (Iran).

Paula Wang Rich and David Rich, ca. 1985: "Marc always wanted to prove to his father that he could be as successful—or even more successful—than [his father] was," said longtime family friend Ursula Santo Domingo. Paula is remembered as a typical Jewish mother—caring, encouraging, and overprotective.

Gabrielle Rich Aouad, the second daughter of Marc and Denise, died of leukemia in 1996 at age twenty-seven in Seattle. Rich knew that if he wanted to see her one last time, he would be arrested. "Please don't come home," begged Gabrielle when he told her that he would travel to her. "If you do this I will be so angry with you."

Marc Rich married Gisela Rossi, his lover of many years, six months after the divorce from Denise in 1996. Gisela had to convert to Judaism before the marriage. They divorced in 2005. "I regret marrying Gisela," said Rich.

Together with his most loyal friends on a trip to Germany: *(from left to right)* Former Mossad officer Avner Azulay, Marc Rich, legendary New York financier Michael Steinhardt, and Isaac Querub, longtime president of the Jewish Community of Madrid. "My friends always supported me because they knew better," said Rich.

Prominent Israelis such as Shimon Peres *(left)*, Nobel Peace Prize Winner and today's President of Israel, and former Prime Minister Ehud Barak *(not shown)* personally lobbied President Bill Clinton for Rich's pardon.

Marc Rich was awarded an honorary doctorate by the Bar-Ilan University in 2007 for his philanthropic support of educational, cultural, and welfare institutions in Israel and the world. "Wealth always means independence and comfort, of course," Rich said, "but it also means that I can help the less fortunate through my foundations."

With girlfriend Dolores "Lola" Ruiz on his estate in Marbella, Spain: Ruiz is the granddaughter of communist leader Dolores Ibárruri, known as La Pasionaria, the legendary heroine of Spain's Civil War.

Skiing in St. Moritz with daughters Ilona *(left)* and Danielle *(right)*, December 2007. "I never spoiled them; I wanted to teach them that you have to work to make money," Rich said. He wanted to pass on "honesty, hard work, responsibility, and some knowledge of the Jewish religion" to his children.

Marc Rich today.

As countries recognized the value of the services he provided, Rich was able to save his existing contracts and business contacts in various countries even though there had been a change of regime. This is true of Cuba after Fidel Castro's Communist revolution, Iran after Khomeini's Islamic revolution, and even in South Africa after the end of apartheid. The ability to maintain contacts in Cuba and Iran was something that American foreign policy had not been able to duplicate.

Rich went where others feared to tread—"the road less traveled," as an employee told me. This was true not only in a geographical sense, as was the case in countries such as Angola or Zaire where markets had yet to be developed, but also in a moral and legal sense. Rich had no qualms about supplying countries such as Cuba, Iran, or apartheid South Africa—all countries that were subject to either American or international embargos. These contracts represented very lucrative deals for Rich, as these countries were willing to pay a premium for Rich's risks in order to meet their own demands. Rich soon developed a reputation—he would do just about anything for money.

Rich was a mediator who brought together business partners who officially wanted nothing to do with one another. Iran and Israel. Arab states and South Africa. Marxists and capitalists. A further example that has remained a secret to this day: Nicaragua under Daniel Ortega's Sandinista government brought in Marc Rich to sell the cheap oil it received from "socialist brother nations" such as Libya or Algeria on the global market. "I wanted the oil, and they needed the money," one of Rich's employees who was involved in the deal in the 1980s told me. It is a paradoxical situation that helps illustrate the fact that many of the aspects of the commodities trade are not as they appear. While the Left decries Rich as an exploiter of the third world, it was actually his company that helped ensure the financial survival of the Sandinistas, who were idealized as "freedom fighters" by many of the same left-leaning people.

Ayn Rand

If you ask traders about their business, you will hear the same expression over and over again, "The concept of trading is giving a service." "Trading is a service business. We bring sellers and buyers together and earn a service charge," as Rich himself describes the trade. It is the realization of the trader principle that the libertarian philosopher Ayn Rand defined as follows: "In any proper deal, you act on the trader principle: you give a value and you receive a value."[6]

Ayn Rand's philosophy has had a major influence on Rich's life. She advocates the virtue of "rational egoism," which holds that one's own life is one's most important value and achieving happiness is one's most important purpose: "Selfishness means to live by the judgment of one's own mind and to live by one's own productive effort, without forcing anything on others."[7] In her roman à clef *Atlas Shrugged*, first published in 1957, businesspeople are represented as courageous "capitalist heroes" who are driven by their own will to create and are capable of bringing about prosperity.[8] One of the book's protagonists, Hank Rearden, is an industrialist who begins his career as a simple worker and becomes the director of the largest steel factory in the fictional United States described in the book. He is later taken to court for failure to follow state-mandated sales regulations, and the media denounces him as "a greedy enemy of society." The similarities between Rich's fate and Rearden's are striking.

You give a value and you receive a value. Rich and his traders took this theory to the point of perfection, and with it they obtained the long-term contracts they desired. "Marc Rich's people were always prepared to make a counteroffer such as prefinancing, a contact, or a bank account," an industrialist from Ghana told me. Marc Rich + Co. took this concept to the point where the company soon began to serve as a kind of investment bank for several developing countries. These were countries that would have had difficulties obtaining credit on the regular financial markets, usually as a result of their poor credit ratings.

Even if they could find someone who was willing to offer them credit, the interest rates were exorbitant. Rich's company financed the construction of mines, smelters, and refineries or the production of oil in Jamaica, Zaire, South Africa, Namibia, and Angola. In return Rich asked for exclusive rights to sell all commodities produced in the country for a period of one year or more.

"You need us and we need you. This is the way we have to establish our relationship." These were the words used by one of Rich's most successful traders to explain the position he adopted when approaching a prospective client. This strategy of offering valuable services in order to obtain long-term contracts is clearly illustrated in Rich's dealings with four countries in particular: Marxist Angola; Jamaica, which alternated between socialist and economically liberal governments; South Africa under apartheid; and the East African nation of Burundi, one of the world's poorest. Rich made offers to these four countries, representing nearly all political forms of government, that they simply could not refuse.

The Mysterious Monsieur Ndolo

Monsieur Ndolo was a well-known acquaintance of the National Iranian Oil Company in the early 1980s. The black man was from Burundi, a poor country in East Africa and a former German colony that remained under Belgian administration until its independence in 1962. Monsieur Ndolo was the director of Cobuco (Compagnie Burundaise de Commerce), a state-owned company that purchased commodities for Burundi. Cobuco's offices were located at rue Marie Depage 7 in the center of the embassy quarter of Brussels, the Belgian capital and the seat of NATO headquarters.

Iranian officials only knew the sound of Monsieur Ndolo's voice. He regularly called NIOC headquarters in Tehran from Brussels. If Iranian officials had ever had the opportunity to meet Monsieur Ndolo, they would have been rather surprised: Monsieur Ndolo did not actually come from Burundi, nor was he black. He was a white trader who worked for Marc Rich and only pretended to be from the African country. Nor was Cobuco a Burundian state-owned company, as everyone believed. In reality Cobuco was a joint venture between Rich's company and the Burundian government, each of which owned a 50 percent stake.

The company was founded to trade with postrevolutionary Iran. Rich's trader, who would later take on the role of Monsieur Ndolo, contacted the Burundian government through an intermediary and suggested what one might call a very original deal. Burundi should request a long-term contract for oil deliveries from Iran's revolutionary government. Monsieur Ndolo, who today does not wish to see his real name appear in print, explained with enthusiasm the advantages the company had reaped from this deal. "A Burundian delegation actually did travel to Tehran in order to negotiate an oil contract. I instructed the delegation from the background. I thought it would be possible for a poor country such as Burundi to ask the Islamic government in Iran for favorable terms of payment. I told the delegation they should offer to pay Iran the official OPEC price, but they would only be able to pay one year after delivery—and with no interest payments." Monsieur Ndolo knew that the Iranians advanced an Islamic economy based on the rules set forth in the Koran, which forbade the charging of interest. After a long series of negotiations, Iran finally agreed to the deal proposed by the Burundian delegation, and the two parties signed a long-term contract for the delivery of crude.

Rich chartered ships to collect the oil from the Iranian harbor of Bandar Abbas in the Persian Gulf. NIOC believed the ships would transport the oil to a refinery in Kenya. There it would be refined and transported by tanker truck to inland Burundi, where it would help to get the Burundian economy running and aid in the development of the country. The reality, however, was completely different. "We made a fortune," Monsieur Ndolo told me in his office located in a European capital. He leaned back and drew deeply on his cigarette. "You usually have to pay for the oil within thirty days," he explained. "In this case we had a year before we had to meet the payments, all without having to pay interest."

For Rich's company, it was two good deals in one. It only had to pay the official OPEC price for the oil—a price that was generally lower than the spot market price—and it earned money on the deferred payment because its customers abided by the usual payment terms. In the early 1980s the prime rate was a horrendous 18 percent (it was 3.25 percent in February 2009). That was 18 percent that Rich could add to the price, as only a small portion of the oil actually made it to Burundi. Most of the oil was sold by Marc Rich + Co. for good prices on the spot market. Both parties had a good laugh at the negotiating table as they closed the fantastic deal—just the way Rich liked it. "We wanted oil from Burundi; Burundi wanted money. We both profited enormously," Monsieur Ndolo confided. He switched from French to English. "The Africans know how to do business successfully."

Angolan Absurdities

Angola, an oil-rich nation in southwestern Africa, was the setting for one of the cold war's greatest paradoxes. In 1975, shortly after the nation gained independence from Portugal, Angola descended into a brutal civil war that would last for twenty-seven years. The country was the backdrop for a proxy war between the capitalist West and the Communist East. The Marxist government under the MPLA (the Popular Movement for the Liberation of Angola), which had seized the reins of control after independence, was financed by the Soviet Union and Cuba. Their opponents, the rebel movement UNITA (National Union for the Total Independence of Angola), were supported both financially and ideologically by the United States and South Africa.

The American company Gulf Oil (now Chevron) had been producing oil since 1968 in the South Atlantic off the coast of the small Angolan exclave of Cabinda. After the Marxists seized power, most foreign oil companies left the country, together with their experts, and their production facilities were nationalized. However, Gulf Oil remained, accepted the MPLA government, and continued to cooperate with the Marxists. The American company was thus responsible for a considerable part of the MPLA's public revenue, and this made Gulf Oil's production facilities in Cabinda a prime target for the UNITA rebels. UNITA wanted to wipe out the government's prime source of revenue and thus carried out regular attacks in the exclave.

So it came to be that Cuban troops sent to Angola by Fidel Castro to support the MPLA were stationed in Cabinda. Cuban Communist forces were now responsible for protecting the production facilities of capitalist Gulf Oil, based in Pittsburgh, Pennsylvania, from UNITA attacks that were financed by the United States.

In 1976, the Marxist government founded the state-owned oil company Sonangol, the Sociedade Nacional de Combustíveis de Angola. Sonangol had total and exclusive rights for the production and marketing of Angolan oil, but the company was lacking in trained personnel. Other than those experts working for Gulf Oil, most had already left the country. If the Angolan government were to market the oil on its own, it would need an independent and experienced intermediary. It found just the right one in Zug, Switzerland. "We became the exclusive agent for Angola for quite some time," Rich explains over a coffee in his office in Zug. The fact that Sonangol was actually a joint venture between Angola and Marc Rich has remained a secret to this day. It was once more a win-win situation. "The Angolans wanted to gain experience in the international oil market," Rich says. He wanted nothing more than to earn money—Rich's favorite activity. *You give a value and you receive a value.*

The joint venture led to a rather strange state of affairs. The American oil company Exxon (now ExxonMobil) noted Gulf Oil's successes in Angola and sought to get a foot in the door of the African oil trade. Exxon managers arranged a meeting with Sonangol representatives. They knew nothing of Marc Rich + Co.'s share in the Angolan state-owned company. The representatives sat waiting in a conference room expecting to meet a black Marxist functionary. One can only imagine how they felt when Pinky Green walked into the room and greeted them with a friendly "How ya doin."[9]

Rich also organized something for the Marxist country that it never could have obtained on its own and without which it could never have gotten into the oil trade: access to international banks. Rich's company excelled at solving financial problems, which provided it with a competitive advantage. One of the best Africa experts in the commodities trade told me, "When you go to Africa, your success in the business is not only dependent on the price you're paying, but also on the financial solution you can find for your customer. If you find a financial solution, you can beat all of the competition. You will be the king."

Marc Rich + Co.'s involvement in Sonangol lasted until 1983. By then the Angolans had learned enough to found their own trading company, which was able to take over the task that Marc Rich + Co. had fulfilled. The joint venture with Rich allowed Angola to become Africa's second-largest oil-producing nation. "They knew nothing about the market. We taught them from the first step, no question. Afterward they were able to copy what we had done," one of Rich's directors told me. "We were the ones who gave them the key of knowledge."

Jamaica Me Crazy

There was a great sense of nervousness in the Jamaican department of Marc Rich + Co. in Zug on February 10, 1989. The charismatic politician Michael Manley had just been elected prime minister in Kingston. His socialist People's National Party had won in a landslide, and Rich's people were prepared for the worst. "We were waiting for Manley's people to call and tell us to stay in Switzerland and not to come back to Jamaica," said one of the traders who had feared for his future then. In those days Michael Manley was a hero of the European Left. The former union functionary cultivated an anti-imperialist rhetoric directed against the United States, and he openly admired Communist Cuba as a role model for his nation. One of the main themes of the election was the question of how Jamaica should handle its natural resources. The Caribbean island is one of the world's largest producers of bauxite, the ore from which aluminum is won. Manley was highly critical of Jamaica's cooperation with Marc Rich.

Rich owed his reputation to the oil trade, but as we have seen, his company traded commodities from aluminum to zinc. Bauxite, aluminum oxide, and aluminum made up about a fourth of its income. Rich had been represented there for some years by his company Clarendon, which dealt directly with the Jamaican government. Manley's People's National Party had promised to stop all business with Rich and to closely reevaluate all existing government contracts with his company. Placards with photomontages were displayed at the party's rallies depicting Marc Rich with blood on his hands. He was denounced as an archetypical exploiter and "foreign parasite."

Manley's first appearance in the Jamaican parliament turned out to be a huge disappointment for Rich's critics. He had made a mistake concerning "the Marc Rich matter," Manley admitted during the budget debate of March 1989. His government would "of course" honor Jamaica's contracts.[10] Rich's critics around the world—particularly activists in the antiapartheid movement, a movement with which Manley was closely associated—were crestfallen. They had hoped that Manley would promptly turn his back on Rich. Why, they asked themselves, did Manley make such a staggering 180-degree turn?

The simplest answer to this question was given to me by a banker who worked for Rich. "Marc Rich had saved Jamaica. He had bailed it out." At that time, in spring 1989, officials from the International Monetary Fund (IMF) were in Kingston to inspect the government's bookkeeping, and further IMF credit was dependent on the results of the inspection. The Caribbean island was as reliant on foreign loans as an addict is on his drug of choice. Jamaica was deep in debt, its balance of payments was heavily in the red, and the Jamaican dollar was steadily losing value. In the spring of 1989 it looked as if Jamaica would flunk the inspectors' test. Most significant, the country maintained lower currency reserves than the amounts stipulated by the IMF, which were intended to help Jamaica meet interest payments and obtain further loans. The new government was lacking $45 million in hard currency, and it needed to find it fast; otherwise the IMF would stop the flow of credit into the country. Jamaica would then find itself unable to meet its payments—a development that would have devastating effects for the Jamaican economy and people.

In the end, even socialist beggars can't be choosers. Shortly after assuming office, Prime Minister Manley entered into talks with Clarendon's managers.[11] They explored the idea of Rich helping Jamaica with a loan—and discovered they were preaching to the converted. The IMF forbade countries from borrowing money to cover their currency reserves, so a normal loan was out of the question. Rich's people, however, believed the problem could be solved with a bit of "creative accounting." They offered to give Jamaica the desperately needed $45 million, but not as a loan. Instead, the money was intended as an advance payment on future aluminum oxide deliveries. Jamaica was saved; IMF officials accepted the government's accounts and approved the new credit.

Critics maintain that Rich was thus essentially able to buy Manley and effectively take Jamaica hostage. However, the reality of the situation was that no bank, no international organization, and certainly no other company would have been prepared at that time to lend Jamaica a single cent. The country was over $4 billion in debt and was not even remotely creditworthy. "In any other company it would have been considered crazy to give Jamaica money under such circumstances," a Rich employee who played an important role in the Jamaican negotiations told me, "but we never let down the people who do business with us. We sometimes even took on losses." Of course, Rich's people were not helping Jamaica out of a sense of charity: "For us every situation was an opportunity. We weren't looking for fast money. We were looking for an ongoing relationship."

Rich's companies were willing to accept the smallest of profit margins—and ready to take an occasional temporary loss—in order to break into a market or enlarge their market share. The trade in commodities—and this is particularly true of aluminum—is a cyclical business. A one- or two-year period of high prices can be followed by longer periods of low prices. Those traders who are prepared to operate against the cycle, hold out during dry spells, and even invest during hard times can reap good profits when the prices again begin to rise. There is no better example of this strategy than Rich's Jamaican aluminum trades.

Rich had already helped Jamaica out of trouble four years prior to the island's troubles with the IMF. In 1985 aluminum prices had hit a low of $1,080 per metric ton—the lowest price in years.[12] At the same time, oil prices had skyrocketed, making the complicated and energy-intensive production of aluminum even more expensive. The American aluminum producer Alcoa, which mainly made money as a supplier of aluminum to the aircraft and automobile industry, wanted to shut down its Jamaican production facilities for converting bauxite into aluminum oxide due to increasing production costs. It had become cheaper for Alcoa to purchase aluminum oxide from a third party.

The closing of the Alcoa facility was a catastrophe for the country, which lived mainly from tourism and bauxite. It was a golden opportunity for Rich, and his people immediately approached the prime minister, Edward Seaga. "We knew exactly what we wanted. We had a plan that covered everything from A to Z," Rich's employee explained. "We told the minister of industry, Hugh Hart, he should suggest to Alcoa that they lease the facility to the government instead of shutting it down. We knew Alcoa would agree, as even a closed facility would have cost them a lot of money. We simultaneously guaranteed Jamaica that we would continue to purchase their yields at fixed prices for a period of ten years. We told the government that we would take care of everything; all they had to do was maintain production." Clarendon, the Marc Rich company, even supplied Jamaica with cheap oil.

In early 1986 Seaga's government signed a ten-year contract with Clarendon for the Alcoa facility's entire annual yield of 750,000 metric tons of aluminum oxide.[13] It was risky for the company to commit itself to a long-term contract while prefinancing the facility's yield in the midst of a crisis. Metals experts assumed that prices would continue to fall. It was a risk that might pay off only to those who could wait. Marc Rich was someone who knew how to wait.

Two years after Clarendon had signed the ten-year contract at fixed prices, the demand for aluminum began to increase rapidly, and prices began to skyrocket. In 1988 the price for a metric ton of aluminum was at $2,430—more than twice the price at the time of the contract. Rich made a fortune as a result of the simple fact that he had had the patience and the money to wait out the slump in the aluminum market. Jamaica also profited from the rise in prices because the price agreed with Rich was a mix of fixed prices, London Metals Exchange–linked prices, and barter of oil for alumina. Between 1980 and 1990 Rich advanced Jamaica's government almost $320 million in order to secure annual yields of aluminum oxide. Critics bemoaned the exploitation of the nation's natural resources by "assorted private individuals."[14] Rich's employee in Kingston in those days is of a wholly different opinion: "The Jamaicans are eternally grateful to us," he told me. "We gave them back their pride, the Alcoa facility was once more able to turn a profit, jobs were saved, and we made a really good deal." *You give a value and you receive a value.*

South African Stratagems

It seemed to be a normal transport like any other. The *Dagli*, a Norwegian tanker, docked in Odessa on September 21, 1988, where she took on a cargo of Soviet oil. The shipping documents listed the destination as the Italian harbor of Genoa. The *Dagli* sailed across the Black Sea and through the Bosporus Strait past Istanbul. The tanker had just reached the Mediterranean when her captain received a telex advising him of a change of plans. According to telexes in the author's possession, the ship's charterer ordered him to set course for Cape Town in South Africa. From that moment onward, the captain was only allowed to identify the *Dagli* on the radio as "MFI," and all further communications were to be carried out using secret code. He was prohibited from disclosing the ship's cargo or the destination. The telex's wording was quite clear: "Any all communications are to refer only to bunkering operation with no reference whatsoever to cargo discharge, vessels [*sic*] name or loadport. Under no circumstances should vessel use usual call sign." Three weeks later, on October 15, 1988, the *Dagli* sailed into harbor at Cape Town. She was virtually a ghost ship—her name was covered with a tarp, and her Norwegian flag had been taken down. She secretly discharged her cargo of oil in Cape Town before disappearing nearly as soon as she had arrived.

There was a reason, of course, for all of this secrecy. The oil's true owner was Marc Rich, and the arranged purchaser was the government of South Africa. The oil itself came from the Soviet Union, which officially boycotted the racist apartheid regime and had broken off diplomatic relations with the country as of 1956. It was a typical state of affairs in which Rich again served as a sort of "crude middleman" who bought sensitive commodities from sensitive sellers and sold them to sensitive buyers. He was able to bring together countries that no longer maintained an official relationship with one another.

South Africa's survival depended on middlemen such as Rich. The Iranian revolution was a catastrophe for the South Africans. In February, 1979, the mullahs in Tehran broke off all diplomatic and economic contacts with South Africa. The National Iranian Oil Company contractually forbade its customers from delivering a single drop of oil to the apartheid state. In the years before the revolution, South Africa had obtained 90 percent of its oil from Iran.[15] The shah had continually refused to take part in the Arab nations' sanctions against South Africa, such as the 1973 boycott. The shah had wanted to become a powerhouse of the oil trade and was happy to sign large (and independent) contracts with new customers. Furthermore, Mohammad Reza Pahlavi's position could be explained by the special relationship he maintained with the government in Pretoria. His father, Reza Shah, was forced to step down by Great Britain and the Soviet Union in 1941 before being forced into exile. Reza Shah spent his final days in Johannesburg, where he died in 1944. As strange as it might sound, Iranians were granted special status as "honorary whites" under the racist laws of the apartheid regime.

Few countries were willing to continue supplying South Africa with oil. In addition to the Arab boycott, the United Nations General Assembly also enacted an oil embargo against South Africa in a series of resolutions in 1977. In truth it remained a voluntary boycott, and the UN Security Council never made it a binding resolution.[16] Nevertheless, most oil-producing nations enacted embargoes—at least officially—and the larger oil companies stopped dealing with South Africa. In 1986 the United States enacted the Comprehensive Anti-Apartheid Act, which prohibited U.S. companies from supplying South Africa with oil.[17]

South Africa's salvation came in the form of Marc Rich—with a hefty surcharge, of course. Rich's companies had very good contacts in South Africa, and a young Briton living in the former Commonwealth country was in charge of company affairs: Alan Fenton, who had changed his name from Felsenstein. Fenton took care of the company's South African business, mainly in the manganese and chrome trade, in the late 1970s. Alec Hackel, one of the founders of Marc Rich + Co., was in charge of South African affairs back at company headquarters in Zug. Shortly after the Iranian revolution, the apartheid government secretly approached Fenton in order to discuss oil deliveries, and the two parties soon came to an agreement.

On April 12, 1979, South Africa signed a long-term contract with Rich for the delivery of large sums of oil. In order to keep their business relationship as discreet as possible, an unknown Swiss company was named in the contract. Minoil was located only a few hundred feet from Rich's headquarters in Zug. No one knew that Minoil also just happened to be a part of Rich's trading empire. Switzerland again proved to be a clever choice for the headquarters of Marc Rich + Co. In those days the neutral country was not a member of the United Nations and did not generally participate in economic or political sanctions.

Under the terms of the contract, Rich was obliged to deliver oil to South Africa for a period of at least one year. The contract stated that Minoil would deliver 2.4 million metric tons of oil in the first six months followed by 1.6 million metric tons in the second half of the year. Together these deliveries amounted to around one-third of South Africa's yearly oil needs. South Africa paid Rich an average of $32.80 per barrel—$8 higher than spot market prices.[18] This contract for approximately 4 million metric tons—nearly 30 million barrels—was worth almost $1 billion. Rich was able to make an estimated profit of around $230 million.

South Africa was in a desperate situation and was forced to resort to "unconventional means" in order to secure its oil supply. These were the words that appeared in a report from June 27, 1984, by the advocate general of South Africa, Piet van der Walt, who was investigating rumors of massive corruption surrounding the oil deliveries. One of the most important of the "unconventional means" involved government risk premiums of $8 per barrel—the same $8 that Rich made above the spot market price. Van der Walt's report stated, "As a further incentive to international oil companies to supply . . . South Africa with crude oil, $8 per barrel of crude oil was paid under a subsidy scheme during 1980. For each barrel of crude oil imported by a company $8 per barrel, adjusted in terms of oil quality, was repaid to the company."[19] South African president Pieter W. Botha later admitted that South Africa, to be able to get oil supplies, had paid between $1 billion and $2 billion each year above the normal price as a result of the boycott.[20]

South Africa under apartheid is the best example of the double moral standards that are still prevalent in the discussions about ethics in the commodities trade. The list of countries from which the oil for the apartheid regime was obtained reads like a complete list of all oil-producing nations. The oil came mainly from Iran, Saudi Arabia, the United Arab

Emirates, and Oman.[21] Oil deliveries also came from Dubai, Angola, Nigeria, Ecuador, Brunei, and the Soviet Union. All of these countries were vocal opponents of the apartheid regime and had loudly proclaimed that they would maintain the boycott against South Africa.

In reality, however, profit triumphed over principles in these countries. Islamic Iran, the Communist Soviet Union, and capitalist Ecuador were all looking for hard currency. They all made, via Marc Rich, lucrative secret deals with the apartheid regime in South Africa. Rich was used in order to conceal the contradictions between these nations' political rhetoric and economic deeds, and they were content to let him take the political heat. Today there is absolutely no doubt that Rich was the ostracized regime's most important oil supplier from 1979 to 1994 (when Rich sold his company). His company was responsible for at least 15 percent of the identified oil deliveries, according to the Dutch Shipping Research Bureau's conservative estimates. These deliveries consisted of 149 tanker loads—a total of 26.2 million metric tons, or around 200 million barrels, of oil.[22] From information gathered during the extensive interviews that I conducted for this book, I have come to the conclusion that the true sum was actually more in the region of 400 million barrels.

Rich made a lot of money in those years. "Believe me, we made huge business with South Africa. Huge business," one of Rich's close cadres with access to the company's books admitted to me. At first he did not wish to tell me the exact sum, so I wooed him with numbers. "A billion?" I asked him. He shook his head and laughed. "One and a half billion?" I asked. Without uttering a noise he mouthed the word "more." I shook my head in disbelief, whereupon he nodded and said: "Two billion dollars. We made a profit of over two billion dollars in South Africa." Two billion dollars was an unbelievable sum in those days. Proof that this sum is no mere overestimation can be found in the debates that took place before the South African parliament in April 1984. During these debates it was discovered that the state Strategic Fuel Fund had paid Marc Rich $306 million above the spot market price for one large oil delivery alone.[23]

"I don't know," Rich said when I asked him about the $2 billion. It seemed as if he were trying to avoid the question. I asked him if he no longer wanted to remember, whereupon he finally answered that he had never calculated how much money he had earned in South Africa over the course of those fifteen years. He did confirm, however, that the trade with South Africa had been his "most important and most profitable" business.

There are good reasons for viewing Rich as something of a Karl Marx figure, "who made all of the oil countries aware of their interests," as Rich's business partner and friend Isaac Querub commented. One can see him as someone who provided third world countries with their "first opportunity to play a role in the global market," as the trader in Jamaica put it. One can view Rich's traders as profit-oriented development workers "who gave the key of knowledge," as the expert on Angola believes. Angola and Jamaica are good examples of this thesis, whereas apartheid South Africa is the exact opposite. Angola and Jamaica were able to assert themselves and develop, but the opposite was true in South Africa, for in the end Rich's services helped to support a regime that oppressed its black citizens.

Dealing with Dictators

How does one do business with racist, dictatorial, and corrupt governments? Is it possible to do so without becoming an accessory to these governments' crimes? I spoke with Rich about these questions in his office in Zug. The rain ran in streaks down the widowpanes and lent a fitting atmosphere to our discussion. Rich's desk, which was usually quite orderly, was covered in open medicine packages. He sneezed continuously throughout our discussion.

Is it possible to remain neutral when doing business in such countries?
    Yes, business is neutral. You can't run a trading company based on sympathies.

Iran, Cuba, South Africa. You were always a crisis profiteer.

Whatever we did, we did legally. We were doing business with Iran, Cuba, and South Africa as a Swiss company. These businesses were completely legal according to Swiss law.

The law is the only criterion?

The law is the only objective standard.

In the case of South Africa you indirectly supported apartheid. Your critics maintain that, thanks to you, apartheid was able to survive longer.

I don't know if this is true. I doubt it. I was fundamentally against apartheid. We were all against apartheid. I just was doing normal business with South Africa.

How do the two fit together?

I'm not a political person. We were not a political company. We just wanted to be an excellent trading company for our customers. The South Africans needed oil, and people were reluctant to sell it to them because of the embargo. We agreed to do it because we felt it was nothing illegal.

Many people—including some businesspeople—would cite ethical reasons for not making some of the deals that you have made. Is that naive?

I think so.

Why?

Because it was perfectly legal to do the business we did do.

Can you understand some of your critics' arguments?

They like to pick on me. By making dramatic statements they have a better chance to sell their newspapers or to create publicity for themselves. The politicians always want to be in the media.

You feel absolutely no remorse whatsoever?

No, no.

It is not as if Rich does not see or does not wish to see the dictators' crimes or the racism of apartheid. He does not ignore them. He was appalled by the fact that the Cuban people allowed the Communists into power. He was disgusted by the rampant corruption in Nigeria and was aware of the fact that the people have in no way benefited from the nation's oil wealth. Although Rich believed the system of apartheid in South Africa was fundamentally wrong, he also believes that business had nothing to do with politics. He does not understand that his business strategy of making profits in crisis regions and his willingness to do business anywhere that such business is legal can cause offense among others.

In the United States, Marc Rich was branded a traitor primarily because of his dealings with Iran and Cuba. Other countries took a more pragmatic view. Remarkably, a striking example of this pragmatism was the new democratic government in South Africa. Rich continued to do business with South Africa after the end of apartheid despite all of the anti-Rich rhetoric from the African National Congress, which won the first democratic elections. The new government under Nelson Mandela relied on Rich's services. "We continued to do oil business with the new government," Rich told me. "It was completely normal for us to continue the business. We think in the long term."

15

SURPRISING SERVICES

How Rich Helped Israel and the USA

Israeli tourist Anita Griffel was spending the weekend of October 5–6, 1985, in the Sinai Peninsula together with her five-year-old daughter and a couple of friends. On Saturday afternoon the group climbed up a sand dune near the resort town of Ras Burqa just before 4:00 P.M. to watch the sunset. The mountains of the Sinai threw their long, violet-colored shadows across the valley. At 4:20 P.M. they suddenly spotted a uniformed man running toward them. He was an Egyptian policeman. Without warning he began wildly firing his rifle at the group of Israeli tourists.

Griffel immediately threw herself on top of her daughter, Tali, in order to protect her from the hail of bullets. "She whispered to me, keeping me calm," Tali Griffel explained years later. "I can still recall the feeling of the jolt as she got shot. Yet she continued to hold me and talk to me."[1] Her mother was struck by two bullets and bled to death. Hidden under the lifeless body of her mother, Tali was the only member of the group to survive the attack, but she was seriously injured, hit in the back by a ricocheting bullet. All told, seven people died that day in Ras Burqa.

The terror attack put a serious strain on the fragile relationship between Egypt and Israel. Only six years earlier, in March 1979, Egypt and Israel had signed the Camp David Accords, which had finally put an end to the state of war that had existed between the two countries since 1948. In 1982 Israel had returned nearly all of the parts of the Sinai Peninsula that it had occupied during the Six-Day War of 1967. Only the border town of Taba remained as a point of contention. However, the attack at Ras Burqa soon led to a grave diplomatic crisis. The families of the Israeli victims sought financial compensation from the Egyptian government as a symbol of its willingness to set an example against the spread of terror. Egypt was not prepared to meet what it saw as excessive demands. The negotiations over Taba were soon put on hold.

Tali Griffel, the sole survivor of the attack, was also a United States citizen, and this meant that the U.S. State Department had become involved in the delicate and discreet settlement negotiations. The United States was particularly interested in finding a quick solution to tensions between Egypt and Israel, as the two nations were the United States' most important partners in the Middle East. Both countries received billions of dollars in U.S. aid.

After years of negotiations, the State Department's efforts finally appeared to pay off—or so it seemed in the eyes of the public—and in January 1989 Egypt agreed to pay the victims' relatives generous compensation. A trust fund was set up for Tali Griffel to pay for her medical treatment and education in the United States. It was a solution that was agreeable to everyone, and relations between Israel and Egypt were soon back on track. The negotiations surrounding the future of Taba resumed, and a solution amenable to both parties was reached. In March 1989 Egyptian president Hosni Mubarak personally raised the Egyptian flag over the border town.

Reconciliation Between Israel and Egypt

The public was unaware of the true story behind the compensation paid by the Egyptians. In reality it was Marc Rich who made it possible for

Egypt and Israel to reconcile their differences. As luck would have it, the State Department recommended Rich's lawyer Leonard Garment to represent the interests of Tali Griffel in the compensation negotiations.[2] The State Department trusted Garment and was aware of the contacts he maintained in the Middle East. After serving as special counsel to President Nixon, Garment was appointed U.S. delegate to the United Nations Human Rights Commission, where he was often involved in issues dealing with Egypt and Israel.

The Ras Burqa negotiations threatened to break down over the issue of the amount of compensation. Egypt insisted on a sum based on its own standards, which the victims' families believed was insufficient. Neither side was prepared to back down from its own position. As it was not feasible for the United States to secretly add funds to the Egyptian offer, the State Department began to look for a third party who could discreetly sweeten the deal. Discussions between Garment and the State Department soon turned up a rather controversial name: the "fugitive" Marc Rich.

Rich, who had supplied Israel with large amounts of oil and also done business with Egypt, was ready to offer his assistance the moment Garment asked him. "Rich gave me discretionary authority to commit up to $500,000 of his funds if I needed it," Garment remembers.[3] Thanks to Rich, the damages that Egypt was prepared to pay were more than doubled by the addition of $400,000 of Rich's own money. The State Department was not concerned with the fact that Rich was on the run from U.S. authorities and named in an outstanding international arrest warrant, and State Department officials had absolutely no qualms about accepting Rich's money. "We saw no impropriety to having Marc Rich contribute to the settlement," said Abraham Sofaer, a former legal adviser to the State Department.[4]

"In the end, decent regrets were expressed and decent payments made to the Israeli families of the Ras Burqa victims," Garment remembers. "This closure in turn proved to be the key to unlocking the Taba issue and bringing about a reconciliation between Israel and Egypt—a precondition for more progress in the peace process. The bone was out of both countries' throats."[5]

Egypt was particularly thankful to "the European partner" who had allowed it to save face on the international stage. Osama El-Baz, President Mubarak's most important political adviser, sent Garment a letter of thanks: "The assistance we received from your European partner was a critical factor for solving the controversy on Ras Burka [*sic*]. We wish to express our gratitude, to you also, especially in view of the fact that, one week later, the solving of the Ras Burka issue helped create the climate contributing to the solving of the difficult controversy surrounding the Taba issue. I want you to know that Mr. Mubarak greatly appreciates your input and your substantial contribution to helping the two sides to finalize this matter."[6]

Sealed Documents

On January 23, 1989, the U.S. Justice Department secretly added a sealed document to Rich's court file with the docket number 1:83-cr-00579-SWK. The contents of this document are considered secret, and it could only have been opened had Rich's case been tried before a court. The sealed document confirmed Rich's involvement in the Ras Burqa affair and was intended to serve as a mitigating factor in the event of his conviction.

There is, however, a second sealed document in Rich's court file dated March 1, 1994, concerning American financier Tom J. Billman. The former chairman of the Community Savings and Loan Association in Bethesda, Maryland, was suspected of embezzling millions of dollars in depositors' savings. Billman fled the country, and federal prosecutors suspected he was in hiding somewhere in Europe—most likely Switzerland—where he held various bank accounts. In early 1992 Marc Rich's lawyers were approached by the Justice Department, which wanted to know if Rich had any information regarding Billman and asked for his assistance in the search for this particular fugitive financier. Rich agreed and assigned Avner Azulay to the complicated task of finding a needle in a haystack.

The reason was clear. "We hoped the Justice Department would treat Marc differently," Avner Azulay told me. "We contributed to the search for this fugitive, and we provided a lot of information on his whereabouts with the help of American and European detective agencies," he says. "I made a huge effort to find this man and transferred the relevant data to the official American agencies. The operation was completely financed by Marc. He spent somewhere between half a million and a million dollars." United States prosecutors had no qualms accepting the aid of one fugitive from justice in order to catch another. "His budget for that case was bigger than ours," as postal inspector David P. Cyr put it succinctly.[7] Billman was, in the end, recognized accidentally by a friend in Paris, arrested, extradited to the USA by the French authorities, and sentenced to a forty-year prison term in 1994. The authorities managed to catch Billman without Rich's support. Rich's assistance in the hunt for Billman is nevertheless officially recognized in this second sealed document.

Secret Cooperation with the U.S. Government

Marc Rich told me that he regularly helped the country that considered him a traitor and was diligently trying to track him down and put him behind bars. As Rich freely admits, he had his own self-serving reasons for offering his assistance. "I felt if I was helpful to them, they might be helpful to me and change their attitude," he says. Over twenty-five years ago, in June 1983, Rich hurriedly fled the United States and took up residence in Switzerland. He has not set foot in the United States since. When I spoke to him about his case, I could sense the deep resentment he felt toward those responsible for the "witch hunt" and the "crusade" against him. Yet Rich harbors no hatred of the country that took him in when he was a refugee on the run from the Nazis during the Second

World War. "I was always very pro-American," Rich says over a cup of tea. "It's a generous country that accepted my parents and me. I'm still very pro-American."

The U.S. State Department benefited from Rich's continual support, and its agents were in regular contact with the fugitive trader—a fact that has remained shrouded in secrecy to this day. They wanted his opinions on various "key people in power" in some of the politically sensitive countries where he did business. State Department officials especially sought details concerning politicians and business people in Iran, Syria, and Russia. He gave them what they asked for. "That's normal," Rich says, as if he had only been quoting the Americans a few commodities prices. When I ask for names, he shakes his head. "I promised not to tell," he says.

Rich maintained contacts in precisely the same countries in which the United States had hardly any contacts left. It was indeed a remarkable network. He knew Iran, Africa, and the Arab nations better than nearly any other businessman in the Western world. He had direct contact with the inner political circles of countries such as Iran, Syria, Angola, and Cuba—countries that, at least officially, wanted nothing to do with the United States, and vice versa. His business dealings were proof of just how good his sources truly were. "Our intelligence gathering was the most sophisticated in the world," a longtime employee of Rich's company proudly told me. "Sometimes we knew critical information before the CIA, especially regarding events in Iran." Marc Rich and some of his employees regularly shared this knowledge with U.S. and Israeli officials. I have spoken with several traders who were involved in this exchange of information, and they have substantiated this version of events. They were following the trader's proven motto: Give and you shall receive.

The State Department's willingness to cooperate with a fugitive suspect (and his traders), who was at the same time being hunted by other governmental agencies, might be interpreted as cynical and hypocritical. Yet any intelligence service in the world would have been interested in maintaining a relationship with a man such as Marc Rich—a man who had both the contacts and the ability to bring such disparate partners together time and time again.

The true value of such contacts and the trusted information that only they can provide becomes tragically clear when they are no longer available. In its 2004 report, the 9/11 Commission, created by the U.S. Congress to investigate the September 11, 2001, attacks, criticized what it saw as a series of "intelligence shortcomings." The report explicitly mentioned "limited intelligence collection and strategic analysis capabilities" and "a limited capacity to share information both internally and externally."[8]

In light of such criticism, there is only one rational approach for the U.S. government when it comes to using a network of informants like Rich's, even though they viewed him as a fugitive from justice. The word for this approach is "realpolitik."

Helping Israel's Mossad

Realpolitik is one of Israel's greatest strengths. The Jewish state was completely surrounded by its enemies, which had imposed a boycott on the country. None of the Arab states maintained official diplomatic relations with Israel, but there were, of course, a number of clandestine contacts—sometimes quite close. It was the Mossad's duty to establish and maintain such contacts, for Israel's intelligence service was the very master of realpolitik. Had the Mossad ignored Rich and his contacts in Iran, Syria, and the Persian Gulf states, the agency would not have been doing its job. The Mossad established its first contacts with Marc Rich back in the 1970s.

"I'm not giving any names," Avner Azulay said flatly when I asked him for details. "This would be much too dangerous." We had been talking about Rich for several hours in a hotel in downtown Lucerne. Azulay explained to me that the Mossad is much more than a traditional intelligence service. It also helps Jews who live in countries where they are in danger or even subject to persecution. It supports Jewish communities in their efforts to organize and defend themselves from anti-Semitism. "We have this duty of solidarity," Azulay told me. "We have been persecuted. History has not been very kind to us. We have a duty to help each other, especially since the Holocaust. Had the State of Israel existed then, perhaps history would have turned out differently." Wherever Jews are living under threat, the Mossad helps them to leave the country by covert means and settle in Israel or wherever they wish. Azulay explained how Rich had helped the Mossad with his business contacts as well as with money during such evacuation operations. Thanks to Rich, Jews from Ethiopia, Yemen, and Israel's enemies could be rescued and brought to Israel in the 1980s and 1990s.

After Azulay left the Mossad in 1983 and went to work as a security expert for Marc Rich, his former colleagues began to ask him if Rich would be willing to help them in the evacuation of Ethiopian Jews—known as the Beta Israel or Falasha—who had been separated from other Jewish communities for centuries. This was before the famed Operation Moses that rescued tens of thousands of these Jews and flew them to Israel in 1984–85. Many of them had fled to the north of Ethiopia—now Eritrea—and to neighboring Sudan in the early 1980s in the wake of civil war and catastrophic famine. The Mossad believed it had a duty to save them.

The Israeli government knew it would have to do the Ethiopians a favor if they were to consent to the evacuation. Yitzhak Rabin met with Ethiopian president Mengistu Haile Mariam. "What do you need?" he asked the Marxist, who had ruled the country with an iron hand since 1974. "Medical assistance," Mengistu answered. "Fine," Rabin said. "We will build a complete emergency unit for you in Eritrea." The Israeli government did not have the money to finance the emergency facility, so Azulay asked Rich if he would be willing to take on the costs. Rich agreed immediately. Azulay soon met with the Israeli minister of health at Rabin's request. The plan was for Azulay to fund the purchase of used medical equipment in good condition from various Israeli hospitals and have the Israeli air force transport it to and install it in Ethiopia. "We set up a full emergency department in Eritrea," Azulay recounted to me. "This was a wholly humanitarian operation funded by Marc. All these activities had nothing to do with espionage," Azulay is keen to point out. The trade-off was that a number of Ethiopian Jewish families were allowed to emigrate to Israel. They were thus able to avoid the famine of 1985 that brought Ethiopia such tragic fame.

Escape from Yemen

Ten years after the rescue of the Beta Israel of Ethiopia, Rich agreed to finance a similar operation at the behest of the government of Israel—this time in Yemen, in the south of the Arabian Peninsula. In 1949–50, forty-nine thousand Jews had been flown out of the country and taken to the newly founded nation of Israel in the clandestine Operation Magic Carpet. By the mid-1990s there were only a few hundred Jews living in Yemen. They were not allowed to leave the country, although they repeatedly suffered from anti-Semitic attacks.

"Marc gave me contacts in Yemen, very high officials," Azulay said. Again, he wanted to avoid getting into details for reasons of security. "It's too delicate," he explained. "I don't want anyone who helped in these activities to be hurt. They don't deserve it." Azulay negotiated with the Yemeni officials. They were willing in principle to allow the Jews to leave the country, but they wanted money in return for their consent and services—a per head fee. "Marc was willing to fund whatever was necessary to help the project," Azulay said. The former Mossad agent first wanted to ensure that these officials would keep their promise. He decided to carry out a trial run and chartered an airplane with which he intended to fly out two large Jewish families of fifteen persons each. It worked—Rich's contacts, the Yemeni officials, escorted the two families past the Yemeni customs agents, who had not been informed of the plan. The families were able to fly to Israel by way of Rome.

"We saved thirty people. It was a big success, but in the end it was a very sad story," Azulay said while regretfully shaking his head. The operation should have been the beginning of an even larger operation aimed at evacuating the entire endangered Yemeni Jewish community. However, the operation was sabotaged by the Satmar, an ultra-orthodox Jewish sect that refuses to recognize Israel or any form of Zionism. When the Satmar got wind of the evacuation of the Yemeni families, the sect threatened Azulay and Rich: "If you continue to do this, we will make public that there are traitors in the Yemenite government." This put an immediate stop to the operation.

Years later, Rich's involvement in the evacuation of Yemeni and Ethiopian Jews was finally confirmed by high-ranking officials. In a very unusual step, Shabtai Shavit, the head of the Mossad from 1989 to 1996, actively campaigned for President Clinton to pardon Rich, thus breaking the Mossad's code of silence. In a letter to the president, Shavit explicitly wrote, "As head of the Mossad, we [sic] requested his assistance in looking for MIA's [soldiers listed as missing in action] and help in the rescue and evacuation of Jews from enemy countries. Mr. Rich always agreed and used his extensive network of contacts in these countries to produce results sometimes beyond the expected. Israel and the Jewish people are grateful for these unselfish actions which sometimes had the potential of jeopardizing his own personal interests and business relations in these countries."[9] Shavit knew what he was writing about—he had been personally involved in some of these operations.

"It's not healthy to get into this," Azulay said to me and paused for a moment. He obviously wanted to avoid answering my question. I had asked him about information that I had received stating that Rich had helped in the search for missing soldiers (who had been captured by Shi-ite militias) in Lebanon, Syria, Iraq, and Iran. According to my sources, Rich used his contacts in Iran and Syria to this effect. Azulay would only confirm that Rich had provided him with "some contacts with senior officials." These "senior officials," he told me, were able to bring him together with people who knew more about the fate of the missing soldiers. "Marc funded my travel, not the government," he explains. "It was dangerous for him and dangerous for them." Azulay then said that he would prefer not to discuss these operations. "Every time the press mentions Marc's name in connection with the Mossad, this makes him a target." According to one article in the British *Observer*, Rich "routinely allowed agents to use his offices around the world as cover"—a claim Azulay says is just a rumor spread by the Americans to "undermine" Rich's business.[10]

Informal Mediator Between Israel and Iran

Rich himself also wishes to avoid getting into details when I ask him about the assistance he provided the Mossad. When I ask him why he was eager to help, Rich takes a sip of Diet Coke and hesitates before answering. "First of all, I'm Jewish. Second, Israel is a country I'm involved with. I'm a citizen. It's a natural thing for me to help Israel." I ask him if it was dangerous for him to ask high officials in "enemy countries" about missing Israeli soldiers. Rich again remains silent for quite some time, as if considering what he could safely tell me. His answer was not as concrete as I had hoped. "There were not many people that I could talk to about it, but a few people who I felt I could talk to I did talk to." How did they react? Rich raises both his hands, shrugs, and says, "It was no problem." "In which countries?" I ask. He shakes his head. Mainly Iran and Syria? "Yes," he says. I notice that this line of questioning is making Rich increasingly uneasy.

As a final question I ask him if he had served as an informal mediator between Iran and Israel. "To some extent I guess I was, but it wasn't a position I was officially looking for. I just wanted to be helpful on a case-by-case basis." One case was about the secret pipeline, the joint venture between Israel and Iran (see chapter 6). After the Islamic revolution in 1979, Iran cut off all contact with Israel and stopped supplying it with Iranian oil. Six years later, the National Iranian Oil Company filed lawsuits against Israel.[11] Iran claimed about $500 million for unpaid oil deliveries. Negotiations through lawyers reached a dead end. Iran objected to direct contact with Israel. So Marc Rich met in Jerusalem with Prime Minister Yitzhak Rabin in 1993 and proposed a possible solution—that his company would buy Israel's shares and negotiate a solution with Iran in a businesslike way. "Rabin agreed," Avner Azulay, who was present at this meeting, told me, "but the affair was torpedoed by the bureaucrats who made the conditions so complicated that Marc Rich eventually lost interest. I'm sure, today they are sorry."

Marc Rich was not a Mossad agent, as some have occasionally claimed. He was not a spy in the true sense of the word. He regularly offered his services as a volunteer, and he was of great use to the Mossad. He organized contacts in places where the Mossad had none. He offered money in situations where Israel officially could not. That is why Rich has been personally acquainted with all Israeli prime ministers from Menachem Begin to Ehud Barak. The Mossad refers to people like Rich as *sayan*—the Hebrew word for "helper." It is a fitting name for the commodities trader, who above all considers himself a provider of services.

16

The PRIVATE LIFE *of the* RICHES

O
n September 8, 1996, a Sunday, Gabrielle Rich was lying in a hospital bed at the Fred Hutchinson Cancer Research Center in Seattle. She had been diagnosed with acute myelogenous leukemia, an extremely aggressive form of cancer that prevents the body from producing normal blood cells and renders it powerless to fight off infection. There was no longer any hope. Gabrielle, Marc and Denise Rich's second daughter, was dying. She was twenty-seven years old.

"It was horrific," Denise Rich says, "all this pain." The emotion in her voice makes it seem as if she is talking about events that had happened yesterday. She reaches out with her arm for her daughter Danielle's hand while fighting back the tears. The three of us are sitting in her nineteenth-floor penthouse—once estimated to be worth $40 million—on Manhattan's Fifth Avenue. The floor-to-ceiling windows offer a breathtaking view of Central Park. Denise Rich sits underneath Andy Warhol's interpretation of *The Birth of Venus,* the Renaissance masterpiece of Sandro Botticelli. The name of the Italian artist means—how fitting for the ex-wife of a billionaire oil trader—"little barrels." Denise is dressed casually in a light blue V-neck sweater and leggings. It was at a fund-raising dinner in this very same penthouse that President Bill

Clinton referred to Denise as one of his "closest friends."[1] It was another era—the era before Marc Rich's pardon.

Before I met Denise I had no idea to how I should broach the subject of her daughter's death. I only asked her after we had spoken about a variety of issues and only when I was sure that she would not misinterpret my asking as mere voyeurism. There is nothing worse for a mother—or father—than a child's death. Such an experience can change a person forever—and it had definitely affected Marc Rich, who was already divorced from Denise when his daughter died. I thought it was important to ask how he and the family had dealt with the loss.

Gabrielle was not alone during her final hours. Her family—including Philip Aouad, whom Gabrielle had secretly married—was sitting with her in the hospital room. Her mother, Denise, who had already lost her own mother and sister to cancer; Ilona, Gabrielle's older sister; and her younger sister, Danielle, were all there. Her father, however, was not—at least not physically. After the doctors had diagnosed Gabrielle's leukemia, the family scoured the globe for the best doctors available. "They found them in the United States," Danielle says. "My father supported this choice even though it was very painful for him not to be able to be with Gabrielle." Rich could only sit in his house on Switzerland's Lake Lucerne and speak to his dying daughter in Seattle by telephone. "He was on the phone up until she took her last breath," Denise explains. "He was with her just as we were, and he couldn't be there. The fact that he could not be there with his daughter was horrific. He was just sobbing on the phone. I finally hung up the phone because he was sobbing so much and I couldn't take it. I wanted to hold her." Shortly past ten o'clock on that very same evening, Gabrielle passed away.

"Don't Come Home, Daddy, Please"

Whoever among his family or acquaintances is asked the single most difficult aspect of the prosecution against Marc Rich gives the same answer: the fact that he was not allowed to travel to the United States in order to see his daughter and hold her in his arms when she needed him most. "The death of a daughter is tragic enough, but on top of that, if you are not able to be there—even though you are so rich and powerful—then what does all that power and money mean?" Isaac Querub asked me. He is one of Rich's trusted associates and a friend who has three daughters of his own. Another friend, the businessman Michael Steinhardt, was Rich's houseguest in the town of Meggen during those sad days. "It was such a tragedy for him not being with Gabrielle. He had very strong feelings for her. She was—and still is—an important part of his life," Steinhardt told me. "You just mention her name and he starts crying," Danielle says.

There is nothing Marc Rich would rather have done than visit his daughter in the hospital. Robert Fink, Rich's longtime lawyer in Manhattan, discussed the issue with Assistant U.S. Attorney Patrick Fitzgerald. "I told him Rich's daughter was dying," Fink remembers. "I asked him if there was a way Marc could be allowed to visit his daughter without jeopardy." The answer was no.

Thirteen years had passed since Rich had fled the United States, and for thirteen years he had managed to avoid falling into the traps that U.S. agents had set for him. Rich knew that if he wanted to see his daughter one last time, he would be arrested the moment he stepped off the airplane in the United States. "Then so be it," Rich said to himself. It was worth it. He called Gabrielle. "He said to Gabrielle, 'I'll come,'" Danielle tells me in her mother's apartment. "Gabrielle told him, 'Please, I beg you, don't come. I beg you, don't come home.' He said, 'I will, I will.' She said, 'Please, Daddy, I love you so much. Please don't come. If you do this I will be so angry with you.'" Denise had to promise her terminally ill daughter that she would make sure her father stayed in Switzerland. "He was prepared to take any consequences," Danielle says.

With the heaviest of hearts, Rich decided against traveling to the United States. He stayed in Switzerland and missed his daughter's funeral. Rich's friends still tell each other how agents attended the funeral in the event Rich did decide to come. The U.S. marshals who were tasked with apprehending Rich were convinced that he might try to secretly travel to the United States via Canada.

"Sure. It's very sad," said Sandy Weinberg, the assistant U.S. attorney who had initiated the investigation into Rich. He seemed irritated that I had asked him if it would have been a humanitarian gesture to grant Rich safe conduct. "It's kind of hard to feel sorry for him. He created the situation. Safe conduct? It doesn't work like that. He chose not to play by the rules," Weinberg explained. He is probably right—those were the rules. Any prosecutor or any politician who had granted Rich safe conduct would have faced the toughest of criticism. It is probably naive for a fugitive to hope for such mercy. However, I remember the words of Avner Azulay: "No humane person would have denied such a request. Marc didn't kill anybody. He is not a terrorist."

I spoke about the case with the Swiss minister of justice who was involved in Rich's case in the mid-1980s. I wanted to know how she would have reacted to just such a request. Elisabeth Kopp-Iklé answered without a moment's hesitation, "As minister of justice I would have granted safe conduct in a similar case. Otherwise I would not have been able to face myself in the mirror anymore." I replied by saying that a decision of that nature would have put her under immense political pressure. She looked at me for quite some time, considering, then said, "There are situations in which humanitarian issues must take precedence over political issues. If this is no longer possible, then you have to ask yourself why you are even involved in politics." Her answer echoed in my head long after our discussion had ended. I was happy that I was not a politician.

Daughter's Grave Moved to Israel

"Doesn't help me," Rich says with a bitter tone when I tell him how the former minister of justice reacted. Rich had also missed the death and burial of his father in New York in September 1986. David Rich was always his son's greatest role model both as a father and a businessman. Marc, an only child, wanted nothing more than to prove to his father that he was successful in business. He wanted his father's recognition. Yet Rich was unable to attend his father's funeral and say the Kaddish, the traditional prayer of mourning that only a son can recite. "It is an extremely important prayer," a religious friend of the Rich family explained. "It is the last service that the son can perform for the dead father. For Marc it was a tragedy that he was not able to be there." Rich had no other option than to recite the Kaddish over the telephone.

As I quickly discovered, Rich does not like talking about the deaths of his father and daughter. There was, however, one question that I had to ask. Can one ever be happy again after losing a child? "The pain still lingers after all these years. I'm happy again, but less than I used to be when she was around," Rich says. Not many people are aware that the Rich family had their daughter's grave moved after Rich was pardoned by President Clinton. Gabrielle's grave is now located in Israel near Tel Aviv, where Rich, an Israeli citizen, can visit as often as he likes—and with no one to disturb him. "I regularly visit," he says. The possibility of traveling to the United States to see his family was one of the most important points in the petition for his pardon. The petition states that the pardon "will allow Mr. Rich and Mr. Green to be with their families."[2] Even so, Rich has not set foot in the United States since the pardon (see chapter 18).

Blind Date with Denise Eisenberg

Marc and Denise Rich first met on a blind date, which is not uncommon in Jewish circles. It was December 1965, and Rich had flown back to New York from Madrid to celebrate Hanukkah with his parents. Paula Rich was beginning to worry about the fact that her son had not yet married, so she organized a meeting with Denise's father. Rich was thirty-one years old and running Philipp Brothers' Madrid office. Denise

Joy Eisenberg, a dark-haired, almond-eyed beauty with a cheerful temperament, was a good ten years younger. She was studying French at Boston University.

Denise came from a solid Jewish family that had found prosperity in America. Her father, Emil Eisenberg, was an entrepreneur who owned one of the country's largest shoe manufacturers, the Desco Shoe Corporation. Eisenberg had founded the company in 1942 shortly after the family had immigrated to the United States. The Riches and Eisenbergs had strikingly similar family histories, for the Eisenbergs were also German-speaking Jews from the Austro-Hungarian province of Galicia. Emil Eisenberg was born in Tarnow, an important trading town that is now a part of Poland, in 1912. The town was only one hundred miles from Przemyśl, the birthplace of Marc Rich's father. Just like David Reich, Emil Eisenberg was able to escape the Holocaust and make his way to the United States.

Eisenberg moved to Paris in 1933, the year Adolf Hitler seized power in Germany. There he met Gery Diamant, and the two were later married (their marriage would last for fifty-three years). At the young age of twenty, Eisenberg, together with three of his brothers, founded a fur-trading company with offices in Paris, London, and New York. In the spring of 1940 the Nazis invaded Western Europe, and the Eisenbergs decided to flee Paris. It was in that same spring that David Reich and his family fled Antwerp for the south of France in a used black Citroën. The Eisenbergs were somewhat more well-to-do than the Reichs, and the family was able to board a ship for New York. In 1942 they settled in Worcester, Massachusetts, approximately forty miles west of Boston.

Half a year after their blind date in New York, in the late summer of 1966, Denise Eisenberg traveled to Spain to visit Rich. Their parents had done well—the match was a success. "Marc proposed to me after two weeks of touring in the north of Spain. We had dinner in the *parador* of Santiago de Compostela. It was very romantic," Denise remembers. Built in the fifteenth century, the *parador* is a former royal hospital with four cloistered courtyards and an impressive dining room. "I had like two seconds, and I said OK. I called my parents and told them I was engaged. My mother wanted to have a nice wedding in Massachusetts. Marc said no. He wanted to get married in two or three weeks. My mother said she couldn't organize a wedding in two weeks, so they negotiated back and forth. Guess who won?" Just a few weeks later, on October 30, 1966, the couple married in Worcester's Temple Emanuel.

The pair flew to Jamaica for their honeymoon, where it rained the entire length of their stay. As he would tell me ruefully so many years later, Rich stepped on a sea urchin on the very first day and had to keep his infected foot raised for the rest of the honeymoon. Exactly nine months later, on August 1, 1967, Ilona was born. The young family settled in Madrid, and Denise devoted her energies to taking care of her young daughter. Gabrielle was born in January 1969.

Family Values

Rich was living in the fast lane. He was working harder and longer than any of his colleagues in the office. He arrived at the office shortly past 7:00 A.M. and he was seldom home before 10:00 P.M. "He was constantly working. It was difficult sometimes," Denise remembers. "His work was his hobby, and his family suffered as a consequence," Ursula Santo Domingo told me. The marquesa became a close friend of the Rich family and came to know them better than almost anybody else. She told me that Denise once complained to her that Rich made too little time for his family. " 'I don't have any time for you during the week,' he told her. 'I can give you a half hour on Saturdays and forty-five minutes on Sundays.' "

The situation did not improve when Rich decided to go into business for himself in 1974. Before moving back to New York, the couple moved to London, where Danielle was born in March 1975. At that point Denise still provided her husband with a great deal of support. "He was building a business, and that's what he had to do. I was there to support him in any way I could. He did what he had to do. I understood. That's what my father did. My father would always say that you have to work for money to really understand what the price of anything is, what the value is." Marc Rich once said of himself, "I guess I'm a business machine."

It was the typical division of labor in those days. Despite her public image as an eccentric jet-setter and flamboyant socialite, Denise was a rather conservative mother and wife with a strong sense of family. Marc and Denise Rich wished to instill traditional values in their children. Marc Rich believed in the classic virtues. "Honesty, hard work, responsibility, and some knowledge of the Jewish religion," he said when I asked him about what he had wished to pass on to his children. (He stopped observing the Jewish rituals at the age of fourteen, he told me. He doesn't believe in God and doesn't pray.) His daughters had to be well behaved, come home on time, and finish their homework right away. Because he was so wealthy, he wished to teach his children the value of money. "I never spoiled them," he says. "I wanted to teach them that you have to work to make money." Danielle still remembers this. "He did not just give me money or let me buy whatever I wanted as my mother would have done," she says. "Instead I was given an allowance and had to work hard for it. If I wanted a raise, I had to prove that I both deserved and needed one."

Demanding Father, Dominant Mother

Rich admits that he was a strict father. He can also be a strict grandfather, as I myself witnessed during our skiing in St. Moritz. Rich's daughters had come to visit along with their families, and on that day we all sat down to lunch together in Rich's chalet. One of his grandsons kept acting up; he refused to sit still at the table, and no one could get him to calm down. After this had gone on for some time, Rich began to scold the boy. "Listen to your mother! If you don't behave yourself, I'll send you to the kitchen." "Then I'll have to eat in the kitchen?" the boy asked. "Who said anything about eating?" Rich dryly replied.

If you ask friends of the family about Marc Rich's values, they refer to the special relationship that he had to his parents as an only child. "Denise always said, 'His mother comes first, and then it's a while before he gets to me,' " Ursula Santo Domingo commented. Another friend said his mother was too dominant. "He dressed the way she wanted." Denise herself says only, "She was very, very, very controlling. She wasn't too crazy about me." According to Rich's cousin René Traut, an eye specialist in Antwerp who kept in close contact with Paula Rich, Marc telephoned his mother almost daily, and it was the highlight of her day. David Rich, on the other hand, was very strict with his son as a child and expected a lot of him, Ursula Santo Domingo says. She believes that Rich's relationship to his parents was one of his driving forces. "He wanted his parents to be proud of him. He always wanted to prove to his father that he could be as successful—or even more successful—than he was."

Denise, the Songwriter

By the early 1980s Marc Rich had indeed achieved this success. He was a giant of the commodities trade, earning $100 million to $200 million a year. The family now lived in a ten-room apartment at 625 Park Avenue. Princess Ashraf Pahlavi, the twin sister of the ousted shah, owned a three-story, twenty-five-room penthouse in the same building. Rich's daughters went to the best private schools, and the family spent their weekends at their beach house on Long Island's Lido Beach. Their life would never be the same after Rich fled to Switzerland in June 1983. It meant a massive readjustment—even more so as they were caught totally unawares. The family moved from New York, widely extolled as the "capital of the world," to the small village of Baar, Switzerland. It was not exactly the glamorous cosmopolitan hub that the Riches were used to.

Rich was able to continue doing what he loved to do: working from early morning until late in the evening. The children attended elite boarding schools in the French-speaking area of Switzerland and the American International School in Zurich. Cut off from her circle of friends, Denise—the only member of the family who was born in the United States—had to reinvent herself. She tried to make the best of the situation. "I started writing songs professionally at that point also because I was so alone so much of the time," she says. She had been writing songs for years and liked to compose with her acoustic guitar while in the bathtub. She was now ready to seek a wider audience for her music.

She found amazing success. Sister Sledge, famous for their song "We Are Family," recorded one of Denise's songs in 1985. "Frankie" was an international number one hit and sold over 750,000 records. With the success of her own album, *Sweet Pain of Love,* one year later, Denise became a much sought-after songwriter. The list of artists who have performed her songs reads like an all-star lineup of R&B: Aretha Franklin, Mary J. Blige, Patti LaBelle, Natalie Cole, Marc Anthony, Céline Dion, Diana Ross, Donna Summer, Chaka Khan, and Grover Washington Jr. Denise increasingly traveled to London, New York, and Philadelphia—the heart of the Philly soul that she so loved—in order to pursue her career as a songwriter. She was happy that her husband was proud of her success. However, she was also aware of the fact that he was not so happy with her frequent absences. "He doesn't like to be alone," she told me. "Those kind of men don't." Nevertheless, after twenty years of marriage during which Denise had ignored her own ambitions, she was finally ready to move on. "It's my turn now and I'm gonna do it," she said.

That Tall Blond German Woman

The better things went for Denise, the worse they got for Marc. "Marc was depressed, but I didn't want to hear about being depressed. It wasn't my fault we had to leave the country," she explains and throws a look at Danielle. It was the classic crisis that many couples experience when one partner finally decides to step out of the other's shadow. Either they adapt to the new situation or they go their separate ways. In order to cheer him up, Rich's family suggested he get out to the mountains more often and go to St. Moritz. Denise shakes her head at how naive she was back then. "I had no clue," she tells me. "There were women up there in St. Moritz reading *Forbes*, you know, looking for a husband." She assures me that Rich had never had an affair up until that point. "I was a blessed wife. His big affair was his business," she says.

Denise was, at first, not worried about the many good-looking, long-legged young women who tended to congregate in St. Moritz. She had failed to recognize that times had changed and that her husband was suffering more as a result of his voluntary exile than he was prepared to admit. They had been living in Switzerland for six years. It is a beautiful country, but it is also small and provincial. Rich, who loved to travel, could no longer go where his will took him. She, on the other hand, could travel the world. She recorded songs in London and went to Brazil to record a sound track for a film about the legendary mail train robber Ronald Briggs. She had the time of her life. "It was not a good time for Marc," she says. "Things started falling apart."

It was around that time, in late 1989, that people began to notice the tall blond German woman at Rich's side at the social events he attended. Gisela Rossi, née Reininger, was originally from Munich and was the widow of a rich Italian industrialist. She was a member of the European jet set that spent their winters skiing in St. Moritz and their summers in St. Tropez on the French Riviera or in Marbella on the Spanish coast. Rich met Rossi on a trip to St. Moritz.

"Of course, it was a dangerous situation," remembers Ursula Santo Domingo, who often spent her winter holidays with the Rich family in St. Moritz. "There are all these women who come to St. Moritz and end up comforting all the unaccompanied men. Along came Gisela, and she caressed him and ran her fingers through his hair and did everything he wanted." It was the beginning of the end for the marriage. "He fell for her hook, line, and sinker," Denise says. "He was very naive about women. He wasn't cheating, he had no girlfriends. My father always said, 'When you are that naive and that green, you fall into the first trap.'"

The affair began while Denise was in Worcester to be at her mother's deathbed. Danielle found out about the relationship and alerted her. Denise would fight to save their marriage for two years, even though her father had told her, "You won't be able to reverse this." "Don't be ridiculous," Denise replied. "It's over twenty years of marriage." A divorce was out of the question for Denise. That was not the way she had been raised. Her parents had been married for fifty-three years. She thought the affair would remain an affair and her husband would soon come back to his senses. "I wouldn't leave him," Denise says and interlaces her fingers. "I stayed for two years. I did whatever I could. I loved him. I didn't want my kids living in a broken home. Our family made a commitment to stay together. I was trying very, very hard. I really was. But he couldn't get out of it. She was doing everything he wanted, and she was there all the time. She was always on time. This woman was so street-smart and manipulative. So manipulative. She also had a lot of friends helping her. It was fun for them to steal a husband. 'Let's see if we can get this Rich guy,' they would say to themselves. He fell into the trap and he couldn't see it. It happens to men, it just happens."

Don't Be Late

Whereas Denise had spoken from the heart, Marc Rich tried to remain diplomatic when I asked him what had gone wrong with his marriage. "I became unhappy with certain things about Denise, and I met Gisela, whom I liked." Could he not accept the fact that Denise was often away pursuing her songwriting career? "She spent a lot of time with her music, that's true, and she had certain characteristics which bothered me. She is always late, always. Still."

After two years of struggle, Denise finally gave up. The two legally separated, and Denise returned to the United States. She filed for a divorce in April 1992. Denise chose to have the trial in Switzerland, as she knew that according to Swiss law she might be entitled to half of the fortune that her husband had accumulated during their marriage. She hired the aggressive lawyer Max Lebedkin to represent her in court. Lebedkin was known for doing whatever was necessary to make sure the wives of rich men came away rich from their divorces. As was usually true when he was involved, the Riches' divorce escalated into an all-out struggle. It would be one of the bitterest, most expensive, and most public divorce trials the world had ever seen.

Lebedkin sought a settlement of around half a billion dollars.[3] The crafty lawyer claimed that Denise and her parents had put up a substantial amount of the seed capital that Rich had needed when he had founded his company in 1974. She had supported her husband for over twenty years and had given birth to his three daughters. Thus, Lebedkin argued, Denise had a right to half of her husband's fortune, which amounted to "at least" $1 billion. According to *Forbes*, Rich was worth at that time approximately $800 million, whereas *Fortune* put the sum at $1.1 billion. Only hours after receiving Denise's claim, Rich's lawyers came up with a counteroffer: $3.33 million in cash on the spot.[4] Perhaps Rich thought he could deal with the marriage as if it were just another trade. "Marc is actually a generous person, but his reaction in this case was rather strange," a friend of Rich's said. "The offer was an insult."

"Marc Destroyed Our Family"

Denise also took the counteroffer as an insult, and she soon hit back as hard as a humiliated wife can. She agreed to an extensive interview with one of Switzerland's most widely read gossip magazines.[5] When the magazine hit the streets, the divorce proceedings went dirty. The interview was entitled "I Want Half of My Husband's Billions." In it Denise stated, "Marc Rich destroyed our family. I was a very loyal wife and devoted mother for twenty-five years. We all suffered from the scandals and the insults. People gossiped about my husband. They said he was a criminal. But I stood by him. Now he shows his gratitude by cheating on me with another woman and by publicly embarrassing both me and my children." Denise had never spoken so negatively of Marc, and she would never do so again. Her words reflected not only the anger of a deeply wounded spouse but also the tactics of her aggressive lawyer. Lebedkin had found the exact means of doing the maximum possible damage to Rich. As a weapon Lebedkin chose what Marc Rich feared most: publicity. "He constantly lied when it came to his finances and his fortune," Denise told the gossip magazine. "While we were still together he always wanted to impress me and everyone else with his enormous wealth. The only thing that has changed is that he still wants to impress everyone with his fabulous fortune, but now he wants me to believe that the reality is somewhat different."

Neither party in the proceedings was squeamish in its choice of methods. Denise sued her husband in both Switzerland and New York. She claimed that he had taken advantage of her twice. In 1988, back when the marriage was a happy one, the two had decided to establish a charitable foundation in Switzerland. Both partners planned to donate $40 million of their own money to the foundation, which Denise did.[6] Denise claimed, however, that her husband had never contributed his share. This claim was rejected by the court in Zug. In New York Denise filed a civil suit against her husband and his business partners. She accused them of using the money in a trust fund, which was intended for their three daughters, for their own ends by means of "self-dealing" and "fraudulent transactions."[7] According to court documents, she claimed her husband had attempted to "defraud me in the most vicious and disgusting manner." She lost at trial.

$365 Million for Denise

Rich's company was a confusing network of over two hundred private companies and subsidiaries spread over five continents. Many of these companies—all of which existed under the umbrella of Marc Rich + Co. Holding—were closely connected with one another, whereas others were completely independent. A few of the companies had equitable interest in outside companies. Rich and his partners had originally created this labyrinthine structure because it would allow them both to minimize risks and to make private deals without letting others know that Marc Rich was controlling the show. Now the convoluted network of companies offered a further advantage—it was nearly impossible to determine Rich's wealth.

Denise's father finally intervened in the proceedings and prevented the case from escalating to the point of explosion. Emil Eisenberg was very fond of Marc and continued to stand by him despite the criminal charges against him. Rich, in turn, had great respect for his father-in-law, who reminded Rich of his own father. Eisenberg had also placed a great amount of trust in Rich and had unhesitatingly given him money when he founded his company in 1974. Rich would always be grateful for Eisenberg's help. Eisenberg traveled to Switzerland in order to negotiate a divorce settlement with Rich. "The lawyers made a big mess," he said to his son-in-law. "Let's make sense of the whole thing." Finally someone had spoken in terms that the trader Marc Rich could understand.

On June 14, 1996, Marc and Denise Rich were finally divorced. Their marriage had lasted for thirty years. The terms of the settlement were never made public. Several knowledgeable sources have confirmed to me that Denise Rich received a total of $365 million; of course, they do not wish to be named when speaking about this very private affair. The $365 million was split into two packages. Like all of the four partners' wives, Denise had a stake in her husband's company. She owned 13.91

percent of Marc Rich + Co. Holding. In December 1990—while she was still married to Rich—Denise received $165 million for her 1,070 shares in the course of a capital reduction.[8] In addition, Rich agreed to pay Denise a further $200 million. When I asked him about this sum Rich just smiled and said what he always says when the research is correct but he does not wish to officially confirm the results. "It's not far from the truth."

"My Biggest Failure"

Six months after the divorce, on December 16, 1996, Rich married Gisela—his lover of many years. They had already been living together for quite some time. In July 1993 the couple had relocated to the village of Meggen in the canton of Lucerne. They moved into the stately Villa Rose on the banks of Lake Lucerne. Rich insisted that Gisela convert to Judaism before they married (a fact that did not meet with universal acceptance in Switzerland's Jewish circles).

Rich's marriage to Gisela would not remain a happy one. When I once asked him what had been his greatest failure, Rich thought about the question for some time before asking, "Business-wise, you mean?" I realized that for once Rich was thinking about something other than closing a deal and said that I was not necessarily asking about business. "Next to the case, my next biggest failure was my marriage to my second wife, Gisela," Rich said. For a moment I was stunned by Rich's openness. Then I asked him why the marriage had not worked. "At the beginning it was very good. Then she got spoiled, with money and possessions. She decided she wanted more and I said no," Rich explained. "Do you regret divorcing Denise?" I asked. "No, I don't, but I regret marrying Gisela," he answered. On June 15, 2005, Rich divorced for the second time. I wanted to know if it had been an expensive affair. Friends of Rich's have told me that Gisela received "several tens of millions" in the settlement. "I don't want to remember," Rich said and laughed. "As expensive as Denise?" I asked. "Much less," he replied.

17

The END *of the* KING *of* OIL

If the 1970s and 1980s were Rich's golden age, the 1990s were by far his darkest years. It was a time of death, divorce, and disposal. The death of Rich's daughter in September 1996 coupled with his divorce from Denise marked the lowest point during these sad times, yet in the 1990s Rich also suffered his greatest financial failure—a fact that has remained a secret to this day. A single bad deal cost him $172 million and took his company to the edge of collapse. It was the deal that finally forced Rich to sell his company. One of Rich's former managers told me about this debacle when I asked him about the company's greatest failure. We were sitting in his office, which I will not describe, as he does not want it to be recognized. Before getting into the details, he stood up, shut the door, and asked me to turn off my tape recorder. "Please, don't get the wrong idea," he said and lit a cigarette. "I have the greatest respect for Marc Rich. I am what I am thanks to him, but this megalomaniacal deal also belongs in his biography."

The trouble started in July 1992. David Rosenberg, a young trader described by colleagues as a gambler, decided he was ready to go for the big time. He had racked up a number of successful aluminum deals over the previous few years and had been promoted to director of the company's metals division. Rosenberg now wanted to attempt what several traders before him had singularly failed to do; he wanted to secretly corner a market in an attempt to manipulate global prices for a metal. He sat down with two of his most important rivals, the German Metallgesellschaft AG and the Spanish Asturiana de Zinc SA.

Together the three parties bought a long position on zinc on the London Metal Exchange (LME), the world's largest metals trading exchange. This meant that the three parties had obligated themselves to purchase zinc at a predetermined time and at a predetermined price. Investors who "go long" on a commodity can turn a profit when the prices rise or lose money when prices fall. Rosenberg and his partners simultaneously began buying huge amounts of zinc in an attempt to drive up the market price in the hope of obtaining a higher price for the zinc that they had purchased. It was a gigantic yet incredibly risky operation. Rosenberg and his associates secretly bought around 1 million metric tons of zinc—approximately 20 percent of the annual global production and nearly two-thirds of all the zinc traded on the LME. All told, they spent well over $1 billion in their attempt to reduce the global supply of zinc.

The Worst Deal of Rich's Career

At first everything went according to plan. Within weeks, Rosenberg and his confederates were able to drive prices to a multiyear high. By September 1992 zinc had risen to $1,400 per metric ton. "They were buying and buying and making the price go up," the manager explained. "It was a high-risk, speculative operation." However, they were unable to keep their secret operation under wraps. The trade press soon began publishing articles detailing the inexplicable rise in zinc prices. As was usually the case when inexplicable things were happening on the market, people began pointing fingers at Marc Rich. This time they were right.

As it almost always does in attempts to corner a market—whether it be in silver, aluminum, or tin—the bubble finally burst. The artificially inflated prices were followed by a very real slump. By November 1992 the price of a metric ton of zinc had fallen by 25 percent to $1,050.[1] "There was no way out," remembers one of Rich's directors who had tried to prevent the worst from happening. "We were that close to a disaster," he says, holding his forefinger and thumb close together. "We had to liquidate the long position as quickly as possible to limit the losses." In the end the trader was successful, and his efforts saved the company from ruin. The insane attempt to manipulate the global zinc market ended up costing Marc Rich + Co. $172 million. Rosenberg left the company.

Rich confirmed that the zinc debacle had indeed been the worst deal in his career as a trader. He seems magnanimous about the entire affair today, even though it was one of the reasons he was later forced to sell the company he himself had founded. "The younger people were tempted and didn't have the experience," he says. He does not, however, interpret the devastating failure as proof of the impossibility of cornering a market. "I wouldn't say it is impossible, but I would not try to do it," he tells me. "The risks are too big." Not only did Rich lose a lot of money, but he also came out of the fiasco with his credibility severely damaged. His senior traders with experience in the metals markets had warned him of the adventure. "This is artificial. There is no physical demand. It's a bubble that will burst," they told him. He refused to listen to them and made no attempt to rein in Rosenberg. He was ignoring one of his own most important business principles, for Rosenberg had done nothing to hedge his long position. The company had no way of controlling its losses when the zinc prices began to plummet.

Rich's actions were an affront to his senior traders. They were the metals experts—not Rich. "Not that I want to belittle Marc's knowledge, but he was not in his element," one of Rich's former senior traders told me. "He's not a metals and minerals guy, he's an oil guy." Rich not only lost his managers' support, he also lost their trust.

Defections

Although Marc Rich + Co. had been a close-knit family-like organization for nearly twenty years, things began to unravel. One of the most important indications that all might not be well at the company came in June 1992, during the zinc fiasco. Rich unexpectedly fired Willy Strothotte, a German who had worked for him for fifteen years, the last two as his right-hand man. He had successfully directed the minerals and metals division at Marc Rich + Co. and had made the company into a true market leader. Even Strothotte's rivals were quick to point out his abilities as a brilliant trader and strategist. Rich's official statement claimed that Strothotte's leaving was a consensual decision, the result of "different views on how the company should be managed." "There is nothing sinister about this," Strothotte said when he left. "I am parting with the Marc Rich group and not with Marc Rich himself."[2] In truth, Strothotte had lost out in a power struggle against Rich. "Willy was too up-front," a former director told me. Strothotte had pushed to discuss the company's future after Marc Rich. He wanted the founder—then only fifty-seven—to pull back gradually from active business and give up his status as majority shareholder.

The separation was not nearly as friendly as the company would like the public to believe, as Rich's employees were soon to discover. Rich had Strothotte's office replaced with a lounge. In a company that operated according to the trader's motto "You never close doors," this was taken very seriously indeed. "Sure, everyone who left the company was considered a jackass," one of Strothotte's closest colleagues told me, "but when Marc did away with Willy's office, it was like when Joseph Stalin had his adversary Leon Trotsky retouched out of photographs."

Further evidence of the deteriorating atmosphere at Marc Rich + Co. came only one month later when Manny Weiss and Claude Dauphin, two key managers, left the company. Weiss had successfully expanded the company's aluminum business and had directed its important London office. For his part, Dauphin had been jointly responsible for the company's oil business. It was a time of dramatic changes for Marc Rich. Within a short time he had lost his most important and longest-serving associates. They had stood at his side throughout his career. Suddenly Rich was alone. He was now the only founding member who was still active in the company. Pinky Green had retired in late 1990 after undergoing a heart bypass operation. Alec Hackel, who had been one of Rich's most important advisers, had followed his lead and had also taken retirement. Each had received between $200 million and $300 million for his shares in the company.

Rich was in sore need of his friends. Although he had always been a good judge of character, he suddenly surrounded himself with poor advisers. Much to his managers' horror, Rich brought one of his American attorneys onto the executive board, although he had not the slightest inkling of the commodities trade. This was a hard break with the tried-and-true company tradition of allowing into management only people who had learned the business from scratch. Rich, who had always trusted his employees and given them as much free rein as possible, suddenly began to meddle in all of the company's affairs. The three principles that had served the company so well in the past—openness, team spirit, and limited hierarchy—were slowly fading away.

If You Can't Catch the Fish . . .

"Marc had lost the big picture," a trader who was working for the company at that time told me. He drank too much. Glasses of whiskey began to appear on his desk at noontime. He smoked too much. His friends began to worry about his health. He was insufferable, his employees said. He was "overbearing, unbalanced, and out of control," as one of Rich's friends summed up his mood in those days. There were several reasons for Rich's bad patch. It was obvious that his private problems involving Denise were taking their toll, both on Rich personally and on the business. The U.S. prosecutors were pressing him harder than he was prepared to admit, and federal agents were making his life as difficult as possible. As U.S. Marshal Ken Hill put it, "We stuck to the motto of the SAVAK [Iran's infamous intelligence service under the shah]: If you can't catch the fish, take away the water. We had tremendous success taking away the water." It was the continuation of legal prosecution by other means. "Because the prosecutors were unable to catch Rich, they did their utmost to destroy him," a former business partner, a manager at British Petroleum, told me. Rich's public image suffered greatly as a result.

Competitors and rivals soon realized that they only had to mention Marc Rich's name in order to provoke a public debate that could damage his business—and aid theirs. They knew that Rich cherished discretion above all else and that any publicity would have a negative effect on his business. In the early 1990s, two important events led to Rich's name being dragged through the headlines. First, October 1990 marked the start of a two-year labor dispute at the Ravenswood Aluminum Corporation in Ravenswood, West Virginia, a company partly owned by Rich. Seventeen hundred employees went on strike for higher wages. The workers were locked out by management and their jobs taken over by nonunion replacements. The United Steelworkers of America organized an international campaign that successfully directed the media focus onto Rich's participation in the company. Demonstrations were organized in front of Rich's headquarters in Zug and at the annual meeting of the London Metal Exchange, where the unionists distributed a wanted poster for Rich. They were able to pin the label of "corporate villain" on Marc Rich. As a vilified Jewish capitalist on the run from U.S. justice, Rich was the perfect bogeyman. Indeed, Rich was the only reason that all of the most important international and American news outlets were keen to report on what was fundamentally a regional U.S. strike of little significance.

"A Little Bit of Rich in My Pocket"

One revelation by the United Steelworkers led to the second case of negative publicity, which made Rich the subject of discussion in the

U.S. Congress. The union had discovered that for years Rich's company Clarendon had been supplying the U.S. Mint with copper and nickel for the production of coins. These government contracts were worth $45.5 million to Clarendon. Politicians and media had a field day over the fact that an indicted tax evader on the run from U.S. prosecutors was doing business with the federal government. A congressional subcommittee began investigating the contracts. From a legal standpoint, however, everything was aboveboard. Clarendon had won the contracts in a public bidding process. However, politicians were quick to denounce the federal government's involvement with a suspected tax fraudster. "Every time I reach into my pocket for some change, I have to wonder if there's a little bit of Marc Rich in there," said Robert Wise, the media-savvy congressman from West Virginia who was in charge of the investigation.[3]

Negative headlines were Rich's Achilles' heel, a fact that his detractors were more than happy to use to their own advantage. Even today critics wag their fingers and cite his name whenever one of his former employees' names turns up in a commodities scandal in some part of the globe—toxic waste in the Ivory Coast, for instance, or the oil spill from the tanker *Prestige* that sank in the Atlantic in 2002 and contaminated the coastlines of Spain and France. Various journalists attempted to associate Rich and his companies with these occurrences, but in reality such events had absolutely nothing to do with him.

Every time an embargo was broken, Rich's name was mentioned almost as if by reflex. Perhaps the best example of this phenomenon involved the embargo against Iraq under Saddam Hussein. According to the *Wall Street Journal*, Rich attempted to circumvent the UN embargo against Iraq in 1991.[4] In fact, Rich's company had sought official authorization from the relevant governmental agency in Switzerland and would only have done business with Iraq with the explicit permission of the UN Sanctions Committee. In March 2008 the Office of the Attorney General of Switzerland came to the conclusion that, contrary to the report published in 2005 by the Independent Inquiry Committee into the United Nations Oil-for-Food Programme, Rich's company had not made "unauthorized payments" to Iraqi officials and was not guilty of any misconduct.[5] Although the accusations had made the headlines, only a few newspapers found the exoneration worthy of a few lines of print.

Marc Rich's Departure

By the end of 1992, eleven years after the Southern District of New York began its investigation, Rich's image had taken a serious beating. His name had become a symbol for greedy and unscrupulous dealmakers. He had been indicted in the United States, and prosecutors pursued him all over the world. The U.S. Congress very publicly criticized his businesses. The $172 million loss stemming from the failed zinc deal put him under additional financial pressure. He could no longer hide from the fact that his days as the company's sole ruler had come to an end. "If something were to happen to Marc Rich, what would be the future of the company?" the bankers began to ask. Rich's own traders also worried about the company's future. "Many of us had the feeling that we might not be there the next day," one of Rich's traders told me. They began to pressure their boss to bring back Willy Strothotte. Although he was disliked for his arrogance, Strothotte had earned the traders' respect. They felt that only he could stabilize the company.

At first Rich resisted their pleas to reinstate the man who had previously tried to dethrone him, but many of the company's senior traders threatened to leave. He was now faced with the twofold risk of losing even more good people who would most likely come back to haunt him as tough competitors. Many observers in those days were reminded of the events of 1974 when Marc Rich and Pinky Green left Philipp Brothers as a result of their own boss's stubbornness. It was a move that had proved to be the beginning of the end for Rich's former employer. However, Rich brought one of his greatest qualities to bear in the midst of these troubled times. According to his colleagues, Rich reacts better than most when faced with pressure. Even when he is personally affected, Rich is capable of sober analysis and rational action. He took the course of action that all good traders must take and put his emotions aside. He realized that he had made the wrong decision and that he now needed to—as a trader would say—turn the position.

In early March 1993 Rich picked up the telephone and called Willy Strothotte, who was on a golfing vacation in Florida. "Come back," Rich asked him. "I'll come back," Strothotte answered, "but on my terms." Strothotte demanded that Rich give up his majority stake in the company. It was a condition that he had been prepared for—and accepted. Marc Rich was now ready to sell his life's work. "I came to the point," he says, "where I had enough."

It was a very cold and snowy day in Zug in November 1993. The thirty-nine most important people at Marc Rich + Co. crunched their way through the snow. They had traveled to Switzerland from all over the world for the meeting at the Parkhotel Zug. Willy Strothotte had summoned them all to inform them of the details of the management buyout and to vote on the future of the company. The takeover contract stipulated that Marc Rich would gradually reduce his majority stake in the company over several years. Management and high-ranking employees would in turn purchase Rich's shares. Together with around two hundred of his employees, Rich signed the contract on November 29, 1993.

"I Was Weak"

"I was weak," Rich says about the sale of his company. It was as if he were describing a struggle in the animal kingdom. The old lion had been driven off by the younger challenger, and now the young lion had taken over the leadership of the pride. "I was weak and the others could sense it, so they took advantage," he says and continues in German, *"Sie hielten mir das Messer an den Hals."* "They held the knife to my throat." Rich believes the most important reasons for his weakness were the indictment in the United States and the campaign of persecution led by U.S. prosecutors. He is sure that if it had not been for his legal case, Marc Rich + Co. would be even larger and more successful today—and Rich himself would have remained at the head of the company much longer. This surprisingly unemotional confession must sound like sweet—if somewhat late—satisfaction to the ears of federal prosecutors. They were never able to bring him to court, but their tactic of "taking away the water" had at least brought them a certain degree of success.

"Marc had no choice," one of Rich's most important managers added, "and at the same time he realized that it was the right thing to do." Even if the separation—which one trader described to me as a "shotgun divorce"—was forced, the future of his life's work was still dear to his heart. It is perhaps the only explanation for why Rich was so generous to the same people who held the knife to his throat: The company's new owners were allowed to pay off the price of Rich's majority stake over the course of several years (it was, in effect, an interest-free loan). The deferred payments allowed them to generate the necessary capital for the management buyout with money earned during the normal course of business. They did not have to borrow any money or sell any of the company's industrial facilities.

The value of Marc Rich + Co. at that time was estimated at $1 billion to $1.5 billion.[6] The company was active in 128 countries, had an annual turnover of $30 billion, and brought in an estimated profit of $200 million to $400 million each year. It was the market leader in the oil, metals, and minerals trade. As is the Swiss habit, the parties agreed to strict confidentiality regarding the final selling price. It's time to disclose this secret here. Rich could have demanded much more for his stake in Marc Rich + Co. In the end he settled for the book value and set the price at $480 million. "Marc sold cheap," one of the buyers told me.

He had two conditions, though. First, Rich didn't want the management to quickly sell on the shares at a higher price to a third party. He could have done that himself. Second, a so-called postclosing adjustment was inserted into the contract. Should a subsequent revaluation of the assets (among them Ravenswood Aluminum Corporation) show that they were worth more than agreed in the contract, Rich would get additional compensation. Marc Rich found out a bit later that the new owners had secretly sold around 20 percent of the shares to Hoffmann–La Roche, the Swiss pharmaceutical giant. Furthermore, the assets were revalued to a higher value. Following an almost amicable dispute, Rich received an additional $120 million. As several shareholders have unofficially confirmed, Rich came away with a total of $600 million from the sale of his company. "Not far from the truth," he said when I asked him to corroborate this sum.

On Monday, November 7, 1994, Rich finally sold the last of his shares in the company that he had founded and stepped down from the administrative board. The name Marc Rich + Co., the name that had made history in the commodities trade for twenty years and continued to stir up so many negative associations, vanished from the scene. As soon as possible, so it seemed, the new owners renamed the company Glencore. Today, the company is still the world's largest commodities trader, and in terms of annual turnover, it is the largest firm in Switzerland. No competitor, no former employee, no spin-out has managed to become bigger and more powerful than Glencore, formerly known as Marc Rich + Co. Nevertheless, there is not a single mention of Rich's name on the company's Web site—not even under the category "history." He was purged.

Unlucky Comeback

It seemed to be the end of an era for the King of Oil. "It would have been the perfect time for Marc to say to himself, 'Now it's time to retire and just enjoy life,'" a friend of Rich's told me, but Marc Rich could not let go. Rich, who when asked about his passions always answers, "My work," could not bear idleness. "I told him many times, 'Just stop and make a nice life for yourself,'" Ursula Santo Domingo remembers. "He told me, 'It has to go on. It has to go on.' The fact that the telephone no longer rang only depressed him." Not even two years had passed since his supposed exit from the commodities trade before Rich was back in the game. In the spring of 1996 he founded Marc Rich + Co. Investment AG and traded in oil, metals, and grains. The company employed 150 people, mainly in Zug and London, and turned over $7.5 billion. The business did not go as well as planned, however, and insiders spoke of massive losses. "We suffered from a lack of size," a company employee explained. "We suffered as a result of the meager trading volumes." The banks threatened to reduce the company's line of credit when trading losses caused its equity base to melt away. Rich was forced to inject tens of millions of dollars of his own money in order to preserve the line of credit, but success continued to elude the company. Eventually, Rich liquidated a part of Marc Rich + Co. Investment AG in 2002 and sold the rest to the management. It was the end of the commodities trader Marc Rich. Together with the Marc Rich Group, Rich now invests in the financial markets and builds commercial centers and residential buildings mainly in Russia and the Czech Republic as well as in Spain, France, and Switzerland.

The Fear of Dying Poor

"Why was he trying to do it all again?" one of Rich's associates of many years asked himself and told me: "He reminds me of Lot's wife. Marc turned around." In the First Book of Moses, Lot's wife ignores the angel's command and turns around to look upon the burning city of Sodom—and is transformed into a pillar of salt. "He has to trade," one of Rich's close friends said of his restlessness. "It's not about making money. People like Marc Rich don't want to earn money just to become even richer. They do it out of passion." There is something about the feeling of success that is highly addictive. "Success is measured fairly easily in his business. It is measured by the amount of money he makes," Rich's friend the hedge fund pioneer Michael Steinhardt told me. These conversations reminded me of George Mallory, the English mountain climber who died while attempting to be the first person to climb

Mount Everest. He is immortalized for the answer he gave when asked about his insatiable desire to climb the world's highest mountain: "Because it is there." When I ask Rich why it is impossible for him to stop trading, he answers, "I love business. Every dollar I make is like the very first."

There is, however, another reason for his obsession. "Marc is afraid he could lose his entire fortune and die poor," a friend confided in me. It is a statement that might seem absurd at first. Rich has more money than he could ever spend—even in the course of several lifetimes. He owns real estate and works of art that, regardless of whatever happens on the stock exchange, are worth tens—if not hundreds—of millions of dollars. Rich's fear of poverty is completely illusory, yet it is a fear that Rich shares with many refugees who have experienced what it is like to lose everything. It is also a typically Jewish fear—one the entire Rich family was well aware of. As Rich's daughter Danielle explained, "It was always made clear to us that we were lucky for what we had and that we must not take it for granted because we could not depend on it always being there. It could be lost or taken away, just like during World War II."

Philanthropist

It was exactly this experience that also made him such a generous philanthropist. Rich has founded three charitable foundations and has donated more than $150 million during the past thirty years. Over four thousand projects in the area of education, culture, social services, scientific research, and health care primarily in the USA, Israel, Spain, and Switzerland have benefited from Rich's philanthropy. "That is a part of our Jewish culture: When you are doing well, do charity," one of Rich's employees told me. "Naturally there was a charity piggy bank in the company at the end of the year. We could write on a piece of paper how much we wanted to donate to a particular organization, and the company would double the sum. It was Marc's idea." Another of Rich's employees remembers how he once sat down together with Rich after receiving a promotion. "After a while Marc suddenly stuck his hand in his pocket and came out with a roll of dollars. 'You will soon be earning a lot of money,' he told me and put the roll in my hand. 'Start by giving this money to the first poor man on the street.'"

"Wealth always means independence and comfort, of course," Rich answered when I wanted to know what his fortune meant to him, "but it also means that I can help the less fortunate through my foundations. It's moving and utterly satisfying to see the effects of a school or hospital in a deprived area or to help along young gifted artists, especially in the field of music." What is he most proud of when it comes to his philanthropy? "The money has an effect and is not wasted."

Rich's "extraordinary" charity was one of the arguments that was used in his pardon application.[7] His critics maintain that Rich became involved in philanthropy only in order to help save his reputation. "Even the good things Marc does are used against him. That really hurts," Avner Azulay told me. He then mentioned that Rich's first foundation was active as early as 1979—long before the indictment. "We couldn't know then," Azulay said sarcastically, "that decades later a President Bill Clinton would pardon him."

18

The PARDON

On Friday, January 19, 2001, Jack Quinn was at a dinner party in Washington, D.C., when his mobile phone rang. It was only shortly past nine, but when Quinn looked at the display to see who was calling he knew the party was over for him. It was "POTUS"— the president of the United States. It was Bill Clinton's last night in the White House, and the president wanted to speak with Quinn about the pardon application that Quinn had submitted a month ago for his clients Marc Rich and Pincus Green.

"The president had obviously read and studied the petition," Quinn told me. He excused himself from the dinner table and made his way to an empty room. He and the president knew each other well, as Quinn had served as Clinton's White House counsel. The conversation lasted around twenty minutes. "It was a good, thorough discussion that was entirely about the merits [of the pardon], not about the politics," Quinn remembers. As he listened to the president speak, the words seemed to course through him like a jolt of electricity. "I persuaded the president," he thought. "I persuaded the president that this was a case that should have been handled civilly rather than criminally." On that evening it was clear that Clinton was seriously considering pardoning Rich and

Green. However, the president had one precondition, and that was why he had called Quinn. Rich and Green would have to agree to face a civil hearing and waive their rights to avail themselves of the statute of limitations. Quinn immediately accepted the president's terms. Clinton wanted to have a written waiver "within one hour."

Quinn looked at his watch. It was 9:30 P.M. He immediately called Robert Fink, Rich's lawyer in New York, explained the situation, and asked him to write up a waiver for Rich and Green in accordance with the president's request. Fink was surprised. He had no longer expected a presidential pardon to come through. "We had no indication," Fink later told me. He immediately sat down at the table and typed up a waiver declaration for the president on his wife's laptop. About thirty minutes later, Fink unplugged the laptop so that he could go into the next room and print the document. The screen immediately went black. Fink had not known that his wife had removed the battery from her laptop.

"Oh my God," Fink exclaimed. "I lost it." He had not even bothered to save the document. He hurriedly plugged in the laptop, rebooted, and began typing a much shorter letter. The hour that the president had given him had nearly run out. Fink printed the waiver and reread what he had written. "Specifically they will not raise the statute of limitations or any other defenses which arose as a result of their absense." A spelling mistake! Fink had written "absense" instead of "absence." There was no longer any time to correct the mistake—a fact that still bothers him to this day. He faxed the letter as quickly as possible and nervously awaited the transmission confirmation. Nothing happened. He faxed the letter again, and this time the fax went through. Fink took a deep breath. Marc Rich had nearly missed his opportunity for a presidential pardon because of something as mundane as a missing laptop battery.

"Nothing else can go wrong," Fink thought to himself and went to bed. At 2:00 A.M. he got a second call from Quinn. Beth Nolan, Clinton's White House counsel, had asked him if Rich had been involved in arms trading, as claimed by the FBI's National Crime Information Center. The president wanted to know if the information was correct. Fink waved the idea aside and told Quinn, "No way. Rich wouldn't know a bazooka from a BB gun." Quinn called Beth Nolan back and told her that none of Rich's lawyers had ever heard of any "arms trading charges." Such accusations, he added, were nothing more than rumors that had first appeared in, of all places, *Playboy*.¹ After Nolan informed the president of the conversation, Clinton replied, "Take Jack's word." On the morning of January 20, 2001, President Bill Clinton granted Marc Rich and Pincus Green "a full and unconditional pardon."

The Furor

Marc Rich was asleep in his Villa Rose in Meggen on the banks of Lake Lucerne when the telephone began to ring. It was Saturday, January 20, around 11:00 P.M. in Switzerland, 5:00 P.M. in Washington, D.C. Rich looked at his gold Rolex. "Who could that be?" he thought to himself. Robert Fink had news that would excuse his calling at such a late hour. "I bring very good news, Marc. President Clinton pardoned you," Fink told him. It took a moment for Rich to realize what exactly Fink had just said. After seventeen years as a fugitive and life in exile, after seventeen years of pursuit by federal prosecutors, Rich was a free man. "I was extremely pleased," Rich said to me. "Nobody had actually expected that." I wanted to know what he had done to celebrate on that evening. "I didn't celebrate," he answered. "I went back to sleep."

At about the same time, Sandy Weinberg was sitting in front of the television in his Tampa home halfheartedly watching the inauguration of George W. Bush in the middle of a Washington downpour. Weinberg, who as an assistant U.S. attorney had led Rich's investigation, was a dyed-in-the-wool Democrat. He had actively supported Al Gore's candidacy, and he was deeply frustrated over the election recount fiasco in his home state of Florida. He was in an even worse mood after he received a call from Michael Isikoff, a reporter for *Newsweek*. "Hi, Sandy. What do you think of the pardon?" the reporter asked. "Michael Milken got pardoned?" Weinberg asked with little sign of interest. "No, Marc Rich," Isikoff answered. "I uttered a vulgarity," Weinberg tells me. " 'This is outrageous,' I thought. 'This is just outrageous.' " In a staccato voice—one, two, three, four—he proceeds to list the four points that from his point of view made it impossible for the president to pardon Rich. "One, it was the biggest tax fraud. Two, he was a fugitive. Three, he renounced citizenship in order to avoid extradition. Four, he traded with the enemy Iran. You cannot pardon a person like that," Weinberg says.

News of Rich's pardon spread among politicians, journalists, and judicial officials. Their reactions were unanimously negative. Rich's case had once more taken on "historic" proportions. According to an article in the conservative *National Review,* the pardon was "one of the most disgraceful chapters in the history of the Justice Department. Not the *modern* history, the *entire* history."[2] For William Safire, a Pulitzer Prize–winning columnist for the *New York Times,* the pardon was "the most flagrant abuse of the presidential pardon in U.S. history."[3] *Vanity Fair* even ventured to suggest that the pardon "may have damaged President Clinton's reputation forever."[4] Those who were involved in Rich's case were particularly disgruntled with the pardon. Rudy Giuliani was "flabbergasted." "It took me about a day to actually absorb the fact that the President of the United States actually pardoned one of our most notorious fugitives," he said. Howard Safir said he was "outraged because this sends a message to the criminals around the world that if you have influence, if you have money, and if you have access, you can put out a sign that says 'Justice for Sale.' "[5]

Organizing a Pardon

Safir was right on one point. Access to the president was a decisive factor in Rich's pardon. It was not only about getting the president's ear but also about explaining Rich's side of the story. The idea of seeking a presidential pardon first came up in early 2000, after U.S. Attorney

Mary Jo White had again informed Rich's lawyers that it was the "firm policy" of the Southern District of New York "not to negotiate dispositions of criminal charges with fugitives" (see chapter 13). Quinn told me that at that time he almost took the refusal as an affront. "It was like— you know—drop dead." All attempts to have the case legally reassessed were thus doomed to failure.

"Why not try a pardon at the end of the Clinton term?" Michael Steinhardt first came up with the idea. Avner Azulay liked it. "What are the chances?" he asked Rich's lawyers. Azulay remembers how they all just shook their heads. "Five percent, they said." He then asked, "Do we have a five percent chance with another solution?" The lawyers were silent. "Then let's go with the five percent," Azulay said.

Rich agreed and gave his permission to seek a pardon. "I kept looking for solutions. I kept trying and nothing succeeded, so the pardon seemed to be a solution," Rich told me. According to Azulay, one of Rich's most trusted employees, the system was "blocked." "The best lawyers created the biggest mess. They just created more aversion. Eventually, the thing developed into a legal monster. It became a political case," Azulay explained. "There was no legal solution. That's why it needed a political solution—an unconventional one."

The Israeli Avner Azulay and the American Jack Quinn were the masterminds behind the application for a presidential pardon. They quickly put together a two-pronged strategy that—at least internally— was described as an "avenue of last resort." One aspect was based on the facts; the second was personal in nature. Quinn would take care of the legal issues, write the petition, and present it to the president. Azulay would be responsible for the personal networking and would try to find as many dignitaries as possible who were willing to put in a good word for Rich and Green.

It is no stretch to say that without Quinn's involvement, Clinton would never have pardoned Rich. Quinn had more contacts in Washington than almost anyone else—and he had a direct line to the president as a holdover from his days as Clinton's White House counsel from 1995 to 1997. Prior to taking on his position in the White House, Quinn was Vice President Al Gore's chief of staff—a position that made him Gore's most important adviser. After leaving the Clinton administration, Quinn founded a public relations firm in Washington, D.C., and in late July 1999 Rich hired Quinn's company to represent him. Quinn had been recommended to Rich by Gershon Kekst, the well-known New York communications consultant. Michael Steinhardt had asked his friend Kekst to see what he could do to help with Rich's case. During our interview in his Madison Avenue office in Manhattan, I asked Steinhardt why he had been willing to help. "Over all these years Marc has never publicly defended himself against the most fallacious and terrible rumors. He never used the power of his wealth to carve his image," Steinhardt explained. Kekst visited Rich in Switzerland and returned with a piece of advice for Steinhardt. "Marc should hire Jack Quinn," he said. As would soon become clear, Quinn was an excellent choice and well worth the retainer of $55,000 per month his law firm was paid for some time.

Crucial Discretion

Avner Azulay, the second mastermind behind the pardon application, was a gifted negotiator and strategist with high-ranking contacts in Israel's political establishment. The former Mossad officer, who had been responsible for Rich's personal security and later went on to direct Rich's humanitarian foundations in Israel, was the one who came up with the plan to directly petition the president for Rich's pardon.

According to the Department of Justice, a presidential pardon is usually obtained in the following manner.[6] The petition is first submitted to a special pardon attorney at the Department of Justice, who, after an initial examination, passes it on to the associate attorney general—the number three in the department—for further consideration. The attorney general then advises the president as to whether he should accept or refuse the petition. Rich's lawyers had intended to follow this path in petitioning for Rich's pardon. Azulay, however, had a fine nose for political and bureaucratic realities, something he had developed while working for Israel's intelligence service. He recognized the risk in the lawyers' plan. "If we do this, the story would immediately explode in the media," Azulay told Rich's lawyers. He advised, "We have to bypass the bureaucratic channel." Rich had a bad reputation, and many even considered him "the biggest devil," as Rich himself says. If it were to become widely known that he was seeking a presidential pardon, his people could no longer control what would happen next.

Rich's lawyers decided that it was legally possible to go around the Department of Justice and take their petition directly to the president. "The pardon attorney doesn't like it, the attorney general doesn't like it, but it is legal," they said. In late October 2000, only three months before Clinton's final day in the White House, Rich's lawyers made the definite decision to take this avenue of last resort. "I tell you we didn't have a sophisticated plan. It was rather a cowboy mission," Azulay assured me. Rich's legal team, including the experienced New York attorney Bob Fink, began to put together a petition. Discretion was of the utmost importance. "We tried to keep a low profile," Fink told me. "I was concerned that the petition would become public. If it did the press would start to attack."

Rich's team was able to keep its efforts out of the media spotlight. In late November the two-inch-thick petition was finally ready. Jack Quinn sent it to "the Honorable William Jefferson Clinton, President of the United States" on December 11. It contained a legal argument combined with a personal and emotional appeal. The legal argument maintained that Rich and Green had been "wrongfully indicted" and "unfairly singled out."[7] "This case was grossly overprosecuted," Quinn emphasized during our telephone interview. All comparable cases in the past, he said, had been tried in civil instead of criminal courts. It was the same argument that Rich's various lawyers had unsuccessfully made over the last sixteen years in order to come to some sort of arrangement with the Southern District of New York (see chapters 10 and 13).

Avner Azulay was responsible for the personal and emotional aspect of the petition, and his efforts to this effect were quite impressive. According to the first lines of the petition, "Mr. Rich and Mr. Green are extraordinary businessmen and philanthropists who have lived exemplary lives since the alleged offenses." Rich's charitable foundations had donated "over 100 million dollars to charitable, cultural and civic organizations."[8] Attached to the petition were letters from dozens of prominent figures offering testimony of Rich's generosity. The petition was supported by several prominent Israelis, including Prime Minister Ehud Barak, Nobel Prize winner Shimon Peres, Foreign Minister Shlomo Ben-Ami, former director general of the Mossad Shabtai Shavit, mayor of Jerusalem (and later prime minister) Ehud Olmert, and several other Israeli and Jewish dignitaries such as Anti-Defamation League national director Abraham Foxman and U.S. Holocaust Memorial Museum Council chairman Rabbi Irving Greenberg. From Switzerland came letters from the well-known art collector Ernst Beyeler, Zurich mayor Josef Estermann, and top UBS banker Pierre de Weck. King Juan Carlos of Spain also put in a good word for his countryman Rich and in the process offered a form of official recognition for the important services that Rich had provided for Spain in the 1960s and 1970s (see chapter 6).

Ehud Barak's Support

Azulay's greatest tactical masterstroke was that he had been able to convince Ehud Barak to personally lobby President Clinton on Rich's behalf. The timing could not have been better. On December 11—the same day that Clinton received Rich's petition—Barak made a telephone call to the White House. According to the White House transcript, the call was made at 6:16 P.M. and lasted exactly nineteen minutes.[9]

"One last remark," Barak said to President Clinton. "There is an American Jewish businessman living in Switzerland and making a lot of philanthropic contributions to Israeli institutions and activities like education, and he is a man called Marc Rich. He violated certain rules of the game in the United States and is living abroad. I just wanted to let you know that here he is highly appreciated for his support of so many philanthropic institutions and funds, and that if I can, I would like to make my recommendation to consider his case."

Clinton responded, "I know about that case because I know his ex-wife. She wants to help him, too. If your ex-wife wants to help you, that's good."

"Oh," Barak said. "I know his new wife only, an Italian woman, very young. Okay. So, Mr. President, thank you very much. We will be in touch."

Azulay had known Ehud Barak well for quite some time. They had served in the same unit together—the Aman, Israel's Directorate of Military Intelligence, which Barak had directed from 1983 to 1985. Barak, Israel's most highly decorated soldier, was active in Lebanon at the same time as Azulay. In November 2000 Azulay asked Barak for his support in obtaining Rich's pardon. "Ehud Barak knew this was an honest request and that I would not lie to him or ask or do anything which would compromise him," Azulay explained. The former Mossad officer told Barak that Rich had supplied Israel with oil in its most difficult times (see chapter 8) and was thus of great importance to Israel's national security. Azulay also explained how Rich had helped the Mossad (see chapter 15). After Barak had verified this information with the Mossad, he told Azulay, "This man had done nothing but good for this country. Why should I not support him?"

Financier of the Peace Process

Azulay proceeded in a similar manner with Shimon Peres, the former prime minister and foreign minister. He asked Peres to give President Clinton a call. "You remember," Azulay reminded Peres, "you asked us for Marc Rich's help in the peace process." He was referring to the Oslo Accords of 1993–94, which had offered a major breakthrough in relations between Israel and the Palestinians when both parties agreed to officially recognize one another for the first time. The accords also envisaged a plan for Palestinian self-government. During the negotiation process, Peres approached Azulay, who at that time was already serving as the managing director of the philanthropic Marc Rich Foundation. Thanks to his work with the Mossad, Azulay was personally acquainted with both the Israeli and Palestinian participants. "Peres asked me, 'What can you do to help this process?'" Azulay explained.

Azulay informed him that Rich had come up with the idea of financing a Palestinian investment bank in order to speed up the economic development of the Palestinian areas. He also suggested developing the border area shared by Israel, Jordan, and the Palestinian West Bank for tourism. Azulay discussed these plans in Jerusalem and Ramallah with the Palestinian economic expert Ahmed Qurei (who would later serve as "prime minister" of the Palestinian Authority). A group of Palestinians, including an economic adviser for Yasser Arafat, traveled to Zug to meet with Rich in 1994, a meeting that until now has remained a secret. "We discussed how Marc could help them," Azulay said. A further suggestion was made that Rich assist in training programs for the Palestinian Authority. Rich was prepared to invest $1 million to help train executive members of staff in the areas of education and social welfare.

"I was willing to do anything they needed," Rich told me. "'Define your needs,' I urged the Palestinians, 'come back to me, and tell me what I can do.'" Yet he waited in vain for concrete suggestions to make their way back to him. He heard nothing more from the Palestinians, who in the meantime had succumbed to a bitter internal power struggle. Thus the Marc Rich Foundation developed its own series of plans for various projects, mainly in the area of establishing a public administration service to manage the international funds and donations as well as health services, which the foundation would later finance to the tune of several million dollars in cooperation with the World Bank.

It was these projects that prompted Foreign Minister Shlomo Ben-Ami to intercede on Rich's behalf. Ben-Ami wrote a letter on official Foreign Ministry paper to President Clinton, stating that Rich's foundation "was among the first private entities to support the Oslo Accords by sponsoring education and health programs in Gaza and the West Bank in cooperation with the Palestinian Authority. Many of these projects of people to people between Israelis and Palestinians would not have been possible without Marc Rich's generous involvement."[10] Sidney Blumenthal, President Clinton's brilliant senior adviser, was not far from the truth when he wrote in his book *The Clinton Wars*, "In short, Rich was a financier of the peace process."[11]

Azulay reminded Shimon Peres of this fact in December 2000. Peres played a central role in the Oslo Accords, and for his efforts he shared a Nobel Peace Prize with Yitzhak Rabin and Yasser Arafat. "If you could just say a few good words about the character of this man," Azulay asked Peres. "Say that he is not the devil that he is painted to be in the media." Peres did not have to think twice about putting in a good word for Rich. He had already lobbied the U.S. government on Rich's behalf in the mid-1990s. He was enthusiastic about the idea of Israeli and Palestinian economic cooperation and wanted Rich to be able to move about more freely without running the risk of arrest.

So Peres called Clinton on the same day as Ehud Barak. It was December 11, 2000—the day that Clinton received the petition for Rich's pardon. Peres also asked the president to pardon Rich and extricate him from the legal impasse his case had reached. According to an e-mail from Azulay to Jack Quinn, President Clinton "took note of his intervention."[12] Rich's importance to Israeli politicians is further illustrated by the fact that Barak spoke to Clinton about a possible pardon on two additional occasions.[13] In a telephone call of January 8, 2001, Barak again stressed Rich's importance to Israel's security: "He helped Mossad on more than one case." "It's a bizarre case, and I am working on it," Clinton answered. "I really appreciate it," Barak said. On January 19, 2001, the same day that President Clinton finally attended to the presidential pardons, Barak called again and asked, "Might it move forward?" "I'm glad you asked me about that," Clinton answered. "The question is not whether he should get [the pardon] or not but whether he should get it without coming back here."

"He just told the truth," Rich said when I asked him about Barak's support. "He knew about me. I've met him. We talked about my case, and he knew I was a positive element for Israel. They appreciated what I was doing for and in Israel, so he decided to be positive."

The Role of Denise Rich

As soon as the pardon had been made public, the media began their descent on a single individual: Denise Rich. She was the perfect subject for a story. She was a member of the international jet set who was worth hundreds of millions of dollars and owned a luxurious penthouse on Manhattan's Fifth Avenue, an extrovert socialite who had once flooded her penthouse terrace to form an ice rink for one of her fabulous parties. She was a successful songwriter known throughout the music industry. She was also a woman who was prepared to stand up for her ex-husband, even though he had left her for another woman.

Denise's involvement in Marc Rich's pardon was particularly scandalous as she was one of the biggest and most loyal supporters of the Democratic Party, to which she had donated more than $1.1 million since 1992. The list of leading Democratic politicians whose campaigns she had supported reads like a roster of the U.S. Senate. Geraldine Ferraro, Edward Kennedy, Tom Harkin, Barbara Boxer, Charles Schumer, and Barbara Mikulski all received donations from Denise Rich. She was particularly close to Bill and Hillary Clinton, whose election campaigns she helped finance, and she donated $450,000 to Bill Clinton's presidential library in Little Rock, Arkansas. Politicians and members of the media soon began to voice the opinion that Marc Rich's ex-wife had managed to "buy" her ex-husband's pardon.

The House Government Reform Committee, which was tasked with investigating the circumstances surrounding Rich's pardon, described Denise as a "key figure in the effort to obtain a pardon."[14] In truth, Denise did enjoy a special relationship to the president as a result of her generous donations. During the Clinton administration, she visited the White

House on no fewer than nineteen occasions, and President Clinton once even described her as one of his "closest friends."[15] In 1998, when the president appeared in public for the first time after the publication of independent counsel Kenneth Starr's report on the Monica Lewinsky affair, it was at an event held in Denise's penthouse. Clinton also appeared as a speaker at a fund-raiser for the G&P Foundation, a cancer research organization Denise founded after Gabrielle's death. (The *G* stands for Gabrielle and the *P* for Philip, Gabrielle's husband.)

A letter from Denise Rich dated December 6 was the first personal letter attached to the pardon petition. "I am writing as a friend and an admirer of yours," Denise wrote to the president. "I support this application with all my heart." Her letter, which Jack Quinn helped write, was a masterpiece. It appealed to the president's emotions while referring to Clinton's own bad experiences with aggressive prosecutors.

The pain and suffering caused by that unjust indictment battered more than my husband—it struck his daughters and me. We have lived with it for so many years. We live with it now. There is no reason why it should have gone on so long. Exile for seventeen years is enough. So much of what has been said about Marc as a result of the indictment and exile is just plain wrong, yet it has continued to damage Marc and his family. . . .

Because of the indictment, I have seen what happens when charges are falsely—even if just incorrectly—made against those closest to you, and what it feels like to see the press try and convict the accused without regard for the truth. I know the immense frustration that comes when the prosecutors will not discuss their charges, and when no one will look at the facts in a fair way. My husband and I could not return to the United Sates [sic] because, while the charges were untrue, no one would listen—all the prosecutors appeared to think about was the prospect of imprisoning Marc for the rest of his life. With a life sentence at stake, and press and media fueled by the US Attorney, we felt he had no choice but to remain out of the country.[16]

One week after President Clinton received the petition for Rich's pardon, Denise also spoke directly to the president about the issue. On December 20 she was a guest at a dinner in Washington to honor the winners of the National Medal of Arts and the National Humanities Medal. During a quiet moment, Denise pulled the president to one side and told him that the pardon "would mean a lot to me."[17]

It was rather surprising that Denise should make such an effort to stand up for her ex-husband. Her relationship to Marc Rich was virtually nonexistent at that point. The two had not spoken—let alone seen one another—for years after their bitter and nasty divorce. Denise not only resented the fact that he had left her for a younger woman, she also felt that Rich had wronged her financially. She still believed that he had cheated her by not matching the $40 million that she had contributed to the charitable foundation they had founded together in 1988—even though her claims were rejected by a Swiss court (see chapter 16). She was so angry with her ex-husband that she even made a financial contribution of $1,000 to the campaign of Rich's nemesis, Rudolph W. Giuliani.

It had been Avner Azulay's idea to include Denise Rich in Operation Avenue of Last Resort. He visited her in November 2000 and asked for her support. "He screwed me. He owes me money," Denise replied. "I want the money he owes me for the foundation—$40 million." Azulay was shocked. He knew that Marc and Denise did not get along, but he had not expected such deep resentment. Azulay told Denise that it would look very strange if she, the mother of Rich's children, did not stand up for her ex-husband. He promised her, "If you help us now, I will talk to Marc." Only after a number of meetings and many long discussions did Denise finally agree to use her influence with the president to help her ex-husband.

What motivated Denise to throw her weight behind her ex-husband's petition? I asked her this question during our conversation in her Manhattan penthouse. I was sitting next to her on a leather sofa taking notes and was having trouble keeping up with what she was saying. I could record our conversation if I liked, Denise said. "I have nothing to hide." Danielle laughed and said, "That's my mother. Everybody else is worried about themselves and she is worried about you." Denise went on to explain that she had been willing to help because "my children asked me to support the pardon. They're my children. How could I not?" Yes, but you had been so angry with him, I remarked. You had publicly accused him of destroying your family. Denise thought about this for a moment before saying, "Every divorce is bitter. He's still the father of my children." She then told me how Gabrielle's death had changed her feelings about Marc Rich. "Gabrielle would have wanted that I forgive him. She would have wanted that I support him."

A Delicate Financial Agreement

However, it is also true that Denise accepted Avner Azulay's proposal to compensate her for the $40 million she thought Marc Rich owed her. According to an agreement, signed in January 2001 by all parties, shortly before President Clinton finally granted the pardon, Rich and Green would each contribute $500,000 per year to the G&P Foundation. (In order to prevent any possible misunderstandings, let me emphasize that Denise Rich herself was not the beneficiary, but rather the G&P Foundation was.) The foundation would use these funds to cooperate with the Gabrielle Rich Leukemia Research Centre at the Weizmann Institute of Science, which Marc Rich had established separately in Israel to support leukemia research. It was up to a committee of scientists designated by both sides to decide how the money could best be invested.

Denise acknowledged the existence of this agreement. "Gabrielle asked that we continue her foundation. It was my daughter's last wish. She had started it, and she asked for it. She was working on her computer up until she died. I had asked [Marc Rich and Pincus Green] if they would help me, and they had said they would. It had nothing to do with the pardon." In the wake of the public outrage that was sparked by Rich's pardon, Denise decided to waive her right to her ex-husband's money. "I didn't want anything to hurt the foundation, so I decided to accept no money from them. I didn't want the question of money to tarnish the foundation." "She wanted it to be pure," Danielle added.

It was certainly the right decision, as the outrage that followed in the wake of the pardon was tremendous. To this day, Denise Rich still finds herself caught up in the critics' crossfire. The whole affair took on the stench of corruption as a result of Denise's contributions to the Clintons' and various other Democratic campaigns. Denise had to deny even more insidious charges on Barbara Walters's ABC newsmagazine *20/20*. "I never had a sexual relationship or anything else that's improper," Denise explained in her interview with Walters.

There was hardly a single journalist or politician who was prepared to believe that Rich's pardon was completely aboveboard. Eight years later, Sandy Weinberg's blood pressure still rises whenever he looks back on the affair. "They were circumventing the entire process. Nobody asked me about it. Nobody asked the Southern District about it. Not one person that had any knowledge about the case weighed in with the president. It's a complete outrage." I asked Weinberg if he believed corruption had played a role in the pardon. "I don't want to speculate," Weinberg told me. "I don't know whether there was money involved, whether some corrupt purpose was involved. What I do know is that President Clinton was sold a bill of goods by Jack Quinn."

Quinn was taken aback by the outrage he faced. "I considered myself astute politically, and I certainly considered President Clinton to be astute politically, but I think we were both surprised at the extent of the uproar that ensued." I felt that the entire affair had made a much deeper impact on Quinn than he was prepared to admit in public, and I questioned him on this point during our interview. "It was among the most painful parts of my entire life," Quinn confided to me. When I asked him what had bothered him most about the reaction to Rich's pardon, Quinn answered, "Having my integrity questioned."

The Role of Eric Holder

It was not only Bill Clinton, Jack Quinn, and Denise Rich who had to face public outrage over Rich's pardon. Eric Holder soon found himself in the firing line as well. Holder served at the Department of Justice as deputy attorney general at the time of Rich's pardon. He was considered a brilliant, independent, and thoughtful attorney who enjoyed a great amount of respect from both Democrats and Republicans. Quinn had met Holder while serving in the Clinton administration, and the two had been in contact ever since. Holder was one of the first people Quinn had approached regarding the Rich affair in November 1999—long before Michael Steinhardt first came up with the idea of applying for a presidential pardon. Quinn was still trying to convince the Southern District of New York to reevaluate Rich's case. According to Quinn's memos, Holder believed that the federal prosecutor's refusal to meet with Rich's lawyers was "ridiculous." Shortly after their discussion, Quinn sent Holder a memorandum explaining his position. Holder replied that "we're all sympathetic" and that the "equities [are] on your side."[18] However, Holder made it clear that he could not force the Southern District of New York to meet with Rich's attorneys.

When Rich decided to petition for a presidential pardon in the late fall of 2000, Quinn asked Holder for advice as to how he should proceed. "Deputy Attorney General Holder advised that it should be submitted directly to the White House," André A. Wicki, Rich's attorney in Switzerland, told me. Holder would play a crucial role in Rich's pardon on January 19, 2001—one day before Clinton would leave office—when he received a call from White House Counsel Beth Nolan. She wanted to know Holder's position on a possible Rich pardon. When he was later called before the House Government Reform Committee hearings on February 8, 2001, Holder informed the assembled committee members of his opinion. "I ultimately told Ms. Nolan that I was now neutral, leaning toward favorable, if there were foreign policy benefits that would be reaped by granting the pardon."[19] In his testimony, Holder told the committee that it was Prime Minister Ehud Barak's call to the president that had swayed him. He later claimed that he had been unaware that he was the only Justice Department official whose opinion President Clinton had sought while considering Rich's pardon. The deputy attorney general did not seem to have been aware of the importance the president placed on his opinion. Nevertheless, many observers believed that Holder's involvement in the affair spelled the end of his career in public service, and Holder seemed inclined to agree with them. He claimed he wanted to "climb into bed and pull the covers up over my head. I'm done. Public life is over for me."[20] In the end Holder was accused of acting in his own interest. It was claimed that he was seeking the position of attorney general in a possible Al Gore administration and that he had been trying to seek the favor of Jack Quinn, Gore's former chief of staff. (Holder was appointed attorney general by President Barack Obama in 2009.)

As a result of the tremendous public outrage, the Rich pardon was subject to an unprecedented amount of scrutiny. The powerful House Committee on Government Reform initiated an investigation and held hearings in spring 2001 to determine what had actually transpired and eventually published two reports consisting of over 1,500 pages.[21] Hearings were also held by the Senate Judiciary Committee, and the Justice Department's Southern District of New York even saw fit to open a criminal investigation. All of the accusations were thoroughly reexamined. Had corruption played a role? Had Denise Rich "bought" her ex-husband's pardon? Was Marc Rich the true source of the money Denise had donated to the Clintons and the Democratic Party? Did Rich pay Denise for her support? Was Rich an arms dealer? Was Jack Quinn guilty of ethical misconduct? Did Clinton break the law by pardoning Rich?

Instead of the mountain they had hoped for, investigators were left with a molehill. The hearings determined that several White House advisers—including Beth Nolan—had in fact advised Clinton *against* issuing the pardon. Despite the combined efforts of the House of Representatives, the Senate, and the Department of Justice, the investigations were never able to come up with proof of bribery, arms dealing, or any other misdeed. Rich's decision to directly petition the president may have been unusual, but it was by no means illegal. Clinton's decision to pardon Rich without seeking extensive counsel from the Department of Justice was also well within the law. The wording of the U.S. Constitution is quite clear. It explicitly grants the president the "power to grant reprieves and pardons for offenses against the United States, except in cases of impeachment."[22]

President Clinton's Motivation

Clinton sought to explain his decision to pardon Rich in an extensive op-ed article published in the *New York Times* in which he included many of the legal arguments that Rich's legal team had sought to employ over the years (see chapters 10 and 13).[23] Clinton interpreted three of the most important arguments as follows:

> I understood that the other oil companies that had structured transactions like those on which Mr. Rich and Mr. Green were indicted were instead sued civilly by the government; . . .
>
> Two highly regarded tax experts, Bernard Wolfman of Harvard Law School and Martin Ginsburg of Georgetown University Law Center, reviewed the transactions in question and concluded that the companies "were correct in their U.S. income tax treatment of all the items in question, and [that] there was no unreported federal income or additional tax liability attributable to any of the [challenged] transactions"; . . .
>
> The Justice Department in 1989 rejected the use of racketeering statutes in tax cases like this one.

These arguments may have been a good way of legally *justifying* the pardon, but I am not sure they are sufficient to explain Clinton's decision to actually *grant* the pardon. The research and interviews I carried out in the course of writing this book have led me to believe that Denise Rich's role in the pardon has been grossly overestimated. Of course Denise was helpful—after all, she was a friend and admirer of the Clintons. She was able to get the president's attention—something that is always in short supply—and thus open a few doors for her ex-husband. Denise was not the deciding factor, though, and her hefty donations to the Clintons and the Democratic Party were not the reason Rich was pardoned.

Neither was Clinton's decision to pardon Rich primarily a result of *legal* arguments. Instead, the president was swayed by the *emotional* and *political* aspects of Rich's petition. On an emotional level, Clinton allowed himself to be convinced by Jack Quinn's argument that Rich's case had been "grossly overprosecuted" by aggressive federal prosecutors. The president had himself experienced the lengths to which fanatical investigators were prepared to go. Independent counsel Kenneth Starr was originally appointed to investigate the Clintons' role in the Whitewater scandal, but Starr later widened his investigation and delved into the president's affair with Monica Lewinsky. The president soon found himself facing impeachment proceedings as a result of the investigations. Although he remained in office, his reputation had suffered greatly in the aftermath.

The president felt that he had been the victim of aggressive, overzealous persecution—and Rich's team had consciously used the president's feeling of victimization in their petition. "The pardon petition was literally written to the president," Bob Fink told me before popping open a can of Diet Dr Pepper. "It was written to him with the hope that he would personally read it and with the hope that he would recognize his own personal experiences."

When it came to the political aspect of the petition, the support of Ehud Barak and Shimon Peres played a crucial role in the president's decision—a belief that is shared by Jack Quinn and Avner Azulay, the two masterminds behind Rich's pardon application. "Without the support of Barak and Peres, Clinton would not have granted the pardon—no doubt about it," Azulay told me. "The entreaties of Prime Minister Barak weighed very heavily on the president's mind," Quinn explained. Clinton seemed to confirm their opinions in his autobiography: "Ehud Barak asked me three times to pardon Rich because of Rich's services to Israel and his help with the Palestinians, and several other Israeli figures in both major parties urged his release."[24]

Marc Rich was indeed of great importance to the Israelis. Rich's oil deliveries and assistance to the Mossad had contributed greatly to Israel's national security. It is difficult to imagine a U.S. president who would have not have had difficulties ignoring the pleas of so many Israeli politicians and dignitaries. Israel is by far the closest ally of the United States in the Middle East. There is a further factor that could have influenced Clinton's decision as well. On the day he issued the pardon, the Israelis and the Palestinians sat down for important peace talks in the Egyptian town of Taba. Clinton had lent his backing to the negotiations a month prior to this Taba Summit. Israel's foreign minister, Shlomo Ben-Ami, who had also lobbied for Rich's pardon, took part in the negotiations. The talks were Clinton's last opportunity as an American president to help end the Israeli-Palestinian conflict. He almost got his wish, as both sides were willing to make great compromises in the pursuit of peace. Never before had the two sides come closer to a comprehensive peace treaty—and they have never come as close since.

Rationally Right vs. Morally Bad

Hardly any of Clinton's other decisions in office were met with the same amount of extensive and prolonged criticism as his pardoning of Marc Rich. The decision raised hackles in nearly all corners of the nation, and the noise surrounding Holder's confirmation as attorney general is proof that the controversy has not subsided. Yet hardly any politicians or journalists seem willing to seriously and impartially address the reasons for the pardon. Published reactions to the pardon reminded me of the old saying that journalists are like birds on a wire—if one flies away, they all fly away. The opinions were formed long ago: Marc Rich is a villain, and because he is a villain he should not have been pardoned. Seen from this perspective, it might just be true that only angels have a shot at grace. In the eyes of the public, Rich's pardon was never really seen as rationally *wrong*—it was just morally *bad*. This type of criticism quickly gets bogged down at a moral level that does not allow for any form of counterargument.

In retrospect it is not only true that President Clinton enjoyed the unlimited and absolute power of pardon that is guaranteed by the U.S. Constitution. It is also important to take Clinton's words at their face value despite all of the attacks on his reputation: "I may have made a mistake, at least in the way I allowed the case to come to my attention, but I made the decision based on the merits."[25] As I have illustrated in this chapter, Clinton had very good reasons—both political and juridical—for pardoning Marc Rich.

Tax Bargain

On March 1, 2001, six weeks after Rich received his pardon, the New York Department of Taxation and Finance sent out the highest tax invoice it had ever issued, for $137,827,781.90. It was addressed to Marc Rich, Kleinnaumatt 9, CH-6045 Meggen, Switzerland. "It is now time for him to pay the piper," announced state tax commissioner Arthur Roth.[26] The State of New York was demanding $26.9 million in back taxes for the years 1980 through 1982 plus $13.5 million in penalties and $97.4 million in accrued interest. The interest alone added up to $20,000 per day. The delinquent taxes were based on the approximately $100 million in oil profits that—from the State of New York's point of view—Rich had failed to declare. Roth simultaneously froze $5 million in a Citibank account belonging to Rich. He revealed his sense of humor by commenting, "Marc Rich is to asset concealment what Babe Ruth was to baseball." No one seriously believed that Rich would ever pay off his tax debts. For his part, Rich contested the state's demands, claiming that he had already legally declared the profits in Switzerland.

The New York revenue authorities were therefore rather surprised when Rich signaled via his lawyer that he was prepared to pay part of the debt. Ever the trader, he suggested they negotiate a sum. The New York Department of Taxation and Finance declared its willingness to negotiate—under the condition that the talks should remain a secret. To outsiders, the affair seemed to take a rather strange turn. The tax authorities, who were usually quite eager to comment on the most trivial of developments concerning Rich's case, suddenly insisted on discretion. Could they have been embarrassed by the fact that they were negotiating a deal with the "biggest tax fraudster in the history of the United States"? Were they afraid of the public debate that might ensue if their pragmatic stance were to become widely known? Whatever the case, Rich was able to reach a good deal with the tax authorities. A tax collector confirmed to me that in November 2003 Rich transferred approximately $3 million to the State of New York. No one at the New York Department of Taxation and Finance wished to officially comment on this sum for reasons of confidentiality. One of Rich's lawyers said, "It would not be in Mr. Rich's interest to violate an agreement [of confidentiality] he made with a government in the United States." Naturally I wished to discuss the matter with Rich. "I paid even though the charge was completely unjustified," Rich said. He confirmed the agreement with the New York tax authorities but did not wish to name the exact sum. "I'm respecting the confidentiality," he explained. I asked him why he had paid anything at all, since he was of the opinion that he did not owe the State of New York any money whatsoever. "To get rid of it," he replied. "It was the only way to get rid of it."

"I'll Never Go Back to the USA"

In the aftermath of the affair, Rich was able to see which way the wind was blowing, and it was a very cold wind indeed. The pardon was like a boomerang. He had hoped to be able to liberate himself from many of the false accusations. He had hoped he would be given the freedom to return unmolested to the United States. He had hoped his name would finally disappear from the headlines. The reality was the exact opposite of what he had hoped for. The reports were even more scathing than they had been before the pardon. The media and the politicians rehashed all of the same facts, rumors, and defamations. Rich, who had been left in relative peace in the years running up to the pardon, was again described as the "fugitive billionaire," the "most wanted white-collar criminal in U.S. history," the "unscrupulous trader" who "traded with the enemy." In addition to all of these accusations, Rich was now seen as the man who was even capable of manipulating the most powerful man in the world: the president of the United States.

"I regret very much that Bill Clinton got in the line of fire for what he thought was the right thing to do," Rich tells me in his office, "more so because I believe—independently of the pardon—that he was one of the best presidents the U.S. has had in recent history. Smart, able, eloquent and positive." He thinks there was a targeted campaign. "The reactions were completely unjustified. Almost all of the negative reactions came from interested parties who felt that scandalizing Clinton's decision would help their own, usually partisan agenda." "Up to today the main allegation is that you essentially bought the pardon," I say. "I didn't," he answers. "Did you give money to your ex-wife Denise in exchange for her help?" "No," he says. "I would never give money to my ex-wife."

At first, Rich thought that the pardon "gave me back the freedom to travel wherever I want." He had asked for a pardon, according to Avner Azulay, mainly "so he could visit his daughter's grave, he could visit his father's grave, he could visit his family in New York."[27] After the public outcry in the wake of the pardon, though, Rich decided to forgo travel to the United States. "The American law system is peculiar in this respect. It is not possible to get confirmation that all legal proceedings are finished," he says. "They might still have an unpaid parking ticket of mine from thirty years ago and might make a big case out of it." I ask him if he intends to return to the United States someday. "Never," he says firmly. "They would look for some excuse to apprehend me. I don't want to be exposed to that."

Marc Rich had hoped the pardon would allow him to regain his reputation. Now he had again lost control over his own name. Once and for all.

19

The FUTURE ACCORDING *to* MARC RICH

Oil, aluminum, mercury. You became the most powerful commodity trader because you had a knack for creating new markets and for seizing opportunities. Where would you go today? In what commodities would you invest?

All commodities will be good business. The world will produce more products for more people and will thus need more raw materials.

Which will be, in your opinion, the most sought-after commodities in the twenty-first century?

Energy and water will probably become very important.

How do you see the future of oil?

Oil will play an important role for a long time to come, but there is no denying that it is a finite commodity.

Where do you see the oil price going?

Up and down, but up in the long term. Without any doubt.

Do you see a business opportunity in renewable energies?

As much as I like oil, it's obvious that oil has to be replaced in the future. Without doubt renewable energy will play an important role in this process. As it will become more expensive to get the remaining oil out of the ground, its price will inevitably go up. Higher oil prices will motivate innovation in the renewable energy sector, and higher prices will motivate people to switch.

Where would you invest?

I would invest in wind energy, but also in nuclear energy. Global warming and the reduction of carbon dioxide emissions will be important issues in the future.

You know the intricacies of the Middle East better than most other Western businessman. What is your opinion of the Iraq War?

The Iraq War was a mistake. It's mind-boggling that a handful of politicians can lead a nation into full war for such skimpy reasons. Obviously Saddam Hussein was a bad guy, but there are plenty of bad guys in this world and the United States hasn't bothered to remove them. It would seem that George W. Bush was driven by personal reasons, which makes the whole story worse, of course.

What personal reasons do you think of?

Saddam Hussein provoked Bush. Bush rose to the bait. It was such a foolish thing to do. He didn't control his emotions. Terrible. Terrible for a president.

Was it a war for oil?

I don't think so. You could have had the Iraqi oil cheaper simply by lifting the embargo, but the oil argument probably helped to convince some of the decision makers.

Do you think the oil industry had an influence on the decision to invade Iraq?

The oil companies will take business when it's offered to them, but I don't believe the oil industry, as you call it, pushed for that war. I think that perception stems from the fact that some of the Republican hawks were connected to that industry.

How do you judge President George W. Bush?

George W. Bush turned out to be a very bad president, disappointingly bad. His father was much better.

What was bad about him?

The Iraq War was the worst, of course, but I don't know a good thing he did.

What do you think of Barack Obama?

It's wonderful that there was a change. Barack Obama might be a
good president. He already changed the atmosphere in the world.
People again anticipate good things to come from America. I hope
Obama will be a good president; it would be good for the world.
I would have preferred Hillary Clinton, though.

Did or do you support Hillary Clinton financially?

No, I didn't and I don't.

*Barack Obama's unlikely rise to power reminded me of you. You both came
from humble origins and made it to the top.*

Yes, but I'm not black, I'm only the black sheep.

*You both represent the classic American success story. The rest of the world
admires the United States for making such opportunities possible.*

The United States was an open country and still is an open country.
I was able to do many things there that would have taken me longer
elsewhere. Business-wise it was a good thing to do, but practically
it was terrible. In retrospect I should have never gone with my
company to the United States.

*What were, in your opinion, the three biggest mistakes of U.S. foreign policy
over the last fifty years?*

Cuba, Vietnam, Iraq, and the notion of being all-powerful and
thus being able to disregard everybody else's opinion and
interests.

And the three biggest successes?

I think the biggest success story of the Americans is their capability
of renewal.

Where do you see the roots of the global financial crisis?

Too much credit. Too much lending of money. The banks didn't
control the risk.

Because of short-term thinking?

No question about it.

Are you affected by the crisis?

Everybody is affected by this crisis.

How much money did you lose?

I won't tell.

But you would say that it is the worst financial crisis ever for you personally?

Yes.

How will we get out of it?

We will get out of it, but not so fast.

How long will it take to overcome the crisis?

Three to five years, I think.

Can the governments be part of the solution?

Probably. They tried. They provided the banks with capital and credits that the banks should pass on, but the banks don't pass it on, so it was only partly successful.

One of the consequences of the financial crisis will be more regulations and less free markets.

Could be.

Would it be bad?

It goes in the wrong direction. I believe in the free market. Government regulation is often negative, restrictive, and impedes the normal flow of business. Political interventionism is the biggest threat to efficient markets.

Will the world be more free or less free in five years?

Broadly speaking, people will always strive to be free. The quest for freedom is probably as old as humanity.

Let me ask in a different way: Will we see more regulation and less liberalization?

Liberalization and regulation come and go in cycles; they are the product of the economic and political landscape in a given moment. Unfortunately, there seems to exist an underlying trend for more regulation. Whenever there is a problem somewhere, even if it's a single event affecting few people, as long as it gets enough publicity, some politician will clamor for a new regulation or law.

Will the world be more globalized or less globalized?

The world will be more globalized. Whatever people pretend,

globalization is not really a recent invention. Cross-border trade has been around since people started traveling and exchanging goods.

How do you see the Russian policy regarding oil and other commodities?

The Russians are looking firstly for themselves. You can't really blame them for that.

Foreign energy companies in Russia such as Royal Dutch Shell and British Petroleum were forced to sell their stakes to the state companies. Do we witness a renationalization of the commodity markets in Russia?

We are indeed seeing a renationalization of certain strategic sectors.

How should the West react to this policy?

The West is not in a good position to criticize the Russian policy. You have only to read the newspapers to see that other countries are equally protective of their pet companies and "national champions."

How do you see Russia's future?

You have to separate the noise from the music. The music is that Russia will slowly, slowly drift in the same direction—by and large—as most developing nations: toward democracy and market economy. We live in an age of instant and all-encompassing information and relative freedom of movement. This means that politicians can't fool people like they used to.

China has become both a major supplier and consumer of commodities.

The Chinese government needs to provide a billion people with food, energy, housing, transportation, et cetera, and they want to catch up with the developed countries. This means they will want to control as much oil and other commodities as they can lay their hands on.

How will this change the commodity markets and politics?

China is a political and strategic player before an economic one. This will clearly have an impact on the market, as most other market participants are guided purely by economic principles.

You were trading with the Chinese much earlier than others. What is special or easy or difficult about doing business with the Chinese?

They play by different rules than the Western companies. Whoever believes he can force his rules and his values on a Chinese business

partner will be disappointed by the result. If you can play their
game, you can have success.

*China's policy regarding commodities is considered quite aggressive. It is
investing billions in Sudan and Zimbabwe, whereas American companies
generally steer clear of investment. What is your opinion?*

China has the critical mass of a world power. It is simply too big
and economically too important to be bullied or boycotted. The
Chinese are obviously fully aware of this and use it smartly to their
advantage.

*Are the Europeans, when it comes to securing the supply of commodities,
naive?*

They are not naive, but contrary to the centralistic-run China,
where the political power is largely in sync with the economic
power, the Europeans simply cannot speak with one voice or act as
one entity.

*Why do you think it is acceptable to do business with countries and govern-
ments that are not exactly beacons of democracy and human rights?*

Take China or Vietnam as an example. If you sell them computers,
mobile phones, and TVs, they will be able to see what is going on
in the world. They will be able to form their own independent
opinions, which is the most important thing for any democracy. By
trading goods with these countries, you actually help their citizens.
The more contacts there are, the better the chance for everybody to
improve.

*One could argue that doing business with such regimes is morally wrong
because it only supports them.*

The Cubans as a people, for example, are not "bad," but because of
the U.S. embargo many children and old people must suffer unnec-
essarily. Yet the forty-seven-year-old embargo has not succeeded in
removing Fidel Castro.

*Can there be democracy without free markets? And vice versa—can there be
free markets without democracy?*

Free markets can exist temporarily without democracy. However, the combination of free markets and modern means of communication such as the Internet, which free markets always adopt immediately, will slowly convert that country into a democracy. As I was saying before, politicians can't fool people like they used to.

Are there any deals that you would not make for ethical reasons?

I would not engage in any illegal activity, of course.

Have you ever traded arms—legally, I mean?

We've been approached to become involved in the arms business a few times over the years. We've always pointed out very clearly that it's our policy not to get involved in such business. Neither I nor my companies sold, traded, or trafficked in arms for any country— including friendly countries.

You are very active as a philanthropist, not least in Israel. After the Lebanon War of 2006 and the recent conflict in Gaza, will there ever be peace between Israel and the Palestinians?

My foundation has made substantial efforts to foster a better understanding between Israelis and Palestinians. It's not an easy task, but I believe the two should be able to live together peacefully sometime in the future.

What are the reasons that there has been no peace yet?

The whole situation is hugely complex, but one of the reasons is certainly the settlers.

What has to change in order to give peace a chance?

Peace is a long-term project, in some cases tremendously long-term. It needs a certain economic well-being of the peoples involved. It needs tolerance and the experience that wars and terrorism don't pay off. All of these need to be learned, and it can take generations until people have accepted it.

Do you see the rise of Islamist fundamentalism in oil-producing countries like Iran or Saudi Arabia as a threat?

Fundamentalism of all colors is a threat.

What would happen to the global oil supply and to the oil price if fundamentalists would take over the power in Saudi Arabia?

The oil price would become even more volatile because of the uncertain and unpredictable behavior natural to fundamentalists and extremists of any type, but even fundamentalists will eventually succumb to the temptation of turning crude oil into easy money to buy themselves the support of their population.

Arabs. Russians. Africans. Chinese. Indians. Europeans. You traded with all of them. How do they differ when it comes to business?

Business everywhere is driven by the same motives, creating and selling things to make an income, but there are differences between different peoples or nations. It's all about local codes. To know and accept them can make a big difference in business.

Who was your toughest business partner?

My toughest business partners were Pinky [Pincus Green] and Alec [Hackel]. That was one of the reasons we were so successful.

What were your three biggest successes analyzing the world markets?

Crude oil, aluminum, and currencies.

What were your three biggest failures?

Not to have had bigger positions of the three best ones.

20

EPILOGUE

The Gray Area

The snow was falling lightly as I drove along the narrow curved road that led down to the Villa Rose. I stopped in front of the massive wrought-iron gate and assumed a pleasant look for the camera installed on a stone pillar. "*Grüezi*," the voice from the speaker called in greeting, before asking for the purpose of my visit. I announced my name, and the iron gate opened slowly in reply. I drove toward the covered parking area next to the villa. It was only then that I noticed the silver Mercedes that had been following me. At the wheel was one of Marc Rich's bodyguards. He nodded toward me with a smile on his face.

It was 8:30 A.m. on a Thursday. I had arranged to have breakfast with Rich and asked if we could meet in his home. "I don't mind," he answered and invited me to meet him at his estate in Meggen on Lake Lucerne, the Villa Rose. A Spanish-speaking servant opened the door and directed me to the living room. I sat waiting on a beige sofa while admiring the valuable cubist works of art hanging on the surrounding walls. There were paintings by the French artists Fernand Léger and Georges Braque and by Rich's fellow Spaniard Pablo Picasso. In the corner stood a slim bronze sculpture by the Swiss artist Alberto Giacometti. Glenn Gould's interpretation of a piano piece by Johann Sebastian Bach could be heard from the tiny speakers mounted on the ceiling.

Suddenly Marc Rich appeared and greeted me. As always, he was wearing a dark suit with a white shirt and red tie. He looked me over and said only half-jokingly, "It's never too early to wear a tie." As we had arranged to meet for a private breakfast, I had decided to leave my tie at home. Before I could come up with a clever riposte, Rich's CEO appeared—bare-necked like me. We sat down to a breakfast of scrambled eggs with black truffles, smoked salmon and horseradish, ripe papaya, and freshly squeezed orange juice.

After breakfast Rich gave me a tour of his estate. We strolled in silence through the gardens. The fig trees, vines, and rosebushes were covered in a thin layer of snow. He then led me to a monumental iron sculpture by the Spanish artist Eduardo Chillida. Lake Lucerne sparkled in the pale light of the sun fighting its way through the clouds. It seemed to be the perfect atmosphere for some fundamental questions. "With the benefit of hindsight, what would you have done differently over the course of your life?" I asked Rich, who turned up the collar of his coat to protect himself from the snow. "Do you have any regrets in particular?" He did not take long to answer my question. "I guess I'd have been more careful to avoid the trouble I had in America," he said. "I didn't need that business. It wasn't necessary at all. I had already made very good business at that time."

If it had not been for that business—a business deal whose legitimacy or illegality has never been determined in court—Marc Rich would certainly never have been painted as the "biggest devil." If it had not been for the (economically counterproductive) price controls imposed by President Richard Nixon, Rich would never have acquired a reputation as "the biggest tax evader in U.S. history." Instead, Rich would still be known today as the "genius in the formerly European dominated metals market," as he was once regarded.[1] Had it not been for Rich's fall from grace, people would speak of him today as the American hero who broke Big Oil's cartel and invented the spot market for the trade in crude oil. He would be described as the embodiment of the American dream, the poor immigrant who would later become a billionaire and a generous philanthropist. For it is the American virtues, the American values, and, yes, the American vices Rich embodies that made him the King of Oil. Work harder. Concentrate on your goal. Think big and bold. Be aggressive. Be successful.

Of course, one can criticize Rich for supplying South Africa's apartheid regime with oil. One can criticize Rich for trading with dictators of every stripe—from Cuba's Fidel Castro to Nigeria's Sani Abacha and Iran's Ayatollah Khomeini—and, of course, one can criticize him for breaking embargos while putting profit above morality. It would be easy to criticize Rich for all of these business dealings were the ways of the world as simple as black and white. The reality, however, is much more complicated than that. Life does not always play out according to preconceived notions; life isn't always what it seems.

A trader who had dealt in virtually every metal for Marc Rich illustrated this point to me quite clearly. I was speaking to him about commodities trading in a bar in a wintry midtown Manhattan. "Ethics." He laughed. Then he pointed at my Diet Coke. "Your Coke can is made of aluminum. The bauxite that is needed to make it probably comes from Guinea-Conakry. A terrible dictatorship, believe me," he said. "The oil that is used to heat this room probably comes from Saudi Arabia. These good friends of the USA hack the hands off of thieves just like in the Middle Ages. Your cell phone? Without coltan there wouldn't be any cell phones. Let's not pretend. Coltan was used to finance the civil war in the Congo." He paused for his words to take effect. "Now, you tell me," he said and pointed his finger at me. "What's the alternative? No trade? Without raw materials the economy would collapse. The world would stand still. Do the people who criticize our work want to know any of this? Or would they rather just pick on us so that they can feel better about themselves?"

These are questions for which only ideologues have an easy answer. Everyone else, the commodities traders most of all, of course, make do with some middle way between a sense of reality and self-deception. Sometimes they look reality in the eye, but sometimes they would rather forget about it. They live in a gray area—sometimes dark, sometimes light. Sometimes it is fair, and sometimes it is exploitative. The name for this gray area is capitalism.

Strolling through the snowy gardens of the Villa Rose, I thought of an intriguing question. The John Templeton Foundation had recently asked leading scientists, economists, scholars, and public figures: Does the free market corrode moral character? "It depends," John Gray, emeritus professor at the London School of Economics, answered. "The traits of character most rewarded by free markets," he said as if he had been asked to comment on Marc Rich, "are entrepreneurial boldness, the willingness to speculate and gamble, and the ability to seize or create new opportunities." Gray added, "It is worth noting that these are not the traits most praised by conservative moralists."[2]

"Yes," a senior Marc Rich + Co. director with vast experience all over the world once confessed to me, "sometimes we had to make a Faustian bargain to clinch the deal." The words resonated in my head for quite some time. *A Faustian bargain.* Nowadays this phrase is usually used to describe self-serving actions and moral sacrifices—a pact with the devil in order to gain power, wealth, or influence—but in *Faust: A Tragedy*, Johann Wolfgang von Goethe's greatest work, the scholar Heinrich Faust is not simply a ruthless egoist. He represents men who strive for achievement and who want to test their own limitations. Faust stands for the scientist who breaks conventions in order to discover "what holds the world together in its innermost." He is also misled— someone who would purchase short-term profit with long-term pain. We may see Marc Rich as a kind of modern Faust of the commodity age. He is, not unlike Faust, a driven individual who strives for success and recognition. He perfected trading methods precisely because he was willing to push the boundaries and break taboos. His power also came from trading with the "devils" of the world.

The air coming off Lake Lucerne was crisp and clear. I could hear the ringing of the sheep bells from the neighboring farm. A mist rose from the surface of the lake, where—despite the weather—a solitary fisherman made his way across the lake. The snowy hills along the opposite shoreline looked as if they had been sprinkled with powdered sugar. It was all bewitchingly beautiful. "You must be a lucky man," I said to the most successful and controversial commodities trader the world has ever seen. Rich looked out over the sparkling surface of the lake and remained silent for some time. Then, almost as if he were speaking to himself, the King of Oil quietly replied, "Sometimes."

NOTES

The following abbreviated citations are used for reports of U.S. House of Representatives committee hearings.

Controversial Pardon   U.S. Congress. House. Committee on Government Reform. *The Controversial Pardon of International Fugitive March Rich.* HR Report 11, 107th Congress, 1st session (2001).

"Take Jack's Word"   U.S. Congress. House. Committee on Government Reform. "Take Jack's Word: The Pardons of International Fugitives Marc Rich and Pincus Green," chapter 1 of *Justice Undone: Clemency Decisions in the Clinton White House.* HR Report 454, 107th Congress, 2nd session (2002).

Thataway   U.S. Congress. House. Committee on Government Operations. *They Went Thataway: The Strange Case of Marc Rich and Pincus Green.* HR Report 537, 102nd Congress, 2nd session (1992).

1: The Undisputed King of Oil

1. Leonardo Maugeri, *The Age of Oil: The Mythology, History, and Future of the World's Most Controversial Resource* (Westport, Conn.: Greenwood, 2006). Maugeri is head of strategy and development for the Italian energy company Eni, the sixth-largest publicly listed oil company in the world.

2. Daniel Yergin. *The Prize: The Epic Quest for Oil, Money, and Power* (New York: Simon & Schuster, 1992).

3. Drivers paid 36¢ for a gallon of gasoline in 1970 (U.S. national average). Today the gallon costs around $2. The record price for regular unleaded was $4.11 in July 2008 (AAA, www.fuelgaugereport.com).

4. Robert Lenzner, "Candidates Need an Economic Clue," *Forbes*, June 9, 2008.

5. Quoted in *Controversial Pardon*, 5.

6. A. Craig Copetas, *Metal Men: How Marc Rich Defrauded the Country, Evaded the Law, and Became the World's Most Sought-After Corporate Criminal* (New York: Putnam, 1985).

7. Rudolph W. Giuliani, the lead prosecutor in the case against Marc Rich, refused to give an interview or even to answer some questions in spite of a very generous time frame.

2: The Biggest Devil

1. The interviews with Marc Rich started in spring 2007.

2. "The 10 Most Notorious Presidential Pardons," www.time.com/time/2007/presi dential_pardons/10.html.

3. *Financial Times*, September 1, 1988.

4. A. Craig Copetas, "The Sovereign Republic of Marc Rich," *Regardie's*, February 1, 1990.

5. According to the Swiss member of Parliament Josef Lang, who made a political career by attacking Marc Rich's businesses.

6. "Marc Rich Indicted in Vast Tax Evasion Case," *New York Times*, September 20, 1983.

7. The superseding indictment of March 1984 lists sixty-five counts. Indictment, U.S. v. Marc Rich, Pincus Green, et al., March 6, 1984, S 83 Cr. 579.

8. As of January 11, 2009.

9. *Controversial Pardon*, 109.

10. Salinger managed to buy 1,200 Petit Upmanns, as he recounts in "Kennedy, Cuba and Cigars," *Cigar Aficionado*, Autumn 1992.

11. BP, Chevron, Esso, Gulf, Mobil, Shell, and Texaco. Enrico Mattei, the legendary boss of Eni, the then state-owned Italian energy company, coined the term "Seven Sisters" in the 1960s.

12. Rich's partners were Pincus Green, Jacques Hachuel, Alec Hackel, and John Trafford.

13. Donella H. Meadows, Dennis L. Meadows, Jorgen Randers, and William W. Behrens III, *The Limits to Growth* (New York: Universe Books, 1992). Marion King Hubbert, a geologist at Shell, coined the term "peak oil" in 1957. The term "Hubbert's peak" is used as well.

14. James Kerr, senior trader with Elders IXL, quoted in John N. Ingham and Lynne B. Feldman, *Contemporary American Business Leaders: A Biographical Dictionary* (Westport, Conn.: Greenwood, 1990), 557.

15. Richard M. Auty, (1993). *Sustaining Development in Mineral Economies: The Resource Curse Thesis* (London: Routledge, 1993); Jeffrey D. Sachs and Andrew M. Warner, Natural resource abundance and economic growth. National Bureau of Economic Research Working Paper 5398, December 1995.

16. "Take Jack's Word."

17. Ibid., 16.

18. Ibid., 14.

19. Quoted in *Controversial Pardon*, 5.

20. "The Billionaires," *Fortune,* June 28, 1993. The magazine estimated Rich's fortune at $2.3 billion.

3: A Jewish Fate

1. Lucy S. Dawidowicz, *The War Against the Jews, 1933-1945* (New York: Bantam, 1986), 33.

2. Fernand Braudel, *The Perspective of the World*, vol. 3 of *Civilization and Capitalism 15th-18th Century* (Berkeley: University of California Press, 1992), 143.

3. David S. Landes, *The Wealth and Poverty of Nations* (New York: Norton, 1998).

4. Eric Laureys, "The Plundering of Antwerp's Jewish Diamond Dealers, 1940–1944," in *Confiscation of Jewish Property in Europe, 1933-1945* (Washington: Center for Advanced Holocaust Studies, U.S. Holocaust Memorial Museum, 2003), 57–74.

5. Raul Hilberg, *The Destruction of the European Jews*, 3 vols. (New York: Holmes & Meier, 1985), 600.

6. Antwerp's remarkable Jewish culture was completely destroyed in World War II. The town was officially *Judenrein* when the Nazis left in September 1944.

7. U.S. Holocaust Memorial Museum, www.ushmm.org. In the course of two days, September 29–30, 1941, a special team of German Nazi SS supported by other German units, local collaborators, and Ukrainian police shot about 34,000 Jewish civilians. The Babi Yar massacre is considered by historians to be one of the largest single massacres in the history of the Holocaust.

8. Toni Falbo and Denise Polit, "A Quantitative Review of the Only-Child Literature: Research Evidence and Theory Development," *Psychological Bulletin* 100 (1986): 176–89.

9. "In KC, Quiet Rich Barely Recalled," *Kansas City Star*, March 2, 2001.

10. Calvin Trillin, *With All Disrespect: More Uncivil Liberties* (New York: Penguin, 1986), 148.

11. Inflation-adjusted purchasing power parity, Bureau of Labor Statistics, www.bls.gov/data/inflation-calculator.htm.

12. Letter from Donald R. Nickerson, then principal of Rhodes School, *Fortune,* February 20, 1984.

4: The American Dream

1. Francis Fukuyama, *Trust: The Social Virtues and the Creation of Prosperity* (New York: Free Press, 1995).
2. Quoted in "The Man Behind Marc Rich," *New York Times*, August 18, 1983.
3. A. Craig Copetas, *Metal Men: How Marc Rich Defrauded the Country, Evaded the Law, and Became the World's Most Sought-After Corporate Criminal* (New York: Putnam, 1985), 71. The same quote appears in "Take Jack's Word" on page 9.
4. "Cuba Speeds Nuclear Project; Marc Rich Is Said to Assist," *Wall Street Journal Europe*, June 4, 1991.
5. Geoffrey Jones, "Multinational Trading Companies in History and Theory," in *The Multinational Traders*, ed. Jones (London: Routledge, 1998).
6. John N. Ingham and Lynne B. Feldman, *Contemporary American Business Leaders: A Biographical Dictionary* (Westport, Conn.: Greenwood, 1990), xxii.

5: The Crude Awakening

1. Daniel Yergin, *The Prize: The Epic Quest for Oil, Money, and Power* (New York: Simon & Schuster, 1992), 555.
2. The term "Seven Sisters" was coined by Enrico Mattei, the legendary boss of Eni, the then state-owned Italian energy company.
3. Edith Penrose, *The International Petroleum Industry* (London: Allen & Unwin, 1968), 78.
4. One gallon was around 35¢ at the pump.
5. The Iranian oil industry was nationalized in 1951 by Prime Minister Mohammad Mossadegh. In 1953 Mossadegh was deposed by Iranian army officers, supported by the CIA and the British Secret Intelligence Service. Mohammad Reza Shah Pahlevi came back from exile and took power again.
6. United Nations Conference on Trade and Development, *World Investment Report, 2007*, www.unctad.org.
7. Lucy Dawidowicz, "Babi Yar's Legacy," *New York Times Magazine,* September 27, 1981.

6: Israel and the Shah

1. Professor Uri Bialer of Hebrew University of Jerusalem just recently managed, based on formerly classified documents, to shed some light on the history of the pipeline. His highly interesting study "Fuel Bridge Across the Middle East—Israel, Iran, and the Eilat-Ashkelon Oil Pipeline" was published in *Israel Studies* 12, no. 3 (Fall 2007). Samuel Segev wrote about the secret pipeline as one of the first in his standard work, *The Iranian Triangle* (New York: Free Press, 1988).

2. Bialer, "Fuel Bridge Across the Middle East," 30.

3. Trita Parsi, *Treacherous Alliance: The Secret Dealings of Israel, Iran, and the United States* (New Haven: Yale University Press, 2007).

4. As of January 16, 2009.

5. Tony Benn, *Against the Tide: Diaries, 1973-1976* (London: Arrow, 1989), 488.

6. Bialer, "Fuel Bridge Across the Middle East," 34.

7: Marc Rich + Company

1. Quoted in "Secrets of Marc Rich," *Fortune*, January 23, 1984.

2. Quoted in "Inside Philipp Brothers," *Business Week*, September 3, 1979.

3. Helmut Waszkis wrote a brilliant company history, *Philipp Brothers: The Rise and Fall of a Trading Giant* (Worcester Park, U.K.: Metal Bulletin, 1992). This book was an important inspiration and a valuable source for me. The quotation is from p. 204.

4. "Hide and Seek," *Wall Street Journal*, August 5, 1983.

5. U.S. Energy Information Agency, www.eia.doe.gov.

6. Geoffrey Jones, "Multinational Trading Companies in History and Theory," in *The Multinational Traders*, ed. Jones (London: Routledge, 1998), 16.

7. Philippe Chalmin, *Traders and Merchants: Panorama of International Commodity Trading* (Chur, Switzerland: Harwood Academic Publishers, 1987), 282.

8. Francis Fukuyama, *Trust: The Social Virtues and the Creation of Prosperity* (New York: Free Press, 1995).

9. Kenneth J. Arrow, *The Limits of Organization* (New York: Norton, 1974), 23.

10. "Secrets of Marc Rich," *Fortune*, January 23, 1984.

11. Daniel Yergin, *The Prize: The Epic Quest for Oil, Money, and Power* (New York: Simon & Schuster, 1992), 722.

8: Trading with the Ayatollah Khomeini

1. Trita Parsi, *Treacherous Alliance: The Secret Dealings of Israel, Iran, and the United States* (New Haven: Yale University Press, 2007), 80.

2. Ibid., 83.

3. Figures from OPEC Annual Statistical Bulletins (www.opec.org), U.S. Energy Information Administration (www.eia.doe.gov), and BP Statistical Review of World Energy (www.bp.com).

4. "The Hustling Price Gougers," *Time*, March 12, 1979.

5. Exec. Order No. 12170, 44 Fed. Reg. 65729 (1979).

6. U.S. Energy Information Agency, Annual Oil Market Chronology, www.eia.doe.gov/emeu/cabs/AOMC/Overview.html.

7. Exec. Order No. 12205, 45 Fed. Reg. 24099 (1980).

8. See Daniel Yergin, *The Prize: The Epic Quest for Oil, Money, and Power* (New York: Simon & Schuster, 1992), 700–706.

9. Exec. Order No. 12205, 45 Fed. Reg. 24099 (1980). Even subsidiaries of American companies abroad were allowed to trade with Iran. United Press International, for example, reported on two major U.S. defense contractors and other U.S. firms that continued legally shipping goods to Iran during the hostage crisis (September 28, 1981).

10. Glencore, the former Marc Rich + Co., is still in business with Iran.

11. "Oil Trader," *Washington Post*, February 15, 1983.

12. "The Lifestyle of Rich," *Fortune*, December 22, 1986.

13. The speech is available at http://www.pbs.org/wgbh/amex/carter/filmmore/ps_crisis.html.

14. The Iranian Consortium was owned as follows: 40 percent BP, 14 percent Royal Dutch Shell, 7 percent Exxon, 7 percent Gulf Oil, 7 percent Mobil (now part of Exxon-Mobil), 7 percent Standard Oil of California (now Chevron, which in the 1980s bought most of Gulf Oil), 7 percent Texaco (now part of Chevron), 6 percent Compagnie Française des Pétroles (now TotalFinaElf), and 5 percent Iricon Agency Ltd. Iricon grouped six U.S. companies, which held the 5 percent as follows: one sixth by each of American Independent Oil, Getty Oil, and Charter Oil; one third by Atlantic Richfield (ARCO—now part of BP); and one twelfth by each of Continental Oil (Conoco) and Standard Oil of Ohio (now part of BP).

15. "Oil Trader," *Washington Post*, February 15, 1983.

16. "Shadow of Khomeini Falls on the Mideast Peace Talks," *New York Times*, February 25, 1979; Uri Bialer, "Fuel Bridge Across the Middle East: Israel, Iran, and the Eilat-Ashkelon Oil Pipeline," *Israel Studies* 12, no. 3 (Fall 2007): 30.

17. "Shadow of Khomeini Falls on the Mideast Peace Talks," *New York Times*, February 25, 1979.

18. "Hearing on the Future of Oil of the House Select Committee on Energy Independence and Global Warming," *Congressional Quarterly*, June 11, 2008, 35.

19. A. Craig Copetas, *Metal Men: How Marc Rich Defrauded the Country, Evaded the Law, and Became the World's Most Sought-After Corporate Criminal* (New York: Putnam, 1985), 115.

20. International Monetary Fund, www.imf.org.

21. Official excerpt from the Zug tax records dated August 12, 1983.

9: The Case

1. The interview with Morris "Sandy" Weinberg took place on March 12, 2008.

2. Marc Rich + Co. AG was a Swiss corporation that did not have to file U.S. corporate

income tax returns. Marc Rich International was a Swiss subsidiary of Marc Rich + Co. AG and did business in the United States. It had its principal offices in Zug, Switzerland, and New York, and it filed U.S. corporate income tax returns.

3. They served ten months.

4. Evan Thomas, *The Man to See: Edward Bennett Williams—Ultimate Insider, Legendary Trial Lawyer* (New York: Simon & Schuster, 1991), 14.

5. Interview with Avner Azulay.

6. Thomas, *The Man to See*, 415–17.

7. Ibid.

8. Letter from Marc Rich to Ruth H. Van Heuven, U.S. Consul General, Zurich, October 27, 1992.

9. "Take Jack's Word," 26.

10. Thomas, *The Man to See*, 415–17.

11. Rich's Netherland Antilles affiliate Richco contributed at least $75 million in purchase money through an irrevocable letter of credit and an undisclosed amount of cash.

12. Quoted in "Dinkins Among 14 Arrested in Protest of Police Shooting," *New York Times*, March 16, 1999.

13. Thomas, *The Man to See*, 416.

14. Leonard Garment, *Crazy Rhythm* (New York: Da Capo, 2001), 394.

15. Article 273 of the Swiss penal code.

16. "Marc Rich Asset Freeze May Halt Its U.S. Business," *Wall Street Journal*, August 1, 1983.

17. U.S. Court of Appeals for the Second Circuit, 84-6033, 6075 at 7.

18. Diplomatic note, handed over by the Embassy of Switzerland, on September 21, 1983.

19. The superseding indictment of March 1984 lists sixty-five counts. Indictment, *U.S. v. Marc Rich, Pincus Green, et al.*, March 6, 1984, S 83 Cr. 579.

20. Quoted in "Marc Rich Indicted in Vast Tax Evasion Case," *New York Times*, September 20, 1983.

21. Indictment, count 7, p. 3.

22. Ibid, count 50, pp. 45–46.

23. *Controversial Pardon*, 109.

24. 15 U.S.C. § 751 et seq.

25. Indictment, page 7. The average world market price of crude oil was around $37 in 1980.

26. Indictment, e.g., counts 7, 9, 10, 11, and 22.

27. Indictment, page 11.

28. Request for Assistance Under the Swiss Federal Law on International Assistance in Penal Matters in the Investigation of Marc Rich et al.: "They also engineered fraudulent transactions whereby $30 million in offshore losses incurred by [Marc Rich + Co.]

AG in Zug were fraudulently billed to International, so that [Marc Rich International] could claim the losses as deductions from taxable income" (5).

29. John Dean, "Why an Investigation of the Marc Rich Pardon Is Imminent," *FindLaw. com*, February 2, 2001.

30. Gerard E. Lynch, "RICO: The Crime of Being a Criminal," *Columbia Law Review* 87, no. 4 (May 1987).

31. Indictment, counts 35–40.

32. "Rich Is Poorer," *Time*, October 22, 1984.

33. Ibid.

10: Rudy Giuliani's Failures

1. Securities Industry Association, *Foreign Activity in U.S. Securities* 8, no. 2 (April 10, 1984): 4.

2. IMAC, Art. 3, Par. 3. "A request shall not be granted if the subject of the proceeding is an offence which appears to be aimed at reducing fiscal duties or taxes or which violates regulations concerning currency, trade or economic policy. However, a request for judicial assistance under the third part of this act may be granted if the subject of the proceeding is a duty or tax fraud." Unofficial translation by the Swiss Federal Office of Justice, www.bj.admin.ch/bj/en.

3. Extradition treaty of May 14, 1900, II.4, II.6; indictment, count 7, p. 3: ". . . and to obtain money and property by false and fraudulent pretenses, representations and promises."

4. "Aussergerichtlicher Vergleich im Fall Marc Rich," *NZZ*, October 12, 1984.

5. "Die Bananenrepublik zeigt ihre Zähne," *Die Weltwoche*, September 29, 1983.

6. Translation of the French note delivered on September 25, 1984, by the Office for Police Matters to the Embassy of the United States.

7. *Annual Report of the Swiss Federal Council, 1984*, 132.

8. Quoted in *Thataway*, 10.

9. "Exporting American Taxes," *Economist*, October 1, 1983.

10. Quoted in A. V. Lowe, "Extraterritorial Jurisdiction: An Annotated Collection of Legal Materials," *American Journal of International Law* 78, no. 2 (April, 1984): 547–49.

11. Harold G. Maier, "Interest Balancing and Extraterritorial Jurisdiction," *American Journal of Comparative Law* 31, no. 4 (Autumn 1983): 579–97; 595, 579 quoted.

12. Ibid., 595–96.

13. A. D. Neale and M. L. Stephens, *International Business and National Jurisdiction* (Oxford: Clarendon Press, 1988), 194.

14. *Thataway*, 11.

15. Ibid., 13.

16. Quoted in "All the Fugitive's Men in Israel," *Los Angeles Times*, February 25, 2001.

17. *Thataway*, 32.

18. Ibid., 37.

19. The Supreme Court wrote in 1895, "The principle that there is a presumption of innocence in favor of the accused is the undoubted law, axiomatic and elementary, and its enforcement lies at the foundation of the administration of our criminal law." *Coffin v. United States,* 156 U.S. 432; 15 S. Ct. 394.

20. Quoted in *The Strange Case of Marc Rich: Contracting with Tax Fugitives at Large in the Alps: Hearings Before the Government Information, Justice, and Agriculture Subcommittee of the Committee on Government Operations,* 102nd Congress, 1st and 2nd sessions, 1991–92 (Washington: GPO, 1993), 8.

21. United States Attorneys' Manual, USAM 6-4.210.

22. United States Attorneys' Manual, USAM 9-110.415.

23. The analysis can be retrieved via www.law.wayne.edu/McIntyre/text/in_the_news/marc_rich.pdf; 23–24 quoted.

24. "Marc Rich's Road to Riches," *Time,* October 3, 1983.

25. Exec. Order No. 12205, 45 Fed. Reg. 24099 (1980). The charges against the companies—but not against Rich and Green—were later dropped.

26. United Press International, September 28, 1981. See note 9 to chapter 8 above.

27. *Controversial Pardon,* 486–87.

28. Ibid., 45.

29. Letter from Jack Quinn to President Bill Clinton, January 5, 2001.

30. Letter to U.S. Attorney Mary Jo White, December 1, 1999.

31. Gordon Crovitz, "RICO's Broken Commandments," *Wall Street Journal,* January 26, 1989.

32. Letter to U.S. Attorney Otto G. Obermaier, November 6, 1990.

33. Hermann Lübbe, *Politischer Moralismus: Der Triumph der Gesinnung über die Urteilskraft* (Berlin: Siedler, 1987).

34. Howard Safir on *Larry King Live,* CNN, February 16, 2001.

35. Quoted in *Controversial Pardon,* 5.

36. Michael Levi, *Regulating Fraud* (London: Tavistock, 1987), 113.

11: "I Never Broke the Law"

1. *Thataway,* 27.

12: The Hunt for Marc Rich

1. Ethan Avram Nadelmann, *Cops Across Borders: The Internationalization of U.S. Criminal Law Enforcement* (University Park, Penn.: Pennsylvania State University Press, 1993), 168–69.

2. *United States v. Alvarez-Machain,* 504 U.S. 655 (1992).

3. *Thataway*, 20.

4. The interview with Ken Hill took place on March 11, 2008.

5. Jeppesen Sanderson officially says it didn't cooperate.

6. Maureen Orth, "The Face of Scandal," *Vanity Fair*, June 2001.

7. For more information about the relationship between Avner Azulay and Ehud Barak see chapter 18, "The Pardon."

8. A. Craig Copetas, "The Sovereign Republic of Marc Rich," *Regardie's*, February 1990.

9. *Wall Street Journal*, January 29, 2001.

10. "Take Jack's Word," 27.

11. Pat Dawson, "The Double Life of Marc Rich," February 12, 2001, www.msnbc.msn .com/id/3071886.

12. Quoted in "The Rich List," *Observer*, May 13, 2001.

13. Editorial, *Regardie's*, August 1985.

14. Answers to Questions Submitted to the Department of Justice by the Subcommittee on Government Information, Justice, and Agriculture Regarding Marc Rich and Pincus Green, 1992, 26.

15. Quoted in "Investigator Tells House Committee That Politics Let Tax Fugitive Go Free," *American Metal Market*, March 6, 1992.

16. *Thataway*, 34.

17. Published as *Thataway*.

18. Parliamentary Motion of June 19, 1992.

19. Howard Safir on *Larry King Live*, CNN, February 8, 2001.

20. *Thataway*, 13–17, 37.

13: Clandestine Talks

1. Web site of Zuckerman Spaeder, Sandy Weinberg's law firm: www.zuckerman.com/ morris_weinberg.

2. Memorandum from Leonard Garment to Otto G. Obermaier, November 6, 1990.

3. Quoted in "Plotting a Pardon," *New York Times*, April 11, 2001.

4. Letter from Jack Quinn to Mary Jo White, December 1, 1999.

5. Letter from Bernard Wolfman to Gerard E. Lynch, December 7, 1990.

6. Letter from Laurence A. Urgenson to Patrick Fitzgerald, June 3, 1994.

7. Letter from Patrick Fitzgerald to Laurence Urgenson, June 27, 1994.

8. Letter from Mary Jo White to Jack Quinn, February 2, 2000.

9. Leonard Garment, "Representing Marc Rich in a Vindictive Time," in *Liber Amicorum Marc Rich* (Lucerne, 2004), 73.

14: The Secrets of Success

1. "Why Marc Rich Is Richer Than Ever," *Fortune*, August 1, 1988.

2. *Financial Times*, September 1, 1988.

3. "Take Jack's Word," 9–16.

4. A. Craig Copetas, *Metal Men: How Marc Rich Defrauded the Country, Evaded the Law, and Became the World's Most Sought-After Corporate Criminal* (New York: Putnam, 1985), 115–19.

5. "The Lifestyle of Rich," *Fortune*, December 22, 1986.

6. Ayn Rand, *Answers: The Best of Her Q&A*, ed. Robert Mayhew (New York: New American Library, 2005), 124.

7. Ayn Rand, *The Virtue of Selfishness* (1964); Rand, *Answers*, 109.

8. Cf. "Capitalist Heroes," *Wall Street Journal*, October 12, 2007.

9. Copetas, *Metal Men*, 115.

10. "Jamaica Eyes Alumina Contracts," *American Metal Market*, March 8, 1989.

11. "Jamaica's Manley Ends Attack," *American Metal Market*, July 6, 1989.

12. Figures from U.S. Geological Survey, http://minerals.usgs.gov/ds/2005/140/aluminum.pdf.

13. "Jamaica Alumina Output Hikes Hit Snags," *Metals Week*, March 23, 1987.

14. Inter Press Service News Agency (IPS), "Jamaica: Rejoicing over New IMF Pact, But . . . ," July 28, 1989, and "Jamaica: Government Blamed for Alumina Plant Closure," February 8, 1985.

15. Associated Press, June 26, 1979.

16. E. S. Reddy, "A Review of United Nations Action for an Oil Embargo Against South Africa," United Nations Centre Against Apartheid, 1981, available at www.anc.org.za/un/reddy/oilembargo.html.

17. HR 4868. President Ronald Reagan attempted to veto the bill but was overridden by Congress.

18. The actual prices were staggered, as is usual in the industry. For comparison: The official OPEC price in 1979 was between $13.34 and $16.75. The international price, paid on the spot market, was $25.

19. Quoted in "Oil Fuels Apartheid," ANC Statement, March 1985, available at www.anc.org.za/ancdocs/pr/1980s/pr850300.html.

20. Twenty-two billion South African rands between 1973 and 1984. Richard Hengeveld and Jaap Rodenburg, eds., *Embargo: Apartheid's Oil Secrets Revealed* (Amsterdam: Amsterdam University Press, 1995), 230; IPS, "Oil Embargo Shows the Heavy Price of Economic Sanctions," August 2, 1985.

21. Hengeveld and Rodenburg, *Embargo*, 274.

22. Ibid., 145.

23. IPS, "Oil Embargo Shows the Heavy Price of Economic Sanctions," August 2, 1985.

15: Surprising Services

1. Quoted in "To Honor Their Lives," February 1, 2005, www.peacenow.org/resources/publications.asp?rid=&cid=228.
2. Leonard Garment, *Crazy Rhythm* (New York: Da Capo, 2001), 376–80.
3. Ibid.
4. Quoted in "A Fugitive's Secret Talks with the Feds," *U.S. News & World Report*, March 12, 2001.
5. Garment, *Crazy Rhythm*, 376–80.
6. *Controversial Pardon*, 1056.
7. Quoted in "Plotting a Pardon," *New York Times*, April 11, 2001.
8. *The 9/11 Commission Report: Final Report of the National Commission on Terrorist Attacks upon the United States* (New York: Norton, 2004), 12.
9. Letter from Shabtai Shavit to President Bill Clinton, November 28, 2000.
10. "The Rich List," *Observer*, May 13, 2001.
11. Yossi Melman, "The Story of Iranian Oil and Israeli Pipes," *Haaretz.com*, October 21, 2007.

16: The Private Life of the Riches

1. "Songwriter Who Doubles as Friend of Bill," *New York Times*, October 11, 2000.
2. Petition for Pardon for Marc Rich and Pincus Green, December 11, 2000, 30.
3. 750 million Swiss francs. The Swiss franc / U.S. dollar exchange rate was around 1.5:1 in April 1992.
4. 5 million Swiss francs at the time.
5. *Schweizer Illustrierte*, May 19, 1993.
6. 50 million Swiss francs at the time.
7. *Denise Joy Rich v. Alexander R. Hackel, et al.* New York State Supreme Court, New York County, Case No. 100710-1993.
8. 215 million Swiss francs. The Swiss franc / U.S. dollar exchange rate was around 1.30:1 in December 1990.

17: The End of the King of Oil

1. Figures from International Monetary Fund.
2. "Marc Rich + Co. Executive to Quit over Disagreement," *Wall Street Journal*, June 4, 1992.
3. Quoted in "Take Jack's Word," 30.
4. "When a Fugitive Marc Rich Flouted U.S. Sanctions," *Wall Street Journal*, February 23, 2001.
5. The report is available at www.iic-offp.org/documents.htm.

6. "A Definition of Richness," *Financial Times*, August 10, 1992.

7. Petition for Pardon for Marc Rich and Pincus Green, December 11, 2000, 4.

18: The Pardon

1. "King of the World," *Playboy*, February 1, 1994.

2. "Opposed to Holder Without Apology," *National Review Online*, November 25, 2008.

3. "Isn't It Rich?," *New York Times*, February 1, 2001.

4. *Vanity Fair*, June 2001.

5. On *Larry King Live*, CNN, February 8, 2001

6. Clemency Regulations, 28 C.F.R. § 1.1.

7. Petition for Pardon for Marc Rich and Pincus Green, December 11, 2000, 8, 28.

8. Ibid., 4.

9. White House Transcripts. Verbatim notes of non-redacted portions of transcripts of Clinton/Barak conversations.

10. Letter from Shlomo Ben-Ami to William Jefferson Clinton, November 26, 2000.

11. Sidney Blumenthal, *The Clinton Wars* (New York: Farrar, Straus and Giroux, 2003), 783.

12. E-mail from Avner Azulay to Jack Quinn, December 25, 2000.

13. White House Transcripts. Verbatim notes of non-redacted portions of transcripts of Clinton/Barak conversations.

14. "Take Jack's Word," 74–83.

15. "Songwriter Who Doubles as Friend of Bill," *New York Times*, October 11, 2000.

16. Letter of Denise Rich to President Bill Clinton, December 6, 2000. Quoted in *Controversial Pardon*, 619.

17. "Plotting a Pardon," *New York Times*, April 11, 2001.

18. Note from Jack Quinn, November 8, 1999

19. Quoted in *Controversial Pardon*, 194.

20. Quoted in "The Threatened Eclipse of a Rising Star," *Journal of Blacks in Higher Education* 31 (Spring, 2001): 69.

21. *Controversial Pardon*.

22. United States Constitution, Article II, Section 2: "The President shall be Commander in Chief of the Army and Navy of the United States, and of the Militia of the several States, when called into the actual Service of the United States; he may require the Opinion, in writing, of the principal Officer in each of the executive Departments, upon any subject relating to the Duties of their respective Offices, and he shall have Power to Grant Reprieves and Pardons for Offenses against the United States, except in Cases of Impeachment."

23. "My Reasons for the Pardons," *New York Times*, February 18, 2001.

24. Bill Clinton, *My Life* (New York: Knopf, 2004).

25. Ibid.

26. Quoted in "Marc Rich Is Sent $137 Million New York Tax Bill," *New York Times*, March 2, 2001.
27. "Head of Rich Foundation Defends Pardon," CNN, February 20, 2001, http://archives.cnn.com/2001/WORLD/meast/02/20/rich.foundation/index.html.

20: Epilogue

1. John N. Ingham and Lynne B. Feldman, *Contemporary American Business Leaders: A Biographical Dictionary* (Westport; Conn.: Greenwood, 1990), xxii.
2. www.templeton.org/market.

INDEX